Return to Sender

Other National Consumer Law Center Publications

LEGAL PRACTICE MANUALS

Consumer Warranty Law

Unfair and Deceptive Acts and Practices

Automobile Fraud

Repossessions and Foreclosures

Truth in Lending

Consumer Law Pleadings

Consumer Class Actions

Fair Credit Reporting Act

Fair Debt Collection

The Cost of Credit

Credit Discrimination

Access to Utility Service

Consumer Bankruptcy Law and Practice

GENERAL INTEREST BOOKS

Surviving Debt: A Guide for Consumers

PERIODICALS

NCLC Reports

NCLC Energy & Utility Update

Return to Sender

GETTING A REFUND OR REPLACEMENT
FOR YOUR LEMON CAR

Nancy Barron

NATIONAL CONSUMER LAW CENTER
Boston, MA
www.consumerlaw.org

For reprint permissions or ordering information, contact
Publications, NCLC, 18 Tremont St., Boston MA 02108,
(617) 523-8089, Fax (617) 523-7398, E-mail: consumerlaw@nclc.org
www.consumerlaw.org

Library of Congress Catalog No. 99-067576
ISBN 1-881793-81-8

This book is intended to provide accurate and authoritative information in regard to the subject matter covered. This book cannot substitute for the independent judgment and skills of a competent attorney or other professional. Non-attorneys are cautioned against using these materials in conducting litigation without advice or assistance from an attorney or other professional. Non-attorneys are also cautioned against engaging in conduct which might be considered the unauthorized practice of law.

10   9   8   7   6   5   4   3   2

Cover design and illustration by Lightbourne Images, copyright ©2000.

Printed in Canada

ABOUT THE AUTHOR

Nancy Barron is a partner with Kemnitzer, Anderson, Barron & Ogilvie. The firm is a leading consumer rights law firm located in San Francisco, San Jose, and Sacramento, providing representation to consumers in lemon law, dealer fraud, deceptive finance, and class actions. (See www.kabolaw.com)

Nancy Barron holds a B.A. from Stanford University, a J.D. from Hastings College of Law (University of California), and was a Fulbright Scholar. She was admitted to the California Bar in 1981, and has contributed to several landmark appellate decisions related to the California Lemon Law. She has been involved in more than 1000 lemon law cases.

She is author of several articles on lemon laws and has spoken at many state and national seminars and conferences on consumer representation. She is a board member of the National Association of Consumer Advocates.

ACKNOWLEDGMENTS

A number of consumer attorneys and experts provided assistance or advice for this project: Mark Anderson, Mark Chavez, Clarence Ditlow, Andrew Ogilvie, James Fishman, Philip Nowicki, Remar Sutton, Ronald Burdge, Kathleen Keest, Bryan Kemnitzer, Steve Kassirer, John Stander, Rosemary Shahan, Patricia Sturdevant, John Lamb, and Jon Sheldon. Jon Sheldon also helped with editing, and Denise Lisio provided editorial assistance. The text was designed and typeset by Ani Associates Design, and Lightbourne Images designed the cover.

CONTENTS

Introduction

About This Book

THE CONSUMER'S RIGHT TO A CAR THAT WORKS

A brand new car, rolling off the showroom floor. For millions of people, that is the real American Dream. However, it's not just the flashy paint job, aromatic leather, and spotless chrome that sells new cars. It's the factory warranty that comes along with those wheels. It's the luxury of security for which we pay.

Ads touting five-year powertrain warranties appeal to the conscious mind even while marketing visuals sell subliminally. The promise of future performance, service networks, and customer satisfaction go to the very heart of the bargain in new car sales. Every auto manufacturer offers a warranty with new cars or it could not compete in the American marketplace. When the manufacturer breaches those warranties by failing to repair a vehicle within a reasonable time, the consumer is entitled to return the defective vehicle and to be made whole — by receiving either a comparable replacement vehicle or a refund of the purchase price.

STATE LEMON LAWS FORCE MANUFACTURERS TO LIVE UP TO THEIR PROMISES

Enforcement of the manufacturer's warranties, in the long run, fosters competition, improves product performance, and invites innovation. In the short run, however, it puts a dent in the automakers' profits, and manufacturers too often are recalcitrant in fulfilling their obligations.

State lemon laws were enacted to insure that car companies honor their own promises and obligations. In the 1970s, beginning with Connecticut and California, states began enacting lemon laws, and by 1993 all fifty states had enacted some form of lemon law. Some are stronger than others. Some are simpler than others. The uniform intent behind these statutes is that a new motor vehicle is a major consumer purchase, that a defective motor vehicle is likely to create hardship, or may cause injury to the consumer, and that the manufacturer must either fix the car or take it back. California's Attorney General (then Assemblyman) William Lockyer, opening committee hearings on amendments to the state's lemon law, powerfully explained the consumer's predicament:

> With incredible distances and very little mass transit, ownership or access to a car is essential. We pay a price, however, for the mobility we enjoy, not the least of which is the fear and loathing we experience when making a significant financial commitment to purchase an auto. Everyone in the room knows the special trauma I'm referring to. . . . Purchasers of new cars occasionally find themselves stuck with a lemon, merchandise that is fundamentally so defective as to be functionally useless.[1]

State lemon laws evidence a concern not just for the buyer's economic hardship, but also for vehicle safety. Defective cars are everybody's problem. Each year, U.S. drivers have an estimated thirty-five million automobile accidents. Defects not only cause accidents, they affect the way a car functions when an accident occurs, even if it is otherwise caused solely by driver error. Frame construction, placement of fuel tanks, and the proper functioning of passenger restraint systems can mean the difference between life and death.

Many consumers labor under the illusion that a new car is bound to be mechanically and cosmetically perfect. Many more are under the false impression that a brand new model is most likely to be defect-free. Anyone can make a mistake. The vehicle may be deficient in design or damaged in the making. Some errors are insignificant, but many others substantially impair vehicle use, value or safety. Manufacturers make these mistakes all the time. Some are more willing to admit their mistakes than others.

HOW THIS BOOK IS ORGANIZED

Return to Sender is written both for car owners and lawyers representing car owners. *Return to Sender* helps consumers effectively confront the car companies when the manufacturer does not live up to its responsibility to fix a defective car. The book explains how lemon laws work and how they can be made to work for the consumer.

Enforcement of lemon law rights takes place in the real world, and all the laws in the world are useless unless an individual can find a practical way to enforce those laws. *Return to Sender* helps consumers decide when they can go at it on their own without a lawyer, when they would be better off with the professional help of a lawyer, and how the lawyer is paid. At the same time, this volume gives advice to lawyers as to whether they should take a lemon law case and how best to pursue it.

Chapters 1 and 2 walk the reader through the standards that must be met for the consumer to be entitled to a refund or replacement under the state lemon law. These chapters detail a lot of hoops to leap through, but that is both the weakness and strength of a lemon law — the lemon law sets out with great particularity exactly when the consumer is entitled under that statute to a refund or replacement vehicle, and exactly when the consumer is not so entitled.

Each state lemon law is the product of legislative wrangling in the face of the industry's well-paid lobbying efforts. With varying degrees of success, depending on the state, these lobbying efforts resulted in certain manufacturer defenses to a lemon law claim. Chapter 3 examines when these manufacturer defenses do and do not trump a consumer's lemon law case.

Chapter 4 sets out the relief the consumer can obtain under a state lemon law. The basic remedy established by every lemon law is replacement of the defective vehicle with a new one or refund of the purchase price. In addition, related damages and the consumer's attorney fees may also be recoverable.

Chapter 5 may be the most practical chapter in the book. It tells consumers when they can handle a lemon law case on their own without an attorney and when they will need a lawyer, how to find a lawyer, how to prepare to meet with a lawyer, and what to ask your lawyer. At the same time, the chapter explains what factors a lawyer should consider in taking on a case and how the fee agreement should work.

Today, the consumer or the consumer's attorney can quickly obtain a great deal of important information about the lemon car even before filing a claim. Just a few years ago, most of the technical information was unavailable to the public, leaving buyers helpless without first filing a lawsuit and initiating the formal, court-enforced discovery process. Chapter 6 reveals much of what this author has learned in more than a decade of handling consumer automotive litigation as to how to find out what you need about your case, even without the manufacturer or dealer's help. For example, you can readily retrieve from the Internet the manufacturer's Technical Service

Bulletins, that set out what the manufacturer tells its dealers about certain systematic vehicle problems.

Many lemon laws were enacted in a climate which was optimistic about alternative dispute resolution. The legislation contemplated informal dispute mechanisms which would expedite warranty claims and which did not require the consumer to hire a lawyer. These out-of-court proceedings have by now gotten decidedly mixed reviews. Nonetheless, many states require consumers to submit their dispute to these IDMs, as they are called, before the consumer can file suit in court. Chapter 7 walks you through the IDM process.

In the event the IDM result fails to give the consumer replacement or refund, the consumer who wishes to pursue the claim has little choice but to go to court. Chapters 8 through 11 set forth the road to success in bringing a lemon law claim in court. These chapters are primarily geared for lawyers, but they are also written for consumers so they can understand what is involved in litigation before they make the decision to go to court to enforce their rights.

Chapter 8 examines the key decisions to be made before any litigation —whether to sue, who to sue, where to sue, and the first steps to take before suing. Chapter 9 sets out in detail exactly what information to demand from the manufacturer and dealer as part of the formal, court-enforced discovery process. Chapter 10 lists a number of additional legal claims to be added to a lemon law complaint that can increase the consumer's recovery, make sure the manfucturer pays for the consumer's attorney fees, and rectify other abuses related to the car sale. Chapter 11 discusses settlement, trial tactics, and recovery of the consumer's attorney fees from the manufacturer.

Chapter 12 is an epilogue of sorts, but not a happy ending. And it is the chapter with which every *used* car owner should start. Several decades after the first lemon laws saw the light of day, many tens of thousands of defective cars have been returned to the manufacturers. Too many of these have been returned to the stream of commerce and the stream of traffic as "laundered lemons." Chapter 12 sets out the consumer's rights if that "peach" of a used car the dealer sold turns out to be someone else's lemon that the manufacturer bought back and never fixed.

Finally, readers will want to be familiar with this book's Appendix that provides the legal citation and summarizes every state's lemon law. There is no substitute for reading the current version of your own law, but this

Appendix helps you find that legislation and provides a quick look at the various features of your state lemon law.

Readers wanting more detailed analysis of their lemon law, the federal Magnuson-Moss Warranty Act, the Uniform Commercial Code, and other warranty laws should refer to National Consumer Law Center, *Consumer Warranty Law* (1997 and Supp.). That treatise is geared for attorneys and provides comprehensive case law discussion and sample pleadings.

---

[1] Assembly Labor, Employment, & Consumer Affairs Committee Hearing on Consumer Protection in re Sale of New & Used Cars (Dec. 1979), Committee Minutes, p.1. Assemblyman (now Attorney General) Lockyer authored significant amendments of the Song Beverly Act. *See* Assembly Bill 3324 (1979).

– 1 –

Types of Vehicles Protected by Lemon Laws

This book is about a consumer's rights under a state lemon law to obtain a replacement or refund for a defective vehicle. But state lemon laws do not apply to all types of vehicles or to all types of purchasers. This chapter explains which types of automotive transactions are covered by state lemon laws and which are not.

If a state lemon law does not apply, the consumer still has remedies available under other laws. The consumer can seek repairs or replacement under an express warranty claim. The consumer can seek damages under a warranty or deception claim. The consumer can even attempt to revoke acceptance and cancel the sale under the Uniform Commercial Code. These other remedies are analyzed in detail in another NCLC publication, *Consumer Warranty Law* (1997 and Supp.). But state lemon laws usually offer a more efficient procedure and clear-cut substantive rights, all to the consumer's advantage, so it is important to determine if a state lemon law applies to the transaction.

In general, lemon laws always apply to a new private passenger vehicle sold for personal use to an individual who still lives in the same state where the individual bought the car. If that is the case, you can probably skip over this chapter, no matter what state you are in, because your transaction meets the threshold of your state lemon law.

This chapter instead deals with five situations where a given state's lemon law *may* or may *not* apply:

1. The vehicle is a motorcycle, snowmobile, motorized wheelchair, moped, driveable lawnmower, truck, tractor, van conversion, dune buggy, mobile home, motorhome, or some other vehicle other than a private passenger car.
2. The vehicle was not purchased brand new, but was bought

as a demonstrator, a late model used car, or even as an older used car.

3. The vehicle's use is not strictly personal, but was purchased for business or agricultural purposes.

4. The consumer is leasing the vehicle, instead of buying it.

5. The consumer did not buy the car in the same state where the consumer now resides.

We examine each of these five situations in turn.

MOTORCYCLES, SNOWMOBILES, MOTOR HOMES, DUNE BUGGIES, AND MORE

All fifty state lemon laws apply to private passenger cars. Less clear is whether they apply to a motorcycle, snowmobile, motorized wheelchair, moped, driveable lawnmower, truck, tractor, van conversion, dune buggy, mobile home, motorhome, or other less standard motor vehicles. The answer will vary depending on the exact language of a particular state's lemon law.

Consequently, the first place to go to answer these coverage questions is the actual language of your state lemon law.[1] Usually the statute will have a scope section and may have a separate section exempting certain vehicles. To further refine what is meant by "motor vehicle" or similar language found in the lemon law, look at the statute's definitions and particularly any definitions found elsewhere in the state's motor vehicle code.

For example, motorcycles are explicitly covered in Virginia and sixteen other states. Vermont specifically excludes motorcycles, tractors, and snowmobiles. Off-road vehicles are categorically excluded in Alaska. Alabama looks instead to whether the vehicle's *primary* use is on public highways, even if the vehicle has off-road capability.

Other states define a motor vehicle as one which must be registered as such, excluding such things as motorized wheelchairs. Gross vehicle weight (GVW) is frequently the determining factor. For example, the lemon laws in Indiana, Vermont, Wyoming and Louisiana exclude from coverage vehicles over 10,000 GVW.

Some states set out long lists of excluded vehicles. Thus you can make the argument that since the legislature was so specific in defining the excluded vehicles, all other vehicles are deemed covered by the statute. For example, Connecticut courts apply the lemon law to motorcycles even though that law does not expressly mention motorcycles.[2]

Because lemon laws are remedial legislation that should be broadly construed, the statute should apply to consumer vehicles that are not explicitly excluded. On the other hand, where a court uses the "objective standard" of whether a vehicle has a consumer purpose (as described later in this chapter), the statute will probably not apply to buses, large trucks, and similar vehicles that are almost always purchased solely for business use.

Motor homes, sometimes known as "RVs," present difficult questions as to lemon law coverage. The exact legislative language will control, and the legislative trend is to include the motorized portion of motor homes, and to exclude the living quarters or non-motorized portion of the vehicle from lemon law protection. That is, if the defect relates to the motorized portion, the consumer is entitled to a new motor home or a refund on the complete purchase. But if the defect relates to the living quarters, then the consumer has no rights under the lemon law, and must use other legal theories to get the quarters fixed.

Questions then arise as to whether a defect relates to the motorized portion or the living quarters. For example, a defect in the heating, air conditioning, and ventilation system should be viewed as a defect in the motorized portion, since the unit was installed in the cab for the comfort of the driver, window defogging is a critical element to the safe mobility of the motor home, and the defect can cause the motor home to stall.[3] The consumer has a good argument that any defect with impairs the driver safety or driveability of the motor home is chassis-related for purposes of lemon law coverage.

California has its own solution for motor homes — one lemon law provision applies to the living quarters and another covers the chassis. You may have to combine these provisions to obtain full relief.[4]

CAN YOU RETURN A CAR PURCHASED AS "USED"?

The classic lemon law applies to new motor vehicle sales. Nevertheless, certain consumers who purchased their cars used can still utilize their state lemon law to return their defective vehicle. Hawaii, Massachusetts,

Minnesota, New Jersey, New York, and Rhode Island have enacted lemon laws that explicitly apply to cars purchased as used. Consequently, in these six states, consumers can return a lemon used car to the dealer in similar fashion that they can return a lemon new car to a manufacturer.

Some used cars are protected
by new car lemon laws.

In the other forty-four states, the rights of used car buyers under the state lemon law are more limited. Nevertheless, there are several situations where consumers can utilize the state's "new" car lemon law even for a used car purchase. A car purchased with significant mileage already on its odometer can still technically be "new." Look to the definition of "new" found in the lemon law or in a state's motor vehicle statutes regulating title and registration. These provisions often define a vehicle as "new" as long as it has not previously been subject to a retail sale or has not yet had a certificate of title issued.

Consequently, the general rule is a car is still "new" even after the dealership has used it as a demonstrator, a loaner, a field vehicle, or a "Brass Hat Special," as long as the consumer is the first retail purchaser.[5] When a manufacturer sends a new car to a dealer, it supplies a certificate of origin, but a title is not issued at that point. A title is first issued when the car is sold at retail. The name of the first person to purchase the car at retail for actual use, instead of for re-sale, is listed as the first title owner. For example, a dealer to dealer transfer does not result in the car being titled.

As long as one or more dealerships are the only owners of a vehicle, the car is still "new" when sold at retail, even if the odometer indicates 5,000 or 10,000 miles, or more. The retail purchaser is the first title owner.

To clarify that cars purchased as demonstrators are covered by a state's lemon law, several states have amended their lemon laws to specifically include demonstrators within their scope. This is logical since there has been no transfer of title and the vehicle is still under the manufacturer's original warranty.

Even when a car has had other owners listed on the title, a state's "new" car lemon law will still apply in certain situations. Those receiving the car as a gift, such as spouses and children of the original purchaser, should be covered by the law. Unless a statute indicates it is limited to legal transferees, transferees who have equitable but not legal title to the car, such as a spouse who after divorce retains a car purchased in the other spouse's name, are also eligible for lemon law protection.

In addition, in some states the "new" car lemon law still applies to a car purchased as used if, at the time of purchase, the car was under the manufacturer's original warranty, no matter how many prior owners the car has had. California and Virginia are examples of two states that apply their lemon laws to used vehicles still within the standard new-car warranty.[6] This approach makes sense because it should not matter to the manufacturer how many owners a car has during the warranty period — the manufacturer has promised to honor its warranty, and car owners should not have fewer rights where the manufacturer fails to do so just because they are not the original owner.

There is one other special case of applying a lemon law to a used vehicle — where the used lemon had been returned to the manufacturer once before. In other words, it is possible that a prior owner experienced many of the same persistent mechanical defects that plague the car's current owner. The prior owner returned the car to the manufacturer as a lemon, and the manufacturer turned around and sold it again to a dealer, who then sells it to the unsuspecting consumer. This is called "lemon laundering" and is becoming more and more widespread as more and more cars are returned to manufacturers as lemons. The victim of lemon laundering has special rights, which are examined in Chapter 12, *infra.*

ARE BUSINESS-USE VEHICLES PROTECTED BY THE LEMON LAW?

Virtually all state lemon laws apply to "consumer" purchases, although a few lemon laws protect anyone entitled to enforce the vehicle's written warranty. The policy behind limiting lemon laws to consumer purchases is clear. The individual consumer stands in an inferior bargaining position when taking on an automotive giant, while business buyers have the commercial skills and economic strength to stand up for their rights — although this distinction breaks down in many cases of small businesses, particularly one or two person businesses.

Where a lemon law limits its protection to cars purchased for "consumer" use, it is often difficult to determine whether a particular car's intended use was for "consumer" or business purposes. Many people buy pick-up trucks that are useful in their work, but are used primarily for personal reasons. What about a salesperson who has a private passenger car that is used for both business and personal reasons? Courts basically use one of two tests to determine if a "consumer" use is present. The *objective test* looks to the nature of the vehicle; the *subjective test* looks to the intent of the buyer of the vehicle.

Objective Test: What Is That Type of Vehicle's Normal Use?

Courts in a slight majority of states use the objective test in interpreting their lemon laws. This is the same test courts generally use in interpreting the federal Magnuson-Moss Warranty Act. This definition looks to whether that type of vehicle is "normally used" or "primarily designed" for consumer purposes. The particular intent or the particular use of the buyer is irrelevant.

If a vehicle itself passes the objective test, it does not matter whether the buyer on title is a corporation or an individual.[7] On the other hand, if a bus was purchased for individual, personal use, this would not be covered under the objective test, because buses are virtually never sold for consumer use, and their "normal" use is therefore commercial.

A vehicle need not be exclusively used, but only "*normally*" used for personal, family, or household purposes, thus applying to private passenger cars and mobile homes.[8] The vehicle can have other uses as long as the vehicle is also "normally" used for personal, family, or household purposes. Vehicles are normally used for personal purposes if their use in that way is not uncommon.[9]

Subjective Test: What Is the Particular Consumer's Intended Use?

A minority of state courts use a subjective test to determine lemon law coverage. The test looks not to the vehicle's normal use by all purchasers, but instead at the intended use of the particular buyer. Did that particular consumer have an intent to purchase the vehicle primarily for personal, family or household purposes? A vehicle used occasionally or even frequently for business or agricultural use should be covered as long as its *primary* intended use is personal. Minnesota uses a variation of this rule: 40% of a vehicle's use should be for personal reasons.

The subjective test can lead to inequitable results and serious problems of proof. Consider the Avon Lady who lives in her motor home: she sells in her living room one day a week, but keeps her samples there all the time and packages her deliveries on the fold-out kitchen table. What is her intended use in purchasing the motor home?

In addition, even if an individual does use a vehicle solely for business use, many small businesses deserve the same protection as individual consumers. The idea that a small business would have any greater bargaining power against, for example General Motors, is pure fiction. The babysitter who drives the children to school and tennis lessons for $8.00 per hour has absolutely no greater bargaining power against Toyota than the mother who drives the same carpool for free. Thus the very same protection that the law extends to the individual should be extended to small businesses in states which employ the subjective analysis of "consumer goods."

The subjective test leads to arbitrary distinctions. The lemon law may apply to a doctor who uses a vehicle to commute to the hospital for work, but not to the same doctor who uses that same vehicle to make house calls in the course of a medical practice. It is time to recognize that the distinction is as obsolete as the very notion of medical house calls.

Some states which utilize the subjective test have struggled to deal with this problem by codifying a "small business" exception. Michigan for example, allows recovery for business use vehicles where the business in question owns a fleet of ten vehicles or less. Vermont, Washington and Tennessee also have small business exceptions for other fleet sizes. California enacted a small business provision as recently as 1998, allowing coverage for businesses owning five vehicles or less.

The variation in fleet size reflects legislative lobbying and compromise. On the other hand, many states do not make such a distinction, but simply cover all retail buyers of prescribed motor vehicles.

CAN YOU RETURN A LEASED LEMON?

A large and growing percentage of car sales are now structured as lease transactions. Consumers who lease view the transaction as little different than a
purchase, just with a different method of payment. They expect the same
warranty rights as if they had purchased the car, and expect the same rights
under their state lemon law.

This makes sense because the lease is based on the same (or higher) purchase price for the car as if the consumer were a purchaser. The price the
consumer pays for the car in a lease is specified on the lease on the same line
as the "gross capitalized cost," being listed as the agreed-upon value of the
vehicle. If you pay the same price for a car, you should get the same lemon
law rights. Moreover, the lemon law's replacement and refund remedies
deter manufacturers from denying warranty repairs, the same deterrence
being necessary whether the consumer purchases or leases the vehicle. The
lessee also has the same needs to enforce the warranty as a car purchaser.

> There is no reason why lemon laws
> should not also apply to leased cars.

Unfortunately, many lemon laws were written before leasing became
popular, and thus did not explicitly cover leased vehicles. Unless specifically
excluded in the language of the law, consumer lessees should get the same
protection as purchasers, under the rule that the statute's remedial purposes
should be broadly construed.[10]

The contrary argument is that the consumer does not own the vehicle,
and it is the leasing company who should enforce the lemon law's rights.
This is a narrow, illogical view of the law. It would make no sense for some
distant bank to decide whether to pursue a lemon law claim. For all practical purposes, only the consumer in possession of the vehicle knows whether
its performance and condition conforms to the manufacturer's warranty; if
only the bank has standing to assert the claim, it is likely the warranty will
not be enforced and will fail of its essential purpose.

More and more lemon laws are explicitly dealing with the leasing issue.
The California and New York lemon laws now state that lessees have the

same lemon law rights as purchasers. Connecticut's lemon law defines "consumer" as including a lessee. On the other hand, Michigan explicitly defines "consumer" to exclude automotive lessees.

WHAT HAPPENS IF THE CAR IS BOUGHT IN ONE STATE BUT PRESENTLY GARAGED IN ANOTHER?

Many state lemon laws apply only to vehicles purchased in that state. Consumers who move their defective car into a state having such a restrictive lemon law will thus have no protection under that state's lemon law. Those consumers may still be able to bring a cause of action under the lemon law of the state in which they purchased the car.

Other state lemon laws restrict coverage in other ways. It becomes important to carefully read the legislative language to determine if a car must be sold *and* presently registered in a state, or only just sold *or* presently registered in a state. If the car need only be sold *or* registered, then protection is offered to *both* consumers who bring a defective car into the state and who buy the car in the state, even if they take it elsewhere. Where ambiguity exists, the consumer is well advised to seek legal advice to resolve the conflicts of law problem.

---

[1] A summary with the legal citations for all state lemon laws is found in this book's Appendix.

[2] Wilson v. Central Sports, Inc., 40 Conn. Supp. 156, 483 A.2d 625 (1984).

[3] Abbs v. Georgie Boy Mfg., Inc., 60 Wash. App. 157, 803 P.2d 14 (1991).

[4] National R.V., Inc. v. Foreman, 34 Cal. App. 4th 1072, 40 Cal. Rptr. 2d 672 (1995).

[5] Chrysler Motors Corp. v. Flowers , 803 P.2d 314 (Wash. 1991); Britton v. Bill Anselmi Pontiac-Buick-GMC, Inc. 786 P.2d 855 (Wyo. 1990). In contrast, states which have a used car lemon law may apply that law to demonstrators instead of their new car lemon laws. *See* American Motor Sales Corp. v Brown 548 N.Y.S.2d 791 (1989).

[6] Jensen v. BMW of North America, Inc., 35 Cal. App. 4th 112, 41 Cal. Rptr. 2d 295 (1995); Suburu of America v. Peters, 500 S.E.2d 803 (Va. 1998)(fourth purchaser).

[7] Results Real Estate, Inc. v. Lazy Days R.V. Center, Inc. 505 So. 2d 587 (Fla. Dist. Ct. App. 1987).

[8] EDP Systems, Inc. v. Mercedes-Benz, 1987 WL 7828 (N.D. Ill. 1987) (available on Westlaw) (car); Narjan Co. v. Fleetwood Enterprises, Inc., 659 F. Supp. 1081 (S.D. Ga. 1986) (mobile home); Drew v. Chrysler Credit Corp., 596 F. Supp. 1371 (W.D. Mo. 1984) (car).

[9] 16 C.F.R. §700.1.

[10] Henderson v. Benson-Hartman Motors, Inc., 33 Pa. D. & C. 3d 6, 41 U.C.C. Rep. 782 (C.P. Allegheny Cty. 1983).

– 2 –

When Can You Return a Lemon?

Every state has a lemon law that gives consumers the right to return a defective vehicle if certain precise conditions are met. Car manufacturers do not like taking back cars, so be prepared for a fight over whether a transaction precisely meets the conditions set out in the state lemon law.

Moreover, the lemon law in every state was passed over fierce industry opposition, and the industry succeeded in inserting certain loopholes into your lemon law unique to your state. Thus, while the remedial intent of lemon laws is similar nationwide, there is variation from state to state as to when you are entitled to return your car to the manufacturer.

This chapter takes you through the basic steps as to when a lemon vehicle can be returned to the manufacturer under the lemon law, and helps you avoid the various traps that manufacturers like to take advantage of in preventing consumers from exercising their rights. But you must in every instance take a close look at your state's lemon law.

The typical lemon law right to a replacement car or a refund kicks in whenever:
- The car does not conform to its warranties;
- The non-conformity substantially impairs the vehicle's safety, use, or value;
- The consumer notifies the manufacturer of the non-conformity; and
- The manufacturer fails to conform the car to its warranties after a reasonable number of repair attempts.

The rest of this chapter examines in some detail these four elements of a lemon law claim.

WHAT WARRANTIES
COME WITH A CAR

In determining whether a car conforms to its warranties, it is important to understand what those warranties are. Obviously, new cars come with a written warranty that sets out specific warranty coverage. Nevertheless, some defects are not covered by the written warranty, and then the question becomes what other warranties come with the car.

Written Warranties

New motor vehicles come with four kinds of written warranties that appear in the owner's manual, warranty booklet, or similar documentation that comes with the car: the bumper-to-bumper warranty, the power train warranty, the corrosion warranty, and the emissions warranty. The "bumper-to-bumper" warranty usually covers just about everything other than tires, but, because the manufacturers are free to define the terms of their own warranties, scrutiny of the warranty itself is imperative.

The "power train" warranty may have a duration several years longer than the "bumper-to-bumper" warranty. The "power train" or "drive train" generally covers engine, transmission, differential and other components of the drive train, but individual manufacturers may include or exclude particular parts. The manufacturer will sometimes try to argue that the particular nonconformity complained of does not fit within the definition of "power train" and thus the claimant is "out of warranty" after expiration of the "bumper-to-bumper" coverage. In pressing a lemon law claim, you should have some general understanding of the mechanical basis for the claim and have a good idea which warranty you contend has been breached.

"Corrosion" warranties cover rust, but usually this means actual holes in the body or frame due to rust, not cosmetic rust impairing a perfect paint job. The "emissions" warranty is defined by very specific state or federal regulations which cover the air quality control system of the vehicle including exhaust and fuel systems.[1] Parts covered by the emissions warranty differ with make and model, and may also vary by state.[2]

Other Express Warranties

A written warranty is one example of an express warranty. Manufacturers can also make express warranties through advertising, pictures, oral statements, and the like. As a general rule, such other express warranties are *not* considered warranties for purposes of state lemon laws, because many state lemon laws limit express warranties to "written warranties." The term "written warranty" typically applies only to (1) a written factual statement or promise that the product is defect-free or will perform at a specified level for a specified time; *or* (2) a written promise to refund, repair, replace, or take other remedial action with respect to a product if the product fails to meet the promised specifications.

A written warranty includes certain written statements beyond the manufacturer's formal written warranty, such as a dealer's pre-delivery inspection form or owner's manual. But other express promises may *not* be considered written warranties, such as sales puffery, testimonials, or perky jingles, even though many of these appear amusing in historical perspective. Recall the Gasmobile which promised to be "The Finest Gasoline Touring Carriage Built in America;" the racy Bates whose motto was, "Buy a Bates and Keep Your Dates;" or the Santos-Dumont whose makers crowed "This One Flies But Never Falters."

In a contemporary twist, Volkswagen recently advertised itself as offering "Fahrvergnugen," an enigmatically unpronounceable word which roughly translates "driving pleasure." The judge in *Volkswagen of America, Inc. v. Dillard* reviewed the abysmal repair history, and was compelled to quip "Fahrvergnugen this was not," and held for the plaintiff.

Implied Warranties

Many lemon laws also provide rights concerning *implied* warranties. An implied warranty is invisible. It is a promise imposed by law based on public policy concerns. There are two types of implied warranties — that the motor vehicle is *merchantable* and that it is *fit for the particular purpose for which it is sold*. Implied warranties are often broader in scope than express warranties.[3]

A Ford Escort that sat on an inventory lot during spring floods may not be merchantable, not being of like quality with its model siblings which stayed dry. Another example occurs where the seller creates an implied warranty of fitness for the particular purpose of performing on muddy roads, even though this is not mentioned in the manufacturer's express warranties. But for a manufacturer, as opposed to a dealer, to create an implied warranty of fitness for a particular purpose, the manufacturer, not just the dealer, must know of the buyer's particular needs.

Dealers often try to sell used cars "as is," that is without any implied warranties. But federal law prohibits manufacturers who offer written warranties from disclaiming implied warranties. Any such attempt to limit the implied warranties not only violates federal law, but has no effect on the consumer's ability to enforce the implied warranty.[4] Breach of an implied warranty thus provides an alternative basis for a lemon law claim to replace the vehicle or refund the purchase price.

Written warranties have a definite time limitation — for example three years or 36,000 miles. Implied warranties, on the other hand, have no explicit time limitation. Nevertheless, the duration of the written warranty has an important impact on the length of the implied warranty for two reasons. Some state lemon laws allow claims for replacement or refund based on an implied warranty only during the duration of the car's written warranty. In addition, manufacturers are allowed by federal law to limit the duration of any implied warranty to the duration of the written warranty they offer, if they do so clearly and prominently on the face of the warranty.[5] Thus, if the written warranty is for three years, the duration of an implied warranty may be limited to three years if the written warranty so states.

Secret Warranties

The implied warranty of merchantability means that new cars must be merchantable *when they leave the manufacturer.* An issue in any case claiming breach of this implied warranty will be whether the defect occurred because of subsequent misuse, or whether it was present when the car left the factory.

While it may be difficult for a consumer to show the car's condition when it left the factory, one effective technique is to point to a "secret warranty," whereby the manufacturer performs free warranty repairs for people who complain loudly enough about defects which the manufacturer knows exist. It is in essence a manufacturer's admission that many units of a like model car were defective when they left the factory. Ralph Nader and Clarence Ditlow, Director of the Center for Auto Safety, claim that "So frequently does this happen that at any one time, there are hundreds of these warranty programs going on throughout the auto industry."[6] Ditlow and Nader point out two serious public policy problems with this practice. First, manufacturers fail to notify owners of known safety defects and eligibility for free repairs. They then apply warranty coverage selectively, rewarding only persistent complainers, while the more complacent consumers pay for the manufacturer's mistakes. The Center for Auto Safety has been a leader in combatting this deceptive practice.

Uncovering a "secret warranty" may turn your case into a slam dunk!

In one notable case, Toyota was found to have been secretly making free repairs for brake pulsation in Camrys. A whistle-blower exposed Toyota's secret warranty whereby certain owners obtained brake repairs for free. Thousands of other Camry owners had to pay anywhere from $790 to $1,380 for brake pulsation repairs, plus the cost of further damages this defect caused the vehicle. The Center for Auto Safety joined the Center for Law in the Public Interest in suing Toyota, ultimately obtaining a settlement for a class valued at around $100 million.

Whether a manufacturer honors a secret warranty in a particular case or not, the very policy of repairing a particular defect at no charge for at least some customers can be viewed as an admission of an inherent defect in the car present at the time of manufacture. Thus the implied warranty of merchantability would apply to the defect.

WHEN DOES A CAR FAIL TO CONFORM TO ITS WARRANTIES?

Nature of the Defect

The majority of lemon laws require that warranty non-conformities involve a "defect or condition." The term "condition" was added to "defect" in some laws to ensure against a possible narrow interpretation of "defect," but is arguably redundant. The terms encompass any characteristic, condition, or performance of the vehicle, as well as the description, model number, engine size, special features and factory-installed options, but not such things as price or delivery terms.

Massachusetts is one example of a state which has taken pains to express a broad meaning of the term. "Nonconformity" is defined as "any specific or generic defect or malfunction, or any concurrent combination of such defects or malfunctions that substantially impairs the use, market value or safety of a motor vehicle."

While the consumer has the burden to prove the defect, this does not mean the consumer must pinpoint the precise nature of the defect, or its cause or source. The car's warranty is a warranty of the whole product, and is breached where the assembled product does not perform properly, even if no individual parts can be identified as defective. In this sense, the proof required to establish a lemon law claim is less than that required in a strict products liability case.

**The consumer is not required
to pinpoint the exact cause of the defect,
only that the problem exists.**

Consider the plight of Nancy Schreidel, who bought a defective 1989 Honda Prelude with manual transmission. "While stopped in traffic, she was unable to shift from neutral into first gear. . . . She was unable to move for one-half to one full minute. . . . This happened numerous times, with cars honking and people shaking their fists at her on about 10 additional occasions. . . ." This testimony coupled with her expert's opinion that the problem lay somewhere in the slave cylinder was sufficient to uphold the verdict against the manufacturer's argument that she had not met her burden of proof that there was a nonconformity. The court held "It was not necessary to pinpoint the exact mechanical detail" to prove her case.[7]

The consumer need present no expert testimony to establish a defect or non-conformity. The owner's own testimony that the vehicle does not properly work is adequate to meet the burden of proof, since the consumer is under no duty to prove the cause of the non-conformity.

Nonetheless, the nonconformity issue may still best be nailed down by expert testimony. Industry defendants have whole corps of in-house experts prepared to state the vehicle conforms to the performance standards of that make and model, that the consumer just doesn't know how to drive, that there was no problem found, that the defect was repaired, that the consumer doesn't know a catalytic converter from a crowbar, that the consumer is just a whiner, etc. Particularly in a case involving intermittent or elusive conditions and a mass of repair orders which state, "No problem found," you may want to engage an expert to validate your side of the story.

Experts may also sort out the sticky issue of whether a nonconformity is in the chassis or coach, is due to after-factory installed equipment, or to counter affirmative defenses such as owner abuse. It is worth the time and effort needed to locate competent, independent experts.[8]

WHEN DOES A DEFECT
CAUSE SUBSTANTIAL IMPAIRMENT?

To return a vehicle pursuant to a lemon law, the defect must substantially impair the use, value *or* safety of the vehicle to the buyer. Remember this is use, value, *or* safety. Any one of the three will trigger the consumer's rights under the lemon law. These are questions of fact as to which the consumer's testimony is very important.

**Even an annoying "shimmy"
or "smelly leather" is enough
to trigger a lemon law.**

Manufacturers may try to dismiss a "no-start" condition as a non-*safety* issue. Courts do not accept this argument.[9] For example, In *Ibrahim v. Ford Motor Co.,* Annamarie Ibrahim tearfully recounted the time she was pregnant when her Mercury Cougar stalled on the railroad tracks. Clearly this impaired the vehicle's safety for her. It also impaired her *use*. In addition, since most consumers could not, in good conscience, think of selling their detested lemon without disclosing its problems to the next owner, the vehicle *value* hits the skids.

A wide range of problems have been found to substantially impair a vehicle's value or use — from obvious safety defects like steering to intangible problems like an annoying "shimmy." Trial courts have found a defective paint job to be a substantial impairment.[10] Los Angeles lawyer, Alan Golden, reports he took a Volvo case to trial in which the sole complaint was "smelly leather." It was so awful, no one wanted to ride in the car. After the entire jury and a skeptical judge exited the courtroom for a "view" and a whiff, they held their noses and returned a verdict for plaintiff.

One very common non-conformity concerns malfunctioning dashboard lights which go on even though there is in fact no underlying problem. This constitutes substantial impairment of the use of a car since the driver would be forced to pull off the road to check the oil or stop at the nearest service station once the warning light came on. In addition, a design defect, not just a manufacturing defect, has been held to constitute an actionable non-conformity meeting the substantial impairment standard.[11]

Pay special attention to whether the lemon law states that the defect must impair the use, safety, or value of the motor vehicle *to the consumer*. If so, the consumer's perspective may be taken into consideration, including the consumer's diminished confidence in the vehicle.[12] The consumer's considerable investment in a new car is, after all, "rationalized by the peace of mind that flows from its dependability and safety."[13]

Substantial impairment need not be proven by an expert witness and may be established by the consumer's own testimony.[14] Sam and Mary Jane Vultaggio, for example, bought a GM truck for the purpose of pulling a trailer, for which the dealer "specially equipped" the unit. Sam testified the transmission could not handle the job. The transmission would

> discharge fluid, emit smoke and a burning odor,
> and the transmission housing would get so hot
> that [Mrs. Vultaggio] could not rest her feet on
> that portion of the floor. . . .

The trial court held this sufficient to overcome summary judgment and GM appealed, arguing that an expert opinion was necessary. The appellate court disagreed with General Motors and affirmed, holding that "unless the subject matter is outside the realm of the ordinary experience of mankind, and requires special learning, study or experience . . . a lay opinion may suffice."[15]

Whether the consumer or manufacturer bears the burden to establish substantial impairment depends on the structure of the particular lemon law. For example, New York's statute follows the majority rule that the manufacturer can try to show that a defect does *not* substantially impair the vehicle value. If it fails to do so, then, once the consumer shows there is a defect, the court presumes the defect substantially impairs value. The consumer need not in that case prove substantial impairment.

NOTICE OF THE NONCONFORMITY

To press a lemon law claim, the consumer should first notify the manufacturer of the defect. Many lemon laws contain a written notice requirement. On the other hand, a California court recently held that no notice is required because it is the manufacturer's duty to replace the vehicle or refund the price once it is unable to repair the problem, without any affirmative request by the consumer.[16] Where a statute is not explicit, it is wise to give written notice to the manufacturer, preferably by certified mail.

You will have to distinguish between a lemon law requirement that you notify the manufacturer concerning defects and a requirement that you notify the manufacturer that you wish to initiate a procedure for informal resolution of your dispute. In some states these are separate notices. In many states, notice of the defect gives the manufacturer one more shot at fixing the car, usually within a fixed period of time, anywhere from 7 to 45 days. On the other hand, in some states, the request for dispute resolution itself is deemed notice of the defect. For example, in Vermont, the consumer provides notice of intent to go to informal dispute resolution, and this simultaneously gives the manufacturer one final opportunity to correct and repair the defect before the dispute resolution procedure begins. The informal dispute process is discussed in detail in Chapter 7, *infra*.

Some lemon laws require that the notice be sent directly to the manufacturer, but most lemon laws indicate notice may be sent to the manufacturer, its agent, or authorized dealer. Where the statute is silent on whether notice must be given directly to the manufacturer, the consumer has a good argument that notice to the authorized dealer suffices, because the dealer's warranty reimbursement claims to the manufacturer put the manufacturer on notice that the vehicle qualifies under the lemon law. Nevertheless, where there is doubt, it is safest to send the notice certified mail to both the manufacturer and the dealer, with a copy to the lender.

A REASONABLE OPPORTUNITY TO REPAIR

Before the consumer can seek a replacement or a refund for a car that does not conform to its warranties, the consumer must give the manufacturer a reasonable opportunity to repair the defect. This repair must be completed within a reasonable time and at no cost to the buyer.

A manufacturer's warranty that requires the buyer to pay a deductible for covered repairs violates the lemon law. Eleven auto manufacturers settled with the State of New York to reimburse consumers to the tune of $10 million for deductibles consumers had paid for repairs covered by the state's lemon law and to pay the state's costs in reaching the settlement.

Moreover, the car need only be returned for repair to an authorized dealer, not to the distant manufacturer itself. In California, manufacturers are required to maintain sufficient repair facilities reasonably close to all areas where its cars are sold. In other states, the accessibility of repair facilities is implicit in the lemon law's "reasonable repair" language.

How Many Repair Attempts Must the Consumer Endure?

Manufacturers of course would like as many repair attempts as possible to fix a defect, because they do not want to provide the consumer with a new car or a refund. Moreover, they know that it is inconvenient for the consumer to take the car in for a repair, and repeatedly lose the use of the car for a period of time. They can plan on a good percentage of consumers just giving up and learning to live with the defect.

Consumers under a lemon law do not have to put up with this abusive strategy. They only have to give the manufacturer a reasonable repair opportunity — after which the manufacturer has to take the car back. Although the term "reasonable repair opportunity" is somewhat vague, state lemon laws provide important guidance as to what that term means.

While there are variations among states, all state lemon laws provide two different standards for a reasonable repair opportunity, being based on (1) the number of attempts to repair a single defect (usually three or four) OR (2) the total number of days out of service within the specified time period (usually 30 days). A consumer has provided a reasonable repair opportunity if either one of the two standards are met.

To keep track of these numbers, you should draw up a repair chronology at the time of making the demand for repair or reimbursement. Calculating the number of repairs may be tricky because it is not always clear what repairs are related to what defect. Frame damage, for example, may manifest itself in electrical problems, leaks, alignment or a cracked windshield. In a given case all of these may relate to attempted repairs of a single nonconformity.

Repair shops may note on a repair order "no problem found," and this can lead to a dispute as to whether this repair attempt counts toward the statutory number of repair attempts or days out of service. But courts are uniform in rejecting the defense claim that if the manufacturer's servicing dealer did not find a problem, it did not exist. The consumer's presentment of the car to the dealer is a repair attempt even if the dealer cannot verify that anything is wrong and thus does not attempt to make repairs.[17]

The phrase "out of service for 30 or more days" means the car is unusable by the consumer for 30 or more days; it need not be in the repair shop for 30 days.[18] Moreover, unless the statute says "business" days, the lemon law standard is out of service for 30 *calendar* days.[19]

The 30-day out of service standard only requires that the car was out of service for 30 days, not that the defect cannot be repaired or still exists.[20] However, the consumer cannot refuse the manufacturer's offer to repair within the 30-day period. Similarly, the consumer has the responsibility to pick up the vehicle promptly after repairs have been completed, in order to accurately count the 30-day period.

The place to begin determining the repair chronology is with the repair orders themselves, since they indicate the date the car came into the shop for repairs. Nevertheless, they are notoriously inaccurate or incomplete in stating the date "out," that is the date the car left the shop. The consumer's own recollection (perhaps supported by phone records or daily diary entries) is needed to fill the gaps.

Numerical Standards
Only Create a Presumption

In many states, the numerical standards as to how many repair attempts a manufacturer is allowed are not absolute, but create a presumption that a manufacturer's attempt to repair more than the specified number is unreasonable. Only rarely can the manufacturer overcome this presumption, and show it should have additional repair attempts. The burden would then be on the manufacturer to prove its failure to correct the nonconformity was caused by conditions beyond its control.

A serious safety defect should not require multiple repair attempts to trigger lemon law remedies

---

More importantly, the consumer can seek a replacement or refund without first waiting for the specified number of repair attempts. It is a common error of the media, and many commentators, to suggest that a car is not a lemon until and unless it is in the shop, e.g., four or more times for a single defect. This might be true in a minority of states, such as Wisconsin, which do not phrase the standard as a presumption, but rather use it in the very definition of "reasonable attempt to repair." In most states, the consumer need only show that the manufacturer was provided a *reasonable* opportunity.

Meeting the numerical standards is *one* way of showing that the manufacturer was afforded a reasonable opportunity. The consumer can provide other evidence that a number short of that specified in the statute is still reasonable. There is *no* presumption that a number less than four is insufficient, only that allowing the manufacturer four attempts is presumed to be more than reasonable.

A serious safety defect or life-threatening non-conformity surely should not require submission of a car for repairs multiple times. If the condition involves brakes or steering, the driver could well be over the side of a cliff before meeting the statutory presumption. Some lemon laws avoid any ambiguity by expressly allowing the manufacturer only one or two repair attempts of a safety defect before the consumer's refund/replacement rights are triggered.

Repairs Made After a Reasonable Number of Attempts

Once the consumer has established that the vehicle was not repaired within a reasonable time, some courts have held *it is irrelevant* that the manufacturer was ultimately able to fix the problem. For example, once a car is out of service for more than thirty days, a subsequent repair does not defeat the consumer's right to demand a refund.[21] These courts take the view that the lemon law "protects against . . . the insecurity of ownership of a vehicle that is perceived to be undependable."

The One Last Chance Rule

Other states allow the manufacturer to have yet another repair attempt (for an additional 10 to 45 days, depending on the state) after the consumer sends the manufacturer notice of the nonconformity and that the consumer has afforded the manufacturer a reasonable number of repair attempts. This is an exception that only applies in a few states, and must be strictly construed against the manufacturer even in those states.

CHECKLIST OF ELEMENTS
IN A LEMON LAW CLAIM

Is the vehicle covered?
   Automobile
   Truck
   Motorcycle
   Off-road vehicle
   Motor home
   Boat
   Other motorized vehicle
   Gross vehicle weight

Was the purchase a consumer transaction?
   Objective test (normal use of the vehicle)
   Subjective test (intended use of the vehicle)

Must the vehicle be sold as new?
   First retail purchaser (first titled sale)
   Sold with remainder of new car factory warranty

Did the manufacturer conform the vehicle to warranty?
   The express written warranty
   Nature of the nonconformity
         Single defect not repaired
         Many minor problems: general poor quality
   Substantial impairment test
   Proof of the nonconformity

Did the manufacturer have a reasonable opportunity to repair?
   Dealer as agent of the manufacturer
   Warranty repair history
   The "no problem found" repair attempt
   Effect of statutory presumption

Has the manufacturer been given the requisite notice?

---

[1] A excellent discussion of federally mandated warranties in Section 207(a) of the Clean Air Act appears in Nader, R. and Ditlow, C., "The Lemon Book" pp. 99-100 (3d ed. 1990).

[2] In California, for example, these regulations are found in the Department of Motor Vehicles Regulations Title 13, Div. 3 (Air Resources Board) (Vol. 17, Barclays Law Publishers). Sec. 1960.1.5 mentions the air and fuel metering system, the exhaust gas recirculation system, air injection system, catalyst or thermal reactor system, exhaust system, evaporative emission control system, and related vacuums, switches, sensors and electronic controls.

[3] For a more detailed analysis of implied warranties, see National Consumer Law Center, Consumer Warranty Law Ch. 4 (1997 and Supp.).

[4] 15 U.S.C. §2308(c).

[5] 15 U.S.C. §§2308(a), 2308(b).

[6] Nader, R. and Ditlow, C. "The Lemon Book" (Center for Auto Safety (3d ed. 1990), pp. 11-12.

[7] Schreidel v. American Honda Motor Co., 34 Cal. App. 4th 1242 (1995).

[8] See Chapter 6, Establishing the Facts.

[9] The occasional failure of the car to start has been held not only to be substantial but even "lethal" under some circumstances. Shea v. Volvo Cars of North America, 1991 WL 71109 (E.D. Pa. 1991).

[10] Russo v. Danbury Auto Haus, Inc., 1994 WL 271866 (Conn. Super. Ct. 1994); Williams v. Chrysler Corp., 530 So. 2d 1214 (La. Ct. App. 1988).

[11] Berrie v. Toyota Motor Sales, USA, Inc., 267 N.J. Super. 152, 630 A.2d 1180 (1993).

[12] See Brinkman v. Mazda Motor of America, Inc., 1994 WL 193762 (Ohio Ct. App. 1994).

[13] Zabriskie Chevrolet, Inc. v. Smith, 240 A.2d 195 (N.J. Law Div. 1968).

[14] Baker v. Chrysler Corp., 1993 WL 18099 (E.D. Pa. 1993).

[15] Vultaggio v. General Motors Corporation 429 N.W.2d 93 (Wis. App. 1988).

[16] Krotin v. Porsche Cars North America, Inc. 45 Cal. Rptr. 2d 10 (1995):

> An automobile manufacturer need not read minds to determine which vehicles are defective; it need only read its dealers' service records … [A] manufacturer is capable of becoming aware of every failed repair attempt. Computerized recordkeeping at dealership service departments could easily facilitate this task, even without any direct contact from the consumer to the manufacturer or any request for replacement or reimbursement to the dealership. It is thus apparent that a manufacturer need not be "clairvoyant;" it need only demonstrate more initiative in honoring warranties.

[17] Chmill v. Friendly Ford-Mercury of Janesville, Inc., 144 Wis. 2d 796, 424 N.W.2d 747 (Ct. App. 1988).

[18] See Vultaggio v. General Motors Corp., 145 Wis. 2d 874, 429 N.W.2d 93 (Ct. App. 1988).

[19] Kletzien v. Ford Motor Co., 668 F. Supp. 1225 (E.D. Wis. 1987).

[20] Hartlaub v. Coachmen Industries, Inc., 143 Wis. 2d 791, 422 N.W.2d 869 (Ct. App. 1988); Vultaggio v. General Motors Corp., 145 Wis. 2d 874, 429 N.W.2d 93 (Ct. App. 1988).

[21] Nick v. Toyota Motor Sales, U.S.A., Inc. 466 N.W.2d 215 (Wis. App. 1991); Pecor v. General Motors Corp. 547 A.2d 1364, Muzzy v. Chevrolet Division, General Motors Corporation 571 A.2d 609 (Vt. 1989).

The Manufacturer Strikes Back: Defenses to a Lemon Law Claim

Manufacturers will not give in easily to a lemon law claim. The claim costs them money, and they are in the business of making money, not giving it back to disgruntled consumers. Manufacturer resistance to your lemon law claim started not at the consumer's doorstep, nor at the repair shop threshold, but in the state legislature. Industry did not take the enactment of state lemon laws lying down.

The lobbyists for various automotive groups — manufacturers, importers, dealers associations — are among the most active in the nation. They are ever present in the halls of state legislatures and of Congress. Depending on their influence in your state when your lemon law was enacted, you may find various loopholes and manufacturer defenses enumerated in your state lemon law.

Whether a consumer is facing an informal dispute panel or a lawyer is evaluating a new consumer case for litigation, it is important to determine if any of these exceptions or defenses apply to your case. Preparation is crucial to winning a lemon law claim, and preparation means anticipating the opponent's attack. A checklist of potential defenses should look like this:

- Owner abuse
- Alteration voiding the warranty
- Lack of substantial impairment
- Consumer's continued use of the vehicle
- Lemon law time period
- Statutes of limitation

- Defective statutory notice
- Failure to submit the claim to an informal dispute mechanism (IDM) before going to court.

OWNER ABUSE OF THE VEHICLE

The owner abuse defense is typically found in a statutory provision such as "It shall be an affirmative defense to any claim under this section that a nonconformity is the result of abuse, neglect, or unauthorized modifications or alterations of a motor vehicle by a consumer." Don't put it past a proud manufacturer to try to shift the blame right back to the consumer. Comments like "You just don't know how to drive this car" are particularly infuriating to consumers who have paid a high purchase price for a high performance or luxury vehicle. This is often pure intimidation. And an independent expert is the best person to debunk the defense.

The manufacturer may also argue that an alleged nonconformity was due to the owner's failure to maintain the vehicle. But there may in fact be no connection between a tardy oil change and a condition, for example, involving faulty steering. Particularly where the defects begin to appear in the early months of car ownership — which is a characteristic of many strong lemon law cases — subsequent failure rigidly to adhere to the maintenance schedule may not defeat the lemon law claim.

The manufacturer has the burden of proving owner abuse, because it is an affirmative defense to the claim. The manufacturer will have to prove not only the consumer's abuse, but that this caused the nonconformity of which the consumer now complains. The term "abuse" should be restricted to abnormal, unforeseeable use of the vehicle, not behavior that merely puts the warranty to its intended test.

Thus, BMW did not get very far with this defense in the case of *Jensen v. BMW of North America Inc.*[1] A few weeks after purchasing her BMW, Lisa Jensen was traveling between 55 and 60 miles per hour on a freeway when the car in front of her braked suddenly. Jensen hit her brakes, and the steering wheel began to shake. She felt like "the tires were going to fall off the car." This condition recurred intermittently and was never repaired.

At trial, BMW claimed the brake shimmy was caused by Jensen's "abusive" driving style and her failure to maintain the vehicle. She is undoubtedly not the first female that has been told she just doesn't know how to handle the "Ultimate Driving Machine." But the jury didn't buy it. Perhaps this was because Ms. Jensen's lawyer, Mark Anderson, produced an internal BMW Technical Service Bulletin which alerted dealers about brake problems like the one Jensen experienced. And perhaps the jury was influenced by the fact the evidence established that no one in the BMW dealer service departments had ever told Lisa Jensen there was a problem with her driving style. This is a significant case in demonstrating how the consumer can effectively combat the owner abuse defense, which may simply be invented after the fact by clever lawyers for the manufacturer.

Nevertheless, many consumers are unaware of the manufacturer's defense of improper use, and walk into an informal dispute mechanism (IDM) proceeding unprepared for what can be an insulting or intimidating attack on their driving habits. There are two ways of preparing for this manufacturer attack — one is to review the car's repair history and all service documents, which will include the car's maintenance records. In addition, at the start of a case it may make sense to hire an independent expert who can verify that the owners' driving habits cannot be blamed for the nonconformity.

UNAUTHORIZED ALTERATION

Manufacturers have two arguments that unauthorized alteration defeats a consumer's lemon law rights. First, the typical manufacturer's written warranty states that certain vehicle modifications void the written warranty. If the defect is not covered by a written warranty, then the lemon law may not apply to the defect — although you may still be able argue that an implied warranty covers the defect, and that breach of the implied warranty can be remedied under the lemon law. Moreover, any language limiting a written warranty for such alterations must be both clear and conspicuous.

The second manufacturer argument is based on the lemon law itself. In some states, the lemon law specifies that it does not apply to cases of vehicle modification. The statute will contain such language as that nonconformity "does not include a defect or condition that results from . . . modification, or alteration of the motor vehicle by persons other than the manufacturer or its authorized service agent."

A warranty can be voided not only by alterations performed by the consumer after purchase, but even by the dealer's after-factory alteration of a car before it is offered for sale. In other words, the manufacturer's written warranty may not apply where the consumer purchases a car that already has been modified, even if the consumer is not told that the warranty has been voided. In this case, the consumer should have other claims against the dealer for not disclosing that the car's warranty had been voided, but the lemon law claim against the manufacturer is in jeopardy.

A vehicle collision or installation of a lift kit, van conversion or alarm or sound system may end your lemon law rights.

Examples of modifications that may void a warranty are lift kits, van conversions, or souped-up exhaust modifiers. A lift kit is a sporty after-installed option which raises the vehicle frame to accommodate oversized wheels. Although performed before original delivery to the consumer, such an alteration may cause the manufacturer to deny coverage. Another example is amateur installation of an alarm or sound system that alters the factory wiring and causes a dashboard fire.

Similarly, if the car is involved in an accident (not only when the consumer owns it, but while it is en route to the dealer or on the dealer's lot) the accident can be the cause of a mechanical defect, and the warranty will not cover this defect either. For example, frame damage may cause irreparable suspension or alignment problems. Steering integrity may be permanently impaired by angled impact.

Before bringing a lemon law case, thoroughly assess the vehicle's history and the impact of after-factory additions or other acts and omissions. You don't want a judge or jury to do it for you many months and miles down the road.

LACK OF SUBSTANTIAL IMPAIRMENT

As explained in the previous chapter, the very guts of a lemon law claim is that some nonconformity substantially impairs the use, value or safety of the vehicle to the buyer. Well-prepared consumers will always introduce evidence that the nonconformity did in fact substantially impair the use, value or safety of the vehicle to them. In some states, the lemon law is written so that the consumer must prove that there is a substantial impairment. On the other hand, other state lemon laws specify only that the consumer must show the defect, and that the manufacturer can defend the lemon law claim by stating that the impairment is not substantial. In the latter case, the manufacturer bears the burden of proof to show the defect at issue did not substantially impair the use, value or safety of the goods to the buyer.

Whether an impairment is "substantial" is almost always subjective and debatable, boiling down to a question of fact. A defect that impacts safety is likely to be found to be substantial, even if minor, such as a minor problem with steering or braking. If the defect only affects value, such as a paint problem, the severity of the defect and the number of repairs may be relevant.

CONTINUED USE OF THE CAR

Manufacturers sometimes argue that the consumer continuing to use the lemon vehicle somehow waives the right to bring a lemon law claim, or that the fact proves that there is no substantial impairment. But this defense should be overcome if the consumer presents proper arguments. For example, a leading California case holds that continued use does waive a consumer's lemon law claim. "This consensus is based upon the judicial recognition of practical realities — purchasers of unsatisfactory vehicles may be compelled to continue using them due to the financial burden to securing alternative means of transport for a substantial period of time."[2]

Lemon law claims can take months or years to resolve, and the typical consumer cannot simply park the car or truck and purchase another. In the case of a safety defect, this is of course necessary and creates additional economic hardship, but most lemon law claims are less severe.

In addition, continued use is sometimes due to the servicing dealer's misrepresentation that the vehicle is fixed, when it is not fixed. Thus in *Vista Chevrolet v. Lewis*[3] the consumers prevailed where a General Motors' dealer made a total of ten unsuccessful attempts to cure an intermittent no-start condition, repeatedly assuring the owners that it was fixed, or that one more repair would do the job. The fact that the unreliable car started sometimes did not defeat the claim.

Similarly, Leonard and Ruth Chmill had driven their defective Ford 78,000 miles at the time of trial, even though the pulling problem, which was never repaired, first appeared as Mrs. Chmill was driving home from the dealer after purchase. The court held "We therefore reject the defendant's argument that because the Chmills drove the vehicle for 78,000 miles, there was, as a matter of law, no substantial impairment within the meaning of the lemon law. Each case must be examined on its facts."[4]

Nevertheless, the consumer's extensive continued use may affect the viability of a case, since it can bolster the manufacturer's argument that the car was not substantially impaired as to safety or use. Similarly, after a car has been driven for several years and tens of thousands of miles, the original diminishment in value that the defect causes has been lessened because the car itself is now worth less money. Consequently, such facts must be evaluated by the trier of fact on a case-by-case basis.

THE VARIOUS RESTRICTIONS LABELED "LEMON LAW PERIOD"

There is considerable confusion surrounding a variety of timing limits involving the right to bring a lemon law claim. Most of these are called the "lemon law period" in the statutes, although sometimes they are referred in statutes as the "manufacturer's warranty period," "statutory warranty period," "lemon law rights period," "period of nonconformity" or "motor vehicle quality assurance period." For simplicity of discussion, these will all be referred to here as the "lemon law period."

Lemon laws in some states have arbitrarily short periods of time within which to act.

All lemon laws restrict the consumer's rights in some way. It is important to understand the differences between these terms on a state-by-state basis. You must determine whether the lemon law period in your state specifies a deadline: for the consumer to first report the nonconformity to a dealer for repair; for all repair attempts to have been completed; or for the consumer to give notice of demand for a refund or replacement to the manufacturer. The differences among states as to what the deadline means can result in a consumer recovering in one state, and not in another even under an identical set of facts.

In states which have a lemon law period shorter than the term of the express written warranty (the result of industry lobbying), statutory protection is weak indeed. On the other hand, ambiguity in coverage should always be construed to preserve rather than inhibit automotive consumer protection, which is the basic legislative intent behind every lemon law.

THE STATUTE OF LIMITATIONS

A second, and completely separate, sort of time constraint is the statute of limitations applicable to the court claim for lemon law relief. Every action at law in our civil justice system is bounded by what is euphemistically referred to as a statute of "repose." Actually, it is the sleep of death. The statute of limitations defines that moment in time when the door to legal relief is closed forever. The statute of limitations differs for different civil claims, and the question here is: what is the statute of limitations for automotive express warranty claims involving breach of the duty to repair?[5]

The Magnuson-Moss Warranty Act does not state a statute of limitations and courts accordingly apply the law of the forum state.[6] Only some state lemon laws expressly state a statute of limitations. Those that do are far from uniform. In a handful of states the statute explicitly sets forth a specified time from delivery of the vehicle.[7] The Arkansas lemon law has a statute of limitations of two years from the date the buyer first reports the nonconformity to the manufacturer or dealer.[8] Hawaii pegs the accrual period to the express warranty itself, requiring action to be brought one year after expiration of the warranty.[9]

Where the state lemon law does not separately set forth a statute of limitations, courts have looked to the Uniform Commercial Code which provides a four-year limitations period for breach of warranty.[10] The question is when the four year period begins to accrue. The general rule under Uniform Commercial Code is four years from the date of delivery.[11] But there is an exception to this rule which comes into play here:

> A breach of warranty occurs when tender of delivery is made, *except that where a warranty explicitly*

> *extends to future performance of the goods* and dis-
> covery of the breach must await the time of such
> performance the cause of action accrues when the
> breach is or should have been discovered.[12]

In *Krieger v. Nick Alexander Imports, Inc.,*[13] the buyers purchased a BMW in December, 1983. Within 24 hours, a portion of the drive train fell out. The car was last serviced in May, 1984, and the buyer filed a complaint with AUTOCAP in October, 1984, but apparently rejected the decision and filed a civil suit February 1988. Critical to the decision allowing this case to proceed was the court's holding that the limitations period begins to accrue, not on delivery, but on the date of discovery that the manufacturers' service dealer was unable to repair the vehicle to conform to warranty. "A promise to repair defects that occur during a future period is the very definition of express warranty of future performance," said the court.

This concept of future performance forms an important exception to the general rule that a cause of action for breach of warranty accrues when the goods are delivered to the buyer.[14] Yet courts have not been consistent in applying the exception to automotive warranty cases.

Even when the statute of limitations appears to prevent a case from being brought, this may not be the case. The statute of limitations may be tolled, or extended, for a number of reasons. Equitable tolling occurs when some action of the defendant lulls the consumer into foregoing legal action and the consumer plaintiff is induced to delay bringing suit solely based upon the defendants' act. This is similar to an equitable estoppel claim.[15] The general rule is that in warranty actions, the statute of limitations is "tolled during the period in which the seller of goods promises to repair and makes attempts to repair faulty goods."[16]

The limitations period may also be tolled during the time the matter is under submission to a qualified IDM proceeding.[17] To avoid the effect of the statute of limitations, the complaint itself should set forth the facts which support the doctrine of estoppel. Sound practice is to do this at the earliest opportunity.

CONSUMER'S FAILURE TO GIVE MANUFACTURER NOTICE OF CONSUMER'S DEMAND FOR REFUND/REPLACEMENT

One of the most frustrating things for the consumer is a requirement in some state lemon laws that the aggrieved buyer give notice to the manufacturer before seeking relief under the lemon law. By this time, the consumer has been complaining for months to the dealer and has lost confidence in the vehicle. Often by this time the consumer is for good reason fearful that the vehicle is no longer even safe to drive.

Yet many states spell out additional notice requirements in detail, the most restrictive providing that the manufacturer must be given written notice of the buyback demand by certified mail, sometimes even then with an allowance of one more repair. The consumer has the feeling that enough is enough is enough.

Nevertheless, always send whatever notice is specifically required by law. Even where there is no separate notice requirement in the lemon law, the consumer is well-advised to contact the manufacturer directly in some form demanding replacement or refund loud and clear. The manufacturer cannot later come back and say, "Gee, we thought you'd be happy with just another repair." Once the statutory requirements for repair opportunity have been met, the buyer's demand for a buyback should be unequivocal and to the point. In states which give the consumer the option of a refund or replacement, the notice should state the consumer's choice.

Where the notice requirement is not explicit, it is safest to provide notice, but failure to do so should not be fatal. The manufacturer has certainly received constructive notice of the problem by the multiple repair attempts by its authorized dealers, and that actual notice is not then required:

> [A]n automobile manufacturer need not read minds to determine which vehicles are defective; it need only read its dealers' service records. . . . Computerized recordkeeping at dealership service departments could easily facilitate this task, even without any direct contact from the consumer to the manufacturer or any request for replacement or reimbursement to the dealership. It is thus apparent that a manufacturer need not be "clairvoyant"; it need only demonstrate more initiative in honoring warranties.[18]

FAILURE TO SUBMIT THE CLAIM
TO AN IDM BEFORE GOING TO COURT

A number of state lemon laws require a consumer to submit a claim to an informal dispute mechanism (IDM) before seeking a court ruling on the consumer's entitlement to a refund or replacement remedy. But this is not always the case. Even when a lemon law does require such submission, an exception will apply where the particular mechanism provided by the manufacturer does not meet certain standards. The consumer can also always go to court to seek money damages or some other relief under a legal theory *other* than the state lemon law. The issue of prior resort to an IDM is discussed in more detail in Chapter 7, below.

---

[1] 35 Cal. App. 4th 112, 41 Cal. Rptr. 295 (1995).

[2] Ibrahim v. Ford Motor Co., 214 Cal. App. 3d 878, 263 Cal. Rptr. 64, 76 (1989).

[3] 704 S.W.2d 363 (Tex. Ct. App. 1985).

[4] Chmill v. Friendly Ford-Mercury, 424 N.W.2d 747 (Wis. App. 1988).

[5] The causes of action explained in Chapter 9 may have different statutes of limitations based on contract or tort claims.

[6] Nelligan v. Tom Chaney Motors, Inc. 479 N.E.2d 439 (Ill. App. 1985).

[7] *E.g.*, Md. Com. Law Code Ann. §14-1502(k) (3 years from date of original delivery to consumer); Minn. Stat. Ann. §325F.665(10) (3 years from delivery date, except 6 months after final IDM decision); D.C. Code §40-1307(b) (4 years from delivery).

[8] Ark. Stat. §4-90-416.

[9] Haw. Rev. Stat. §481I-3(j).

[10] Uniform Commercial Code §2-725.

[11] U.C.C. §2-725(1).

[12] U.C.C. §2-725(2) (emphasis added).

[13] 234 Cal. App. 3d 205, 285 Cal. Rptr. 717 (1991).

[14] *See* U.C.C. §2-725(2)

[15] Uniform Commercial Code §2-725(4) and comment thereto.

[16] *See., e.g.*, Aced v. Hobbs Sesack Plumbing Co. 55 Cal. 2d 573 (1961).

[17] Md. Comm. Law Code Ann. §14-1502.

[18] Krotin v. Porsche Cars North America, 38 Cal. App. 4th 294 (1995)

How the Replacement or Refund Remedy Works

The basic remedy of every lemon law is a replacement vehicle or a refund of the purchase price in exchange for return of the defective vehicle. This simple premise gives rise to a host of questions:

- Who gets to choose whether the consumer receives a replacement or a refund?
- How can you return the vehicle when the bank holds a title lien?
- What constitutes a replacement when new models change from year to year?
- What amount must be refunded in a retail sale?
- What must be refunded in a lease?
- What about interest, insurance, and other incidental expenses?
- In what condition must the car be returned to the manufacturer?

WHO GETS TO CHOOSE BETWEEN REPLACEMENT AND REFUND?

Who gets to choose whether the consumer receives a replacement vehicle or a refund will be determined by the exact language of your state lemon law. Dig it out and read it carefully. The following examples demonstrate the variations you should look for.

Washington State provides that the manufacturer "shall, at the option of the consumer, replace or repurchase the new motor vehicle. . . ." The majority of the states adopt this rule that the consumer controls the choice. Close variations on this are found in language which requires that the replacement must be "acceptable to the consumer"[1] or "the consumer may reject any offered replacement and receive instead a refund."[2] Georgia gives the option to the consumer in a purchase transaction, and to the lessor in a lease.[3]

The minority rule is represented by South Carolina's lemon law which states that the manufacturer shall replace the motor vehicle with a comparable motor vehicle, "or at its option" accept return of the vehicle from the consumer and refund to the consumer the full purchase price. Thus, in South Carolina the manufacturer gets to choose.

Utah's statute merely reads: ". . . the manufacturer shall replace the motor vehicle with a comparable new motor vehicle or accept return of the vehicle from the consumer and refund to the consumer the full purchase price. . . ." without designating the party with choice. In this case, the consumer has a good argument that the buyer may choose since the law was designed for consumer protection and thus any doubt is to be resolved in the buyer's favor. It is reasonable to assume that a consumer has lost all confidence in that make and model which failed to conform to the warranty; particularly in the case of a design defect which was never repaired, the consumer may refuse to trade one lemon vehicle for another of the same make and model.

In states which give the option to the manufacturer, a consumer dissatisfied with the manufacturer's decision to opt for a replacement has no recourse but to bring a Uniform Commercial Code (UCC) Article 2 action for revocation of acceptance. If the defect is a design defect inherent in the subject make and model, the consumer should argue, under the good faith obligations of the UCC, that the manufacturer must provide a different but comparable model.

WHAT IS A COMPARABLE VEHICLE?

Suppose you (or your client) bought a 1998 Taurus in June 1998 and tried to get Ford to repair the subject Taurus for fourteen months before making demand for a replacement. It's now September 1999 and Ford had its year 2,000 models on the lot in August. Since the right to replacement or refund is not triggered until after a reasonable opportunity to repair has passed — and with it a considerable passage of time — a comparable new car, i.e. a new 1998 Taurus, is not available. The manufacturer must then do the next best thing, namely, offer a comparable make and model from current stock.

Even if the manufacturer had an old 1998 Taurus sitting around which had never been sold at retail, it would not be comparable, because it is not good for a car to sit idle for years. Therefore, the Taurus owner has a viable argument that under the remedial intent of the statute, she is entitled to a similarly equipped 2000 Taurus.

The word "comparable" does not mean a car with comparable mileage or use at the time of return, but comparable to the vehicle at the time of original purchase.[4] When a consumer gets a replacement vehicle, the consumer need not reimburse the manufacturer for miles driven in the lemon car. One court awarded a replacement of a brand new car even though the defective car had been driven 78,000 miles at the time of return.[5]

Many statutes contain express language that the replacement vehicle must be reasonably acceptable to the consumer.[6] Even if the statute does not say so specifically, the consumer can argue that the legislative intent behind the lemon law requires the replacement to be acceptable.

REPLACEMENT AT NO EXTRA COST

Loathe to give the consumer the better half of a bargain, the dealer or manufacturer immediately starts to wheel and deal again when the consumer agrees to accept a replacement in kind. They will often offer a "trade assist" package whereby credit for the defective car is rolled into the replacement vehicle which they tout as an "upgrade."[7]

Don't put it past a dealer to insert hidden charges for your "free" replacement vehicle.

Wait a minute. By doing this they are attempting to avoid giving you a true replacement at *no charge*. They may be treating your defective lemon as a trade-in and pocketing the profit. If you do choose to accept a true upgrade, your defective lemon should be valued at its comparable new vehicle retail price, not its wholesale trade-in value as a used lemon, and you should do the same kind of thorough research on the upgrade as you would do on the purchase of any new car.

When a manufacturer offers a leased vehicle in replacement for a purchased vehicle, a comparison becomes even more difficult. The monthly payments are *not* a clue to comparable value. If you were paying $500 under a five year retail installment contract, it is not cheaper to pay $450 or even less per month on a 5-year lease because lease payments build no equity, and the consumer owns nothing at the end of the payment period.[8]

A common manufacturer ploy is to charge the consumer a certain amount for the change in vehicles, but not to disclose this to the consumer, but instead to churn the amount into the lease. This will be noticeable if, but only if, the consumer requests an itemization of the gross capitalized cost at the time of the new lease.

When replacing one lease with another lease, it will be important to ascertain not only whether the monthly payments stay the same, but also whether the lease term and purchase option price do not increase, and that no additional payment is made for the new lease. Otherwise, you are paying extra for the replacement lease.

CALCULATING THE REFUND OF THE PURCHASE PRICE

The refund remedy is intended to return lemon car owners to their position before buying the car, less a dollar amount equal to the benefit the consumer received in using the lemon car until it was returned. To achieve this goal, the first thing you do is pull out the contract. Was it a sale or a lease? Was the sale cash or financed? Then you look to the statutory fine print for a description of charges included in the purchase price, and what recoveries are available under a state lemon law. Variations among states are significant, and a chart summarizing state lemon laws in this area is found later in this chapter.

Before you send your first demand letter, you should scrutinize the purchase contract or lease form, gather all documents reflecting taxes, license, registration (including subsequent year's registration) and document fees paid to the state and others. But don't stop there. If state law allows, painstakingly establish evidence of all other indirect damages associated with ownership and use of the defective vehicle. Only then will the consumer be made whole.

From the outset of case evaluation, it is useful to keep at hand a damage calculation sheet. A sample damage calculation sheet is reprinted at Chapter 8, below. This document must conform to the specific provisions of applicable state law, which as describe below, vary somewhat state by state.

SUMMARY OF STATE LEMON LAW REMEDY PROVISIONS

State	Purchase Price	Tax/LIC	Incidental/ Collateral	Lease Explained	Atty. Fees To Prevailing Party consumer only x either party xx	Civil Penalty
Alabama	x	x	x		x	x
Alaska	x				x	
Arizona	x		x			
Arkansas	x		x		x	
California	x	x	x		x	x
Colorado	x	x			xx	
Connecticut	x	x	x		x	
Delaware	x					
DC	x	x			x	
Florida	x		x		x	
Georgia	x		x	x	x	
Hawaii	x		x		x	
Idaho	x		x			x
Illinois	x		x		x	
Indiana	x			x	x	
Iowa	x		x	x	x	
Kansas	x		x			
Kentucky	x	x	x		x	
Louisiana	x		x	x	x	
Maine	x	x	x		x	
Maryland	x	x	x		xx (bad faith)	
Massachusetts	x	x	x		x	
Michigan	x				x	
Minnesota	x	x	x		x	xx (bad faith)
Mississippi	x	x	x		x	
Missouri	x		x		xx (bad faith)	
Montana	x		x		x	
Nebraska	x	x			x	
Nevada	x	x				
New Hampshire	x	x	x	x	x	
New Jersey	x	x	x		x	
New Mexico	x		x		xx (bad faith)	
New York	x	x	x		x	
North Carolina	x	x	x	x	x	x
North Dakota	x					
Ohio	x	x	x			
Oklahoma	x	x				
Oregon	x	x			x (launder only)	
Pennsylvania	x		x		x	
Rhode Island	x	x			x	
South Carolina	x	x			x	
South Dakota	x	x	x		x	
Tennessee	x	x	x	x	x	
Texas	x		x			
Utah	x		x		xx	
Vermont	x	x	x	x	xx	
Virginia	x		x		x	x
Washington	x		x	x	x	x
West Virginia	x	x	x		x	
Wisconsin	x	x	x		x	x
Wyoming	x		x		x	

Refund of What the Consumer
Paid for the Vehicle

Cash purchases present the easiest case as to how to determine a refund. The full purchase price should be refunded, including the base vehicle price, options and accessories on the vehicle at the time of sale, sales tax and registration fees. The purchase price includes not only hard add-ons, such as sound systems or upgraded wheels, but soft add-ons as well, such as undercoating, document and dealer preparation, transportation, extended warranties and service contracts.

The full purchase price includes the amount paid in cash and also any amount paid via a trade-in. The trade-in is very much a part of the consideration which the consumer paid for the vehicle. That is, the full purchase price to be refunded is not the price after the trade-in credit has been deducted, but the total cost of the car, before the trade-in credit is deducted.

In the case of a retail installment sale, the refundable purchase price is calculated the same way, despite the fact that the consumer may not be out-of-pocket that amount because one must look to the consumer's total obligation. The actual payment of this amount will be "made to the consumer and lienholder as their interests may appear," but first it is necessary to calculate the total obligation of the manufacturer.

In a lease, the matter gets more complicated, particularly in pre-1998 leases which failed to disclose the capitalized cost of the vehicle. See the discussion as to leased vehicles later in this chapter.

Incidental Charges

The purchase price which must be refunded generally includes charges that were "incidental" to the purchase. These include government charges, such as taxes, registration, title and documentary fees, finance charges and insurance premiums.[9]

Sometimes the basis for such incidental charges is explicit in the state lemon law. For example, the Washington State lemon law defines allowable collateral charges as "any sales-related charges, including but not limited to sales tax, arbitration service fees, registration fees, title fees, finance charges, insurance costs, transportation charges, dealer preparation or any other charges for service contracts, undercoating, rust proofing or factory installed options."[10] The California lemon law lists as recoverable costs reasonable repair, towing and rental car costs.[11]

Your refund should include everything you paid for the car and anything else related to the car purchase.

Other times, the lemon law provides for such a refund, but only in general terms. Some laws speak in terms of "collateral" charges, others in terms of "incidental" damages and "pecuniary loss." In interpreting these general terms, statutes such as the Washington lemon law may prove helpful in indicating what is in fact an incidental charge. Not only should finance charges be reimbursed, but any charges related to the extension of credit, such as credit insurance.[12]

Emotional Distress and Substitute Transportation

Do not count on a manufacturer or an IDM awarding a car owner any compensation for aggravation, pain and suffering, or even for substitute transportation caused by the nightmare of owning a lemon vehicle. Moreover, even if you pursue the case in court, your chance of recovering such damages is not great. Courts in many states remain reluctant to extend the scope of relief under lemon laws to emotional distress damages[13] or loss of use.[14]

Nevertheless, this is not uniformly the case. The West Virginia lemon law is the only one to explicitly mention that a consumer, in a civil action, can recover damages for the cost of repairs, loss of use, annoyance, inconvenience, and replacement transportation during any service period.[15] But, where a court will not award damages relating to pain and suffering or lost use of a car under a state lemon law, it might do so based on a simple breach of warranty claim under the Uniform Commercial Code (UCC), a law in effect in every state but Louisiana. The UCC provides one possible bases to award pain and suffering damages, and another to award both pain and suffering and lost use of the vehicle damages.

The first is that damages can be awarded under the UCC for "injury to the person . . . proximately resulting from any breach of warranty."[16] Thus an Alabama appeals court has upheld $8,000 in emotional distress damages under the UCC in a case of a lemon vehicle, construing the words "injury to the person" as including mental anguish. The mental anguish was proximately related to the car defects since purchase of a new motor vehicle is so tied to matters of mental concern that a breach of warranty obligations may reasonably result in mental suffering.[17]

The second basis under the UCC to recover lost use of the vehicle and pain and suffering damages is that a buyer can recover "consequential damages" for "any loss resulting from general or particular requirements and needs of which the seller at the time of contracting had reason to know. . . ."[18] The Minnesota case of *Jacobs v. Rosemont Dodge/Winnebago South*,[19] concerning a defective motorhome, is instructive. It upheld an award of UCC emotional distress damages under this second basis, reasoning that the general needs and requirements of the buyers included the need "to have confidence that their motorhome was safe and dependable for driving." This need is foreseeable to the seller or manufacturer, inherent in the very nature of the warranty sold with the new motor vehicle. Failure to satisfy this statutorily protected and foreseeable need exposes manufacturer\warrantors to damages for the buyer's mental distress in having to drive the defective vehicle when the evidence shows that such harm in fact occurred.

These courts views on the emotional distress that is directly caused by lemon vehicles was well summarized in a statement by California Assemblyman William Lockyer, in proposing amendments in 1979 to strengthen the California Lemon law:

> The Committee . . . convenes today to study problems of significant and sometimes *emotional concern* to California consumers - the problems that arise in the sale of new and used cars. . . . With incredible distances and very little mass transit, ownership or access to a car is essential. We pay a price, however, for the mobility we enjoy, not the least of which is the *fear and loathing* we experience when making a significant financial commitment to purchase an auto. Everyone in the room knows the special trauma I'm referring to. . . . There seems to be *significant evidence that the trauma associated*

with car purchases is caused by more than just under-
standable jitters. . . . Purchasers of new cars occasion-
ally find themselves stuck with a lemon, merchandise
that is fundamentally so defective as to be func-
tionally useless.[20]

OFFSET FOR BUYER'S
CONTINUED USE

When a vehicle is returned under a state lemon law, and the owner, instead
of a replacement, receives a refund, nearly every lemon law allows the manufacturer to deduct from the refund an equitable offset for the consumers'
use of the vehicle. The consumer's use is usually measured only from the
date of delivery up to the date of the first repair attempt which gave rise to
the nonconformity.

For example, if the nonconformity was a faulty transmission for which a
Chrysler Caravan was taken in for repair four times, but not beginning until
the Caravan had 3,269 miles on its odometer, Chrysler would be entitled to
deduct an offset for the consumer's use of the Caravan for 3,269 miles. On
the other hand, if "general poor quality" of the vehicle was the nonconformity for which a Ford Taurus was taken into the shop for thirty-one days in
the first year beginning with a repair for electrical defects at 125 miles, Ford
would have to use the 125 mileage figure for its offset calculation.

A typical formula multiplies the vehicle's purchase price by a fraction
having as its denominator 100,000 or 120,000 and having as its numera-
tor the number of miles the vehicle traveled prior to the time the buyer first
delivered the vehicle to the repair shop. In the Caravan example, if the
Caravan cost $25,000 and a statute used 100,000 in the denominator, the
offset would be .03269 times $25,000, or $817.25.

Other state lemon laws refer to some portion of use allowances set by the
Internal Revenue Service, and still others merely allow an offset for "reasonable" use. The full IRS allowance exceeds the reasonable amount
because it is inflated by such things as gasoline. On the other hand, if the
statute does not specifically provide for an offset, the manufacturer bears
the burden of proof to establish that the consumer was unjustly enriched,
and the failure to meet that burden bars the offset.[21]

MANUFACTURER ATTEMPTS TO RE-COMPUTE
THE ORIGINAL PURCHASE PRICE:
RE-VALUING THE ORIGINAL TRADE IN

Ever alert to ways to reduce its liability under the lemon law, the auto industry has launched a new challenge at the meaning of "purchase price." It argues that the refund owed the consumer should be based not on the lemon's actual purchase price, but on a price adjusted downward to reflect the fact that the dealer inflated both the lemon's purchase price and the consumer's original trade-in allowance.

This issue all starts with the fact that many consumer trade-ins have "negative equity," meaning that they are worth less than the amount the consumer still owes on the trade in. Some industry insiders indicate that 30% of vehicle trade-ins involve negative equity. Negative equity is also discussed at Chapters 7 and 10, below.

Nevertheless, consumers do not like to be told that they will have to pay money to have the dealer take their trade-in off their hands. Moreover, dealers could have trouble with their financiers and with state law requirements if they were to take vehicles in trade and charge the consumer negative equity.

The solution is simple — the dealer gives the consumer a good deal on the trade-in, usually valuing it equal to the outstanding loan on that car. The consumer is happy just to be rid of an old car. The dealer hopes to make up for its generosity through increasing the new vehicle's purchase price and through the sale of options, insurance, and financing.

Down the line, where a new car or truck was purchased with a trade-in where the consumer got a good deal, and that new car or truck turns out to be a lemon, some manufacturers balk at paying restitution for the full purchase price. That price, they claim, was inflated to make up for the good deal on the trade-in. The real purchase price should be lowered to reflect a more accurate value for the trade-in.

Take an example where a trade-in had a negative equity of $2,000, but the dealer called it a wash. The dealer sells the car for $20,000, and the net amount the consumer owes is $20,000. The manufacturer argues that this transaction should be retroactively re-written as a negative $2,000 for the trade-in and $18,000 for the car. The net amount the consumer would owe is still $20,000. The difference is that the manufacturer wants to rewrite the purchase agreement so that it refunds the consumer $18,000, instead of $20,000.

There are both legal and equitable problems with the manufacturers' position,[22] not the least of which is the fact that the consumer was never told or agreed to what the amount of negative equity was, and the manufacturer cannot really prove what that amount is. These figures are malleable in negotiation and are unlikely to appear on the contract face.

No state lemon law specifically addresses the issue of negative equity, but all are intended to make the consumer whole and should be liberally construed to that end. Moreover, certain lemon law statutes expressly provide for recovery of the amount "paid or payable."[23]

The manufacturers' argument that the refund of negative equity would be a windfall to the consumer and unfair to the manufacturer also falls short of the mark. The purpose of creating the negative equity in the first place was for the manufacturer's sales dealer to clinch the deal, make the sale, move the goods. In allowing the practice to proceed, the manufacturers are in essence taking a calculated risk that the vehicle will conform to warranty. The manufacturers have access to their dealers' sales figures on a regular basis and know what their cars are selling for. If the manufacturer wants to prohibit the practice, or else to limit its own risk, the manufacturer is in the best position to control this activity through terms of its dealer agreements.

Instead, the dealer and manufacturer encourage the negative trade practices to grease the wheels of the trade cycle. The simple truth is many consumers would not otherwise purchase a new car until they were able to crawl out from under their existing debt.

CALCULATING A REFUND
FOR LEASED VEHICLES

Refunds for leased vehicles are complicated because the lessor, not the consumer bought the car and owns it. The consumer may have a purchase option, but certainly does not want to exercise that for the lemon vehicle. To make the consumer whole, the manufacturer would have to pay for what the consumer has already paid to date — the consumer's trade-in, down payment, initial payments at lease signing, plus all monthly lease payments made to date. An offset for use may be appropriate.

In addition, the consumer will owe the lessor a sizeable early termination penalty when the lease is terminated prematurely. To be made whole, the manufacturer will have to pay the consumer for this early termination penalty or pay the lessor enough so that it waives this penalty. In addition, to get the car back from the lessor, the manufacturer will have to pay the lessor enough so that the lessor feels itself made whole as well.

When returning a leased lemon, make sure you have no obligation for the early termination penalty!

Unfortunately, many state lemon laws are not clear as to the exact method by which a refund should be computed in the case of a lease. (In a few states, the lemon law will not even apply to leases. See Chapter 1, above.) A number of state lemon laws do provide guidance, though. For example, Vermont sets forth specific separate amounts to be refunded to the lessee and to the lessor, and states that the lessee does not owe the lessor for any early termination penalty.[24] In other states, when arguing that the consumer should recover all payments made to date and be relieved of any early termination obligation, it may prove helpful to point to the formulas found in Vermont and other states.[25] The goal should be to clear the slate of any future obligation for the lessee and make the lessee whole for all amounts paid to date.

CAR OWNER'S OBLIGATION TO RETURN THE VEHICLE

The flip side of the consumer remedy of refund or replacement is that the consumer must give the lemon car back to the manufacturer. While a consumer will like nothing better than to get rid of a lemon vehicle, a number of problems may arise in the delivery of that vehicle back to the manufacturer. The manufacturer may refuse to accept the car if it is in unsatisfactory condition; the vehicle may not be movable, and the consumer may not have clear title to the vehicle, and so cannot transfer it to the manufacturer.

Condition of the Vehicle

Manufacturers may object to a refund or replacement where they claim that the vehicle the consumer is returning is not in satisfactory condition. You should assess objectively the vehicle's condition, and even clean or detail it as a prudent purchaser would prepare a trade-in. If there are problems attributable to the nonconformity itself (such as water damage in the passenger compartment due to irreparable leaks), the manufacturer should not be able to object, particularly if you have notified the manufacturer about these problems from the beginning of the dispute. But unrelated dents, dings and dirt can wreak havoc with a good settlement. Check it out beforehand and be candid about these things in negotiating settlement value. More than once, the consumer is stuck at the dealership with a zone representative refusing to accept a damaged car.

The worst case is when the vehicle is in an accident after the consumer has served demand for reimbursement or replacement. If the accident is caused in whole or in part by the nonconformity complained of, the manufacturer has no claim to quibble about return of damaged merchandise. On the other hand, unrelated accidents should be disclosed with candor, honesty and a willingness to accept a lesser settlement sum. This problem should be dealt with in the initial client interview both as to any past accident history and as to the risk of future driving, pending outcome of the case.

Return of Vehicles that Cannot Operate

It is not unusual for the vehicle to be completely inoperable by the time settlement occurs. Perhaps the Cadillac was towed home the last time it stalled in traffic; perhaps the Jeep Wagoneer has been so long in dispute the battery is dead; perhaps the Ford Bronco which rolled over is unsafe to drive. Demand for the right remedy should include means of returning the vehicle in these difficult circumstances, identify an acceptable delivery destination, and set forth which party will bear responsibility for the towing and delivery charges. These can be significant in motorhome cases, where the vehicle is incapable of being driven under its own power and the factory is in Indiana.

Reconveyance of Good Title

Possession may be "nine-tenths of the law," but it is not everything. You cannot return a lemon vehicle to the manufacturer without also providing the manufacturer with the car's title. This is not so simple where there is a car loan or lease involved. A lender must be paid off for it to remove its lien from the car's title,[26] and a lessor also must be satisfied for it to convey its title to the manufacturer.

These problems are usually solved with the manufacturer's refund check going to both the consumer and lender/lessor. Many states specifically provide that the refund shall be made to the "consumer, lessor or lienholder, if any, as their interests may appear."[27] The lender or lessor should be apprised of the lemon law dispute and be included in negotiations. Where financing or the lease was arranged for by the dealer, you may even want to name the lender or lessor as a defendant in any lemon law litigation, as described in more detail at Chapter 8, below. Even a jury verdict is a Pyrrhic victory if it fails to absolve the consumer of full liability on the outstanding debt.

If the lender has to be paid off, make sure you keep track of the pay-off figure. From the time you make a demand for settlement to the time it is accepted the payoff may change radically.

A large percentage of vehicles are financed via the manufacturer's own captive finance company. General Motors Acceptance Corporation holds title to the Geo in your garage; or Ford Motor Credit Corporation keeps the "pink slip" to your Taurus. It is a mistake to assume informality in the internal financial affairs of the related companies. Before you sign the release, make sure you have some signed statement or other evidence that the manufacturer actually did satisfy the lien with its sister corporation, and that all appropriate title documents were transferred back to the manufacturer in resolution of your claim.

---

[1] Compare the legislative intent section of Vt. Stat. Ann. tit. 9 §4170 with the replacement/refund provision at §4172(e).

[2] Me. Rev. Stat. Ann. §1163(2).

[3] Ga. Code Ann. §§10-1-784(a)(1), (2).

[4] Washington's statute is very specific: "The replacement motor vehicle shall be identical or reasonably equivalent to the motor vehicle to be replaced as the motor vehicle to be replaced existed at the time of original purchase or lease, including any service contract, undercoating, rustproofing, and factory or dealer installed options." Wash. Rev. Code Ann. §19.118.041(1)(a).

[5] Chmill v. Friendly Ford Mercury of Janesville, Inc., 144 Wis. 2d 796, 424 N.W.2d 747 (Ct. App. 1988).

[6] *See* Vt. Stat. Ann. tit. 9 §4170 ("The legislature finds and declares that manufacturers . . . should be required to provide in as expeditious a manner as possible a refund of the consumer's purchase price . . . or a replacement vehicle that is acceptable to the consumer whenever the manufacturer is unable to make the vehicle conform with its applicable warranty.").

[7] "Trade assist" is a loosely defined term which also provides a way for the manufacturer to claim this was not a return under the lemon law at all and thus exempt from resale disclosure requirements. *See* Chapter 12, *infra*.

[8] It is this author's opinion that Remar Sutton's book "Don't Get Taken Every Time" is required reading for any new car buyer and if you didn't read it the first time around, read it before accepting any replacement vehicle to which you are required to add cash. You should also check prices and updated information on the subject make and model by consulting Jack Gillis' *New Car Book* and *Consumer Reports*.

[9] *See e.g.*, Nick v. Toyota Motor Sales Inc. (1991) 160 Wis. 2d 373, 466 N.W.2d 215 (in addition to purchase price, down payment and trade-in, tax and license, plaintiffs entitled to finance charges of $4,549.82); Muzzy v. Chevrolet Division, General Motors Corp. 571 A.2d 609 (Vt. 1989) (credit insurance premiums allowed).

[10] Wash. Rev. Code Ann. §19.118.021(2).

[11] Cal. Civ. Code §1793.2(d)(2)(B).

[12] Muzzy v. Chevrolet Division, General Motors Corp. 571 A.2d 609 (Vt. 1989).

[13] Kwan v. Mercedes Benz of North America, 23 Cal. App 4th 174, 28 Cal. Rptr. 2d 371 (1994).

[14] Bishop v. Hyundai of North America, 44 Cal. App. 4th 750 (1996).

[15] W. Va. Code §46A-6A-4(b).

[16] U.C.C. §2-715(b).

[17] Volkswagen of America, Inc. v. Dillard, 579 So. 2d 1301 (Ala. 1991).

[18] U.C.C. §2-715(2).

[19] Jacobs v. Rosemont Dodge/Winnebago South, 310 N.W.2d 71 (Minn. 1981).

[20] The California Assembly Labor, Employment, and Consumer Affairs Committee Hearing on Consumer Protection in the Sale of New and Used Cars (Dec. 14-15, 1979), Committee Minutes, p. 1 [emphasis supplied].

[21] Page v. Chrysler Corp., 1996 WL 724768 (Ohio App.1996).

[22] Staff counsel for the California Department of Consumer Affairs, John Lamb, has written a 12-page legal memorandum on this subject, dated April 10, 1997, to Peter Brightbill, Chief of the California Department of Consumer Affairs Arbitration Review Program. Lamb concludes that negative equity is "part of the actual price *payable* by the buyer, and that the manufacturer therefore *is* required to reimburse it as part of a repurchase decision . . . that reimbursing 'negative equity' does not unjustly enrich the buyer and is not unfair to the manufacturer." [Original emphasis.] The memorandum further concludes that the very practice of rolling over negative equity "is probably unlawful and may not create and enforceable obligation against the buyer to repay the 'negative equity' amount." Letters on file with the author.

[23] Cal. Civil Code §1793.2(d)(2)(B).

[24] Vt. Stat. Ann. tit. 9 §4172(i).

[25] *See, e.g.*, Ark. Code Ann. §4-90-407(b); Ga. Code Ann. §10-1-784(a)(2); Ind. Code §24-5-133-11.5(a); Iowa Code Ann. §322G.4(2) (no early termination penalty shall be assessed); La. Rev. Stat. Ann. §51:1944(B); N.H. Admin. Code §357-D:3(IX); N.C. Gen. Stat. §20-351.3(b); Tenn. Code Ann. §55-24-204; Wash. Rev. Code Ann. §19.118.041(1)(b).

[26] Laws regarding titles vary by state. Forty states are "title holding," meaning the lender keeps physical possession of the title document until the car is paid off; the other ten are "non-title holding," meaning the buyer keeps physical possession of the title document (Arizona, Kansas, Kentucky, Maryland, Michigan, Minnesota, Montana, New York, Oklahoma, Wisconsin), but the lien is still marked on the title.

[27] *See* Conn. Gen. Stat. Ann. §42-179(d).

– 5 –

What Consumers and Their Lawyers Should Know About Each Other

DO YOU NEED A LAWYER?

The prior chapters explain a consumer's lemon law rights. Unfortunately, manufacturers are not keen on providing consumers with new cars or refunds, even when the lemon law indicates that they should. In most cases, you will have to fight for your rights, either before a manufacturer's informal dispute mechanism (IDM) or in court, or both.

If you decide to fight for your rights, your first question will be "do I need an attorney?" If you are preparing to appear before an IDM, you do not have to have an attorney appear for you. Procedures are informal and you can appear for yourself.

On the other hand, even if an attorney does not *appear* for you at the IDM, an attorney's help in *preparing* the case for IDM may increase your chance of success enough to make a modest fee worthwhile. Some lemon laws also provide that the manufacturer must reimburse the consumer for the consumer's attorney fees where the consumer prevails at IDM. So hiring an attorney may not really cost you anything. This may be the first question you want to ask.

Unlike informal hearings, you should hire a lawyer if you are going to press your lemon law claim in court. Labyrinthine local rules of procedure can be daunting to the layman representing himself. It is very easy for a consumer to lose because a technical procedural requirement is not met, even when the consumer's case on the merits is a clear winner.

HOW TO FIND A LAWYER

Finding the right attorney to handle an automotive dispute is not a simple task. This is not a friendly province for the generalist lawyer. You might want to interview more than one lawyer before signing a fee agreement.

One of the best sources nationwide for finding a lemon law lawyer is the Center for Auto Safety, which maintains a list of lawyers throughout the country who handle car defect litigation.[1] The National Association of Consumer Advocates also has members who handle lemon law claims.[2]

Many county and local bar associations have a lawyer referral system which assigns cases from a list of available attorneys in various categories. The media will not usually give referrals or recommendations, but a local consumer reporter or broadcast producer may *identify* lawyers who have recently appeared on newscasts concerning automotive defects and deceptive practices.

The Internet is an increasingly well travelled road for referrals, and a consumer advocate who seeks to educate on the Internet may be the best litigator or negotiator on your behalf. *See* Chapter 6, *infra*, Establishing the Facts. Finally, the attorney yellow page section of many phone books is now broken down into practice sections.

HOW TO GET READY TO MEET WITH AN ATTORNEY

The discussion which follows is designed not only to help you win your lemon law claim, but to save you and your lawyer time. In the legal context, time is money.

Find out in advance whether there will be a charge for the initial interview and exactly what the lawyer expects you to bring. To maximize the use of time at that interview, fill out the client intake form provided later in this chapter, whether or not the lawyer asks you to do so. Study and bring to the interview the checklist which appears at Chapter 2, above, summarizing the elements of the claim. Also bring the damage calculation sheet, included in Chapter 8, below. You may also want to bring this book for the lawyer to use as a time-saving resource.

You should also take to the interview as many of the following documents as you can locate:

- The warranty(ies) which are sometimes found in the owner's manual;

- The purchase or lease contract;
- All documents concerning your trade-in, if any;
- All documents which were provided to you at the time of signing the contract, including any due bills, waivers, notices, odometer statements, disclosures, transit documents;
- The window sticker;
- Title and registration;
- Car insurance documents;
- Records of all payments to the dealer, bank, registration, insurance;
- Records of all payments for un-reimbursed repairs, tow charges, rental cars for alternative transportation;
- Advertisements you have seen for the vehicle at any time;
- Repair orders;
- Letters you wrote to the dealer or manufacturer;
- Letters the dealer or manufacturer wrote to you;
- Recall notices;
- Phone memos or calls to and from you and the dealer or manufacturer;
- Calendars which note repair shop appointments;
- Written notes of phone calls or meetings with service personnel or zone representatives;
- News articles about the subject vehicle or any related defects.

Put the repair orders and correspondence in chronological order. Your good organization will save money in lawyer's time and make it easier for the lawyer to evaluate your claim.

WHAT YOU SHOULD ASK YOUR LAWYER

At the interview, find out whether the lawyer has any experience representing consumers in general and lemon law claims in particular. Ask whether the lawyer will take your case on a contingent fee basis or expect monthly payments for work done on an hourly basis.[3] Many lemon laws state that the manufacturer must pay the consumer's attorney fees if the consumer prevails. This may be enough of an incentive for a lawyer to take your case, even if you are unable to pay an attorney very much. However, you should clarify with your attorney what you will owe for fees and costs both if you win and if you lose. For example, you should know whether you will have to pay the other side's costs if you lose.

These things should be set forth in a written fee agreement which you both sign. If the lawyer hands you a fee contract you do not understand, make sure the lawyer explains it to you in detail. If you have the feeling the lawyer is just another car salesman, that is probably not the lawyer for you.

Next, find out what that lawyer plans to do for you. Discuss your expectations. A lawyer is not a therapist. Nor should you expect your lawyer to bring General Motors to its knees over a lemon law claim. A review of Chapter Four will explain the potential recovery you can seek under a lemon law. Go over the damage calculation sheet together, noting that it is a sample and all categories of recovery are not available in every state.

Be candid about your expectations. Recognize that in settlement you may have to compromise. You will have to consider what is your own bottom line. Talk to the lawyer about what recovery you think would satisfy you and what your lawyer thinks you will have to do to reach that point.

Discuss timing and procedure with your lawyer. You should know that a letter-writing campaign, even by a lawyer, is generally useless, unless you file an IDM claim or a court complaint to back it up. Too many lawyers are happy to charge a fee for ineffective threatening letters; you should make sure the lawyer you select is prepared to follow-up with litigation if a letter demand gets no result.

Ask the lawyer to evaluate whether your case is strong enough right now to demand your replacement or reimbursement rights, or whether you should give the manufacturer further opportunity to repair. If you have a present right to demand a replacement or reimbursement, a lawyer who vacillates by accepting further repairs may actually injure your ultimate claim.

If the first step is a rescission letter or statutory notice, discuss with your lawyer how soon your lawyer will follow-up with IDM or legal action. Ask what deadlines the lemon law places on you. If you do not act by a certain date, do you lose any of your legal rights? Let your attorney know about your personal need for continued use of the vehicle during the period of resolution, if that is a financial issue for you.

THE LAWYER'S DECISION
ABOUT TAKING ON A CLIENT

The first question for an attorney is: can you work with *this* client to win *this* case? In order to answer that question, make sure the client comes to the initial interview as prepared as possible. Read the preceding section about what a prepared consumer should bring when first meeting with an attorney. For example, ask the consumer to complete the client intake form and send it to your office *before* the appointment.

The attorney should then prepare a potential client file even before the consumer walks in the door. To do this, use the client intake form found in this chapter. Also use the checklist of the elements of a lemon law claim, found in Chapter 2, above. If you do not take the case, you can terminate this file with a closure letter declining the matter. On the other hand, these simple documents will provide you a factual skeleton for opening the case.

In the correspondence scheduling your initial appointment, specifically request that the potential client bring to the interview all of the documents listed earlier in this chapter. If you decide to take the case, have copies made of every document to send home with the client and, except for the warranty and registration, keep the originals for your office file.

Since one of the reasons for the initial client interview is to assess the credibility of the client, discussing the documents will give you the basis for evaluating this person as your primary witness. While many consumers suffer from the inability to articulate automotive concerns, honesty and a positive attitude are important no matter how angry and upset the client is. All lemon owners are frustrated by the time they come to a lawyer, but the obnoxious know-it-all of questionable integrity is not a client you want, no matter how many repair orders are tossed on your desk.

Also try to have the potential client park the vehicle at issue just outside your office. If the complained of defect is particularly subjective, like an engine noise, or passenger compartment fumes, your own impression of the car and the defect will be valuable. You may also want to have the vehicle inspected by an independent expert *before* you agree to take the case.

One important act you must perform before agreeing to accept each and every lemon law case should be a preliminary repair chronology drawn up from the repair orders. Sometimes the expert will do this as part of his report. While this chronology may be supplemented in later discovery, it is essential to focus immediately on the warranty history of the subject

CLIENT INTAKE FORM

BACKGROUND INFORMATION

Name ☐ Mr. ☐ Mrs.				Date	Assigned to

Address				Home Phone ( )	Work Phone ( )

City		State	Zip	Fax ( )	Pager ( )

Year	Make	Purchase Date	☐ New

☐ Used

Model	Current Mileage	☐ Used With Mfg. Warranty

☐ Used With Dealer Warranty

Selling Dealer	Servicing Dealer	☐ Used As Is

☐ Service Contract

Purchase Price With Tax & License	☐ Financed With ☐ Leased With	☐ Retail Buy Back

MAIN UNRESOLVED PROBLEMS

SUMMARY HISTORY

Mileage at First Repair	No. of Visits	Total Days in Shop	Is the Vehicle Useable Now ☐ Yes ☐ No	Demand Refund or Replacement ☐ Yes ☐ No

CONTACTS WITH MANUFACTURER

Verbal   Written

REFERRED BY

☐ Yellow Pages ☐ Former Client DETAIL
☐ Attorney ☐ Media

DISPOSITION

☐ Appointment Made ☐ Client to Mail Docs. ☐ Declined on Phone ☐ Referred to Small Claims vehicle. This will also form the basis of a well-pleaded complaint. A sample form for a repair chronology is included below.

At this point, avoid the temptation to interpret the repair orders. That is, if the service documents report a transmission complaint one time and a clutch problem the next, record it as written. If they are related, your expert

REPAIR CHRONOLOGY

Name: Colleen McCullaugh
Auto: 1996 BMW 318i Convertible
Date of Purchase: 3/30/96

Visit	Date	Mileage	Customer Concern	Repair Attempt	Days In
1.	2.24.96	80	Redelivery Inspection (PDI)	Performed inspection and report required repairs to sales manager.	
			Found rear brake pads defective.	Replaced rear brake pads.	
2.	4.11.96	380	Ignition key would not come out of ignition.	Install SOP; ignition assembly has internal fault; replaced lock cylinder assembly.	3
			Check engine light came on.	Could not duplicate.	
3.	4.23.96	510	Windshield has very bad water leak.	Cannot re-seal windshield; sublet for windshield replacement.	2
			Windshield wiper blades malfunction.	Wiper rubber inserts warped. Replaced windshield wiper inserts.	
4.	6.05.96	951	Glove compartment will not latch.	Replace latch mechanism.	1
			Brakes squeak when applied, gets louder as vehicle slows.	Installed new front brake pads.	
5.	1.01.96	11,011	Brakes squeak loudly.	Inspected brake system; mild squeaking upon brake apply normal at this time.	3
			Rear windows in-op at this time (when hot out).	Performed function test for rear windows; normal operation at this time.	
			Transmission clunks when taking off from stop.	Upon inspection, found front engine mounts loose; re-torqued mounts; inspected transfer gearbox and output shaft; both ok; some clunking noise is normal due to transfer control box design.	
			Glove compartment will not latch.	SOP part for glove compartment latch assembly.	
			Rattle comes out of center of dash; if area above radio is pressed rattle stops.	Re-secured loose radio chassis (rattling).	
			Passenger door squeaks.	Lubricated all doors.	
6.	3.18.97	18,570	Rear window inop at times.	Checked critical grounds; removed center window switch assembly, Glove compartment cubby assembly and checked wiring connectors to rear windows; remove and repair both rear door panels, checked for proper window operations and wiring; removed glove box to repair connector; SOP ECU.	5
			Glove compartment latch is broken.	Installed SOP Glove compartment latch.	
			Re-install left rear bumper tip.	Replaced left-rear bumper end cap and side bulb.	
			Front stub axle seals leaking.	Replaced leaking left front and rear stub axle seals.	

Visit	Date	Mileage	Customer Concern	Repair Attempt	Days In
			Engine leaking oil.	Diagnosed valve cover gaskets leaking oil; replaced valve cover gaskets; resealed oil filler neck and crankcase tube.	
7.	6.10.97	19,116	Power windows, radio, and misc. other electrical parts are in-op and radio has no prompt for CD.	Removed passenger side under dash panel, removed 5 head junctions and found 17 corroded wires; removed and reassembled all wires by splicing them; ordered water shield.	5
			Remote alarm is difficult to activate.	Installed new battery for remote; reprogrammed remote; removed passenger panel side and re-connected antenna lead and remote antenna.	
			Service engine light comes on.	No work done at this time.	
			Re-install cover on rear tail light.	Replaced tail light lamp guard.	
8.	10.20.97	26,675	Water leaks above windshield.	Installed water deflector kit.	2
			Install right rear tail light guard part behind driver's seat.	Straightened lamp guard, repaired hole and installed new "nutsert."	
9.	11.26.97	28,307	Vehicle idles rough.	Replaced ignition cap, rotor and wires, set base idle.	5
			Spark plugs malfunction.	Replaced spark plugs.	
			Install latch for Glove compartment.	Installed.	
10.	12.22.97	30,108	Rear window intermittently inop.	Install SOP: replaced rear window ECU.	3
11.	1.27.98	31,432	Turn off service engine light.	Light turned off.	4
			Front headlight is full of water.	Replaced front headlamp and bulb.	
			Install yellow fog lights with separate on/off switch if possible.	Part not available.	
			Replace broken fog light.	Replaced fog lights.	
			Water leaks in through top of windshield at top.	Sublet to Classic Auto/Teeters for repair; rust on "A" pillar result of original problem with windshield.	
12.	2.9.98	33,566	Car loses power while driving.	Pulled codes and tested relevant systems, found fuel pump relay not switching, 02 sensor heater circuit on, replaced relay.	4
13.	5.4.98	36,572	Vehicle chugs and dies when low on gas, idles rough and loud.	Road test, unable to duplicate, suspect fuel filter, replaced fuel filter, clogged at outlet, brown fluid and dirt came out.	1
			Right headlamp when park lights are turned on and tail works intermittently.	Replaced left parking bump in headlamp, replaced right rear tail light bulbs.	
			Squeak noise out of right front when turning right.	Unable to duplicate.	
			Squeak noise out of steering column when cold.	Unable to duplicate.	
14.	7.19.98	39,823	Steering not responsive.	Exam revealed power steering fluid Power leak. steering hose clamps defective, replaced.	5
			Running rough.	No problem found at this time.	
			Glove box latch broken.	SOP latch.	

TOTAL 43

can make the appropriate connections or deposition questioning can draw the connection out of the service manager as the case proceeds.

Take a hard look at this repair chronology when completed. This is the profile of the claim. Look at its patterns and aberrations. Do the repairs suggest any pre-sale damage? Premature tire wear coupled with multiple realignments, for example, might imply frame damage. What appears to be a recurring paint problem might be covering up Bondo repairs. Pre-sale accidents and transit damage are surprisingly common, even when cars are sold as "new." Such scrutiny may give you clues to dealer fraud or deceptive practices, as well as a mere lemon law claim. See Chapter 10, below, for discussion of these related causes of action.

THE FEE AGREEMENT WITH THE CLIENT

An attorney should have a written fee agreement with the client. Whether or not the fee agreement is based on a contingent fee arrangement, there should be a scheduled hourly rate agreed upon.[4] In fee shifting litigation, the reasonableness of attorneys fees will be based on the hourly rate multiplied by the actual time spent on the case. Discuss the fee agreement, which is ideally written in "plain English" to begin with. Also discuss who will be responsible for paying fees and costs. You want to make sure your client fully understands all aspects of your representation, including the risks.

At the same time, this is a good opportunity to discuss what is expected of the client: cooperation and availability; settlement range; appearance at depositions, mandatory settlement conferences and trial. Apart from candidly exploring settlement expectations, it is important to inform the client that litigation takes time. A frank discussion of all of these matters will make the entire litigation process go more smoothly.

---

[1] The Center for Auto Safety, 2001 "S" St. NW, Suite 410, Washington, D.C. 20009, www.autosafety.org, is a nonprofit organization. Membership is $15 per year. It is not a lawyer referral service, and merely provides this list of practitioners as a member service at no extra charge.

[2] Contact them at 1717 Massachusetts Ave., Suite 704, Washington, D.C. 20036, (202)-332-2500, www.naca.net.

[3] Contingency fee arrangements are widely misunderstood by the public. They are regulated in some states and jurisdictions. Not all contingency fee arrangements are based on a percent of the recovery. Some may state that no fee is earned until the client obtains a net monetary recovery in settlement and then the fee is based on actual time expended at the stated marketable rate. You may negotiate the terms of your fee agreement.

[4] Nightingale v. Hyundai Motor America, 31 Cal.App. 4th 99 (1994).

– 6 –

Establishing the Facts

You may think that the facts of your lemon case are straightforward — the car is defective and you have a number of repair orders to show that the manufacturer has not fixed the problem. Nevertheless, it is a virtual certainty that you will meet stiff manufacturer opposition to your attempt to obtain a refund or replacement, and this makes it imperative that you do a thorough job establishing the facts of your case.

Long before you address your first demand letter to the manufacturer, you should have a firm idea of the strength of your case. You will be amazed at the amount of information relevant to your case that you can develop without any cooperation from the manufacturer or dealer. While some effort will be required, this preliminary spade work is well worth it, both for a car owner preparing for IDM, or for an attorney deciding whether to take on a particular case. Moreover, concrete knowledge that you have a strong case helps establish your credibility from that first encounter with the opposing side.

For attorneys, the time spent in fact gathering is billable, if you do take a case and prevail. It will be reimbursed by the manufacturer if the defendant must pay legal fees. If you eventually file and lose a civil action, you have satisfied your Rule 11 (or comparable state statutory) obligation to proceed in good faith, because you have a reasonable factual basis for your allegations.

The more legwork you do before taking the case, the better you can assess the risks of litigation. Not only is pre-litigation analysis every attorney's ethical obligation, it is good business practice. So where to begin?

GETTING STARTED

For any automotive case, you should keep four facts handy. Write them on the file jacket for rapid reference:
- the make (e.g., Ford)
- the model (e.g., Explorer)
- the year (e.g., 1999)
- the 17 digit alpha-numeric known as the "vehicle identification number" or VIN (e.g., JT3VX39W5R0155869)

The VIN appears on the purchase or lease contract, the registration, and on the driver's side door jamb of the vehicle itself. This not only acts as an identifying serial number, but contains valuable information about the engine, manufacturer series, and factory or plant of origin.

THE CENTER FOR AUTO SAFETY
IS AN INVALUABLE RESOURCE

Since 1970, The Center for Auto Safety has taken a leading role in protecting automotive consumers against unsafe vehicles and industry abuses. Of special relevance, it provides consumers and their attorneys with detailed information about specific defects in particular makes and models. In the late 1960's, Ralph Nader's controversial classic, *Unsafe At Any Speed*, had just propelled his name into every household and projected issues of deceit and betrayal into America's so-called "love affair with the automobile." But Nader could not raise all of his brainchildren himself; so he and Consumer's Union created the Center for Auto Safety and appointed Clarence Ditlow its director. Ditlow has since developed the Center into a powerful watchdog agency and a respected public voice.

Membership in CAS is $15, which Ditlow likes to remind you is less than the cost of an oil change. The Center for Auto Safety is now fully independent and funded solely through membership dues. It is money well spent. Write to The Center for Auto Safety, 2001 "S" Street NW, Suite 410, Washington, D.C. 20009 or visit www.autosafety.org. With membership, you not only contribute to the Center's critical lobbying efforts for protective legislation and regulations, education, publicity, research and pressure for recalls, but you also receive its informative newsletter, *The Lemon Times*.

In its ongoing role as a clearinghouse for automotive defect information, the CAS makes available to its members information packets on various defects it follows. Some of these are general, such as "Toyota Defects (1988-1995)" and some more specific such as "Ford Paint (1985-1995)" or "GM Power Steering Failure (1980-1988)." A full list of publications is available to members.

For an additional moderate charge, CAS researchers will ferret out complaints pertinent to your particular requests. Thus you could ask them to research all that is publicly available or privately known to CAS about engine mount defects in 1998 Ford Explorers. You thus gain access to CAS' invaluable ongoing compilation and analysis of consumer complaints.

In addition, CAS offers several publications, including detailed information packets. *The Lemon Book*[1] has an overview of warranty rights; emphasizes group organization, public action or other "strategies outside the system;" and offers practical advice on how to avoid buying a lemon, as well as how to recognize a lemon as it ripens in your driveway. Bear in mind however, that the purpose of the Center for Auto Safety is first and foremost public advocacy. Thus the emphasis on letter-writing and media attention which serves the broader public does not *necessarily* achieve the individual's private purpose of replacement or refund of a particular defective car. Letter campaigns are sometimes an end in themselves. A lawyer should not charge consumer clients money for writing threatening letters unless that lawyer is willing and able to back up the claim by going to court.

THE NATIONAL HIGHWAY TRAFFIC SAFETY ADMINISTRATION ALSO COLLECTS AUTOMOTIVE DEFECT DATA

NHTSA, the National Highway Traffic Safety Administration, is a federal agency that receives, investigates and researches consumer complaints about motor vehicle defects, and in appropriate cases orders manufacturer recalls. The NHTSA Auto Safety Hotline (800-424-9393) is a rapid-fire way to check on pending investigations or recalls of a particular model defect.

You can obtain more detailed information by filing a request with NHTSA's Technical Reference Division for a computer printout of complaints NHTSA has received concerning model-specific defects, technical service bulletins relating to such defects, and other public documents relating to investigations.[2] Caution: ask about the anticipated volume and cost in advance. This author was flooded with a box of more than 600 actual complaint forms upon making one particular request.

Probably the best way to access NHTSA information is over the Internet, by going to www.nhtsa.dot.gov. Here, right on your desk top, face-to-face with your anxious client, you can pull up the actual bulletin recalling 36,000 1996 Nissan Altimas for rear seatbelt problems. Print out the actual bulletin and your client can take it to the dealership, or you can file it away until the zone representative's deposition.

The NHTSA site not only has recall information, but reports on pending investigations. Most importantly for lemon law litigation, it provides technical service bulletins ("TSBs"), and TSB indices, which just a few years ago could only be obtained through expensive motions to compel discovery in court. Thus, with a few short clicks of the mouse you can learn that there is not just one, but at least three TSBs on problems in the engine cooling system of a 1996 Ford Taurus. Imagine the strength of this information to combat the defense of three repair orders in which the service department noted "no problem found."

OTHER VALUABLE PRINT RESOURCES

You can also learn about known defects which plague existing models by perusing used car buying guides. This may also give you an idea of the loss in value some make and models are suffering because of particular consumer complaints. One such used car buying guide is published by Consumer's Union, *Consumer Reports' Guide to Used Cars*[3]

Another buying guide containing warranty and defect data is *The CAR Book* by Jack Gillis. This annually updated compendium relies heavily on information obtained from the Center For Auto Safety. In easily readable form, Mr. Gillis reports safety ratings, volume of complaints filed with NHTSA, repair cost comparisons, warranty terms, and other information useful in investigating a defect claim. If, for example, your client has a 1996 Toyota Supra, and your refund/replacement demand is meeting Toyota's notorious stone wall, *The CAR Book* informs you that you may not be alone: that model series has an astronomical complaint index based on a ratio of the number of complaints relating to that series compared to sales of that series.[4]

The federal government also provides numerous publications for a modest handling charge, or for free. These publications are listed in the *Consumer Information Catalog.*[5] Your gumshoe work is also incomplete without a glance at that ubiquitous industry weekly, *Automotive News.*[6] This Detroit trade publication provides the latest on competitive practices, recalls, lawsuits, class actions, plant closures and expansions, sales incentives, advertising, sales figures, model changes, joint venture production, mergers and acquisitions, profits and sales figures. You may learn, for example, that the Geo Metro is actually the product of a joint venture between General Motors and Suzuki, a fact which may cause you to more carefully scrutinize the warranties, target your demand letter, choose your defendants and word your complaint.

THE INTERNET: AN INCREASINGLY POWERFUL TOOL

Public access to the information superhighway is making the asphalt highway safer. Masses of information on automotive defects are now instantaneously available through the Internet. Until recently, the auto industry fought doggedly, with abusive and dilatory discovery tactics, from turning over information that is now available in seconds to anyone who is interested.

The Internet has revolutionized how you investigate a lemon problem.

If you do not yet have the Internet at your fingertips, a trip to your local library is an investigative must. Spend an afternoon surfing the worldwide web. To get started, use a search engine such as Yahoo!, Lycos, Excite, Alta Vista or Infoseek. A search engine is itself a website that acts somewhat like a computerized card catalogue. A word search using combinations of "consumer" *and* "automotive" *and* "lemon" or "warranty" will access more sites that you may want to cope with, but you can progressively narrow your search to your customized needs.

A search which includes the automotive name itself, such as "Chrysler," is likely to lead you to an advertising website for the manufacturer. One problem with the web is the plethora of "infomercials;" it can become difficult to separate fact from fiction and marketing.

If you have the name of the website, you can search directly for that address.[7] Earlier in this chapter we discussed NHTSA's website. Another excellent place to begin is "www.consumerworld.org," the website created by Edward Dworsky, an attorney who originally helped write the lemon law in Massachusetts, and who is now with the Federal Trade Commission. Dworsky has assembled an impressive array of more than 1,500 consumer resources, many of which have to do with automotive issues. Through Consumer World, you can order many other publications, many for free or nominal charge. Or you can find out how to file a Better Business Bureau complaint online.

Via Consumer World's access to the Oxbridge Directory of Newsletters, you can locate the address and phone number for numerous sources of ammunition to support your specific claim. The *Consumer Product Safety Review, The Consumer Product Safety Guide*, the newsletter of the Consumer Federation of America, CALPIRG and other agencies may all post news of automotive defects. This website is definitely worth a visit and links you with yet further research tools.

Another outstanding resource is found at www.alldata.com, which provides TSBs, recall and other technical information, and also provides one of the most comprehensive links directory to other automotive sites on the web. At this writing, it had established more than 100 links to other vehicle-related websites. This site alone proves that the unsavory game of "hide the ball" is getting harder and harder for the auto industry to play.

A virtual encyclopedia of auto industry information is found at www.autopedia.com, driving home the self-teaching nature of the world wide web. Using this and other cross-referencing sites, you can corroborate information you have obtained elsewhere. This effort at verification is important when researching online, because it is often hard to determine who sponsors a website and there is a great deal of misinformation on the Internet.

If your vehicle possibly had a prior owner (many cars are sold as "new" or as "demonstrators" while having prior owners), you will want to check out its vehicle history. You can do this in a preliminary way via the Internet. The CarFax system is a nationwide database of (at this writing) 846 million vehicles. While it is not a perfect chronicle of every car's history, it is an extremely useful instrument. For $19.50, you can punch in the seventeen digit VIN number and get a printout of the title and other data CarFax has on that car. Particularly if the vehicle is suspect as a recycled lemon, salvaged car, or odometer rollback, CarFax is a good place to start blazing the paper trail. It can be accessed directly at www.carfaxreport.com or indirectly through www.carprices.com, www.kbb.com, and certain other websites.

A number of private law firms have set up websites which educate the public on matters of automotive interest; at the same time they acquaint potential clients with their expertise. One award-winning site is that of the Alexander Law Firm in San Jose, California. From the home page at www.alexanderlaw.com, you can jump to the firm's Consumer Law Page. Selecting automotive topics, you can learn about recent class action settlements and ongoing cases. The site also provides links to other online resources. On the cutting edge of technology, the content and presentation of this webpage changes frequently and is worth repeated visits.

Specialized lemon law firms also have sites useful to consumers and legal practitioners alike. At www.kabolaw.com, you can read about odometer fraud, deceptive leasing, the California lemon law, co-signing, Spanish language issues, and related topics.

Online chat sessions can even be the source of lemon-aid. One frustrated Chrysler owner voiced his complaint in an automotive newsgroup chatroom. Of about sixteen anonymous unsolicited responses which returned through cyberspace, fifteen told him to go to one law firm. He did. And it wasn't long before Chrysler paid.

Chandra Fienen, who designed one lemon law website, cautions you however to "Be aware that the Internet is not private. The computer quickly figures out what interests you the user, and soon you will see automotive advertising banners displayed." Your web search of automotive issues has revealed your interest to the advertisers and other companies.[8] Thus, in the time it took this author to surf through the information in this chapter segment, the computer assigned the advertising banner for a Ford Lincoln Navigator when I accessed my search engine. A double click on the tempting riddle "What can make going out in the worst weather seem like a day at the beach?" produced a full color display of the advertised vehicle.

There is not space here to examine all the myriad possibilities of the Internet, and the rapidly evolving information interchange may alter course by the time this book enters print. This is the very nature of the information superhighway. The important thing is to open up your inquiry and investigation to include the Internet. One afternoon surfing the net may be an excellent investment.

EXPERT OPINION

An independent opinion early in the game can save you money in lost time and effort, as well as weed out cases that have little merit. An unfavorable report which convinces you not to file a civil action can be as valuable as a strong report that supports a good claim. Some lemon lawyers do not subject the vehicle to independent analysis, on the theory that the consumer does not have the burden to pinpoint the exact nature of the complaint. It is this author's view that hiring an expert immediately is valuable to establish the consumer's credibility and challenge the manufacturer's anticipated defenses. Particularly where the defect's symptoms are intermittent, a qualified technician verifying the problem greatly strengthens the case. Attorneys should even consider not agreeing to take a case until after an expert has inspected the vehicle.

Finding an Expert

How do you find an independent expert? It may not be easy. Ideally, you want someone who can engage a jury the way Tom and Ray Magliozzi entertain their National Public Radio audiences every Saturday on CarTalk. What you might have to settle for is someone who knows a differential from a dipstick and can write a good report.

In metropolitan areas, experts often advertise. The law library or public library may have catalogues listing forensic consultants by category. There are several expert listings already online; for these services the expert pays for the listing and there is no cost for access. On the other hand, professional forensic experts are not always the most credible in lemon litigation. The Internet may lead you to other good independent technicians, as discussed below. Examine the field.

Consider your personal acquaintances, or other clients with the necessary connections. If you have no personal relationship with a repair shop, call local community colleges and vocational schools which teach auto shop and train technicians for the workplace. If an instructor is unavailable or unwilling, ask for referrals to past students who have gone into business on their own.

Interview your expert. Of course, you will want to inquire about education, experience, and special expertise, including attendance at manufacturers' ongoing seminars. Ask what diagnostic tools the expert will use. You will want to know for which manufacturers the expert has worked and whether the expert has testified before. If you are in a state which requires written reports, discuss the fact that such a report is expected. Determine expert witness fees in advance.

THE CAR AS EVIDENCE

Whether you are the car's owner or an attorney, you also want to become familiar with the car itself, and not leave everything to the expert. You may have to remove that gray suit jacket and get dirty. LAVA is not a soap found in most law offices, but it works well to get rid of grease.

If you have never opened up the hood of a car and looked in, you may find it helpful to acquaint yourself with the basic layout of the chassis by using a software program like Auto Insights For Windows — this program will tell you what to look for. Take a camera whenever you have the opportunity to see the car. Attorneys should ask their clients for pictures that may have bearing on the claim.

**A photograph, video, or defective old part
from the car may persuade a jury
far more than a thousand words.**

The video camera is a powerful tool. If water leaks are the problem, videotape a journey through the local car wash. Capture the squishy sound as you wring out the floor mats. Steering vibration, brake fires, electrical malfunction, paint defects, brake shudder, leaks, and uneven tire wear are just some of the many conditions which you can demonstrate dramatically with multimedia. In the course of directing this creative activity, be sure to record the conditions of the documentary, the identity of the cameraman, and any other evidentiary requirements in your jurisdiction.

Finally, you should try to gather any relevant parts which have been removed in the repair process. These are often given to the owner upon return of the car and you should document the chain of possession. That greasy, grimy severed drive shaft sitting on counsel table throughout the trial is bound to intrigue the jury, especially when you roll up your sleeves and explain through a series of witnesses just exactly how it got that way.

Lacking actual parts from the subject vehicle, you should consider alternative means of demonstrative evidence. Local independent mechanics, body shops, or vocational auto repair programs may have similar parts you can use as models. Educate yourself as you will one day educate the judge and/or jury using schematic drawings from AutoInsights software or similar text. Although it is not incumbent on the consumer to prove the exact nature of the defect, a lawyer who can present the pertinent mechanics as a shared learning experience — without being condescending — is apt to win votes in jury deliberations.

KEEPING POSSESSION OF THE VEHICLE; SPOLIATION OF EVIDENCE

Tempting as it may be to default on payments for a defective car which may be unsafe to drive, consumers should do everything possible to prevent repossession, and to retain control over the vehicle. It is best if your expert has unfettered access to the vehicle right up through trial.

On the other hand, you or your expert should be present whenever the manufacturer's expert inspects the vehicle. At the manufacturer's inspection, you want to make sure they do not alter or try to repair the vehicle, thereby destroying the evidence for trial. Take notes regarding what tests the manufacturer's expert did and did not do. Record or make note of comments the technicians make and what literature they refer to in analyzing the problem. Did they use Genesis equipment? Did they take a test drive? If the manufacturer obtains possession of the vehicle, you lose control of the inspection process.

Preservation of the car as evidence is not only in your interest, it is required. Any alteration in the evidence may result in serious sanctions from the judge and may also amount to a tort where the other side can sue the party altering the evidence. In pending or future litigation, the destruction or significant alteration of evidence, or the failure to preserve property for another's use as evidence, is called "spoliation," and is a serious matter indeed.[9]

If a dealer, creditor, or manufacturer gains possession of the vehicle, you should promptly advise the party in possession that any resale or alteration of the vehicle may subject them to a claim for spoliation. The car instead should be stored pending the trial. If opposing counsel balks, send a notice in lieu of document subpoena requiring production of the vehicle at the time of trial.

This notice raises the stakes should the opposition even be contemplating attempted repair or resale of the vehicle. Your notice that you will need the vehicle in the anticipated or pending litigation means that any subsequent alteration or sale of the vehicle is *intentional* spoliation.

---

[1] R. Nader and C. Ditlow, *The Lemon Book* (3d. ed. 1990).

[2] National Highway Traffic Safety Administration, Technical Reference Division, Room 5108, 400 Seventh St. SW, Washington, D.C. 20590. Phone (202) 366-2768.

[3] Available in most book stores, or write to Consumer Reports, 256 Washington St., Mount Vernon, N.Y. 10553.

[4] Center for Auto Safety, *The CAR Book*, which can be obtained from CAS, 2001 "S" Street, N.W., Suite 410, Washington D.C., 20009.

[5] You can find this in a public library or order it from The Consumer Information Center, P.O. Box 100, Pueblo, CO 81002.

[6] Published by Crain Communications, Inc. 1400 Woodbridge Ave., Detroit, MI 48207.

[7] For example, this author's firm website is located at www.kabolaw.com. The National Consumer Law Center's website is at www.consumerlaw.org.

[8] Your search has created what are called "cookie files" because the user has left a trail of crumbs, like in the fairy tale Hansel and Gretel.

[9] Welsh v. United States, 844 F.2d 1239 (6th Cir. 1987); Willard v. Caterpillar Inc., 40 Cal. App. 4th 892 (1995).

7

Informal Dispute Mechanisms: The Good, The Bad, and the Ugly

When you notify a manufacturer that your car meets the statutory standard of a lemon, do not expect the manufacturer voluntarily to offer a replacement or refund. Instead, you will have to force the manufacturer to do so.

Your first step usually is to present your demand for relief to an informal dispute resolution mechanism (IDM), a panel that will consider your claim in a non-judicial setting. Depending on your lemon law, either the manufacturer will arrange for the IDM or your state will establish one. You can always submit a lemon complaint to an IDM if you want to. In many cases, you *must* do so before going to court, even if you would prefer not to. In certain situations, though, you have the option to skip IDM and go straight to court. This chapter examines whether you must first utilize an IDM; whether you should, if you have a choice; how to prepare for an IDM procedure and whether you need an attorney; and what to do after you receive an IDM ruling.

MUST YOU USE AN IDM?

Most, but not all, states require you to use an IDM first if you seek relief under the lemon law. If there is a qualified IDM to hear your dispute, you cannot go to court before completing the IDM procedure.

However, not all lemon law claimants must first resort to IDM. Even though the manufacturer will try to steer you to its program, in many cases the process is not required. First, read your state lemon law. Some statutes do not require prior resort to IDM and you can file an action directly in court.

In a number of states, such as California, the state must certify an IDM. If the manufacturer does not use a certified IDM, the consumer may skip the IDM process entirely. In many states the lemon law requires the consumer to use an IDM only if the IDM complies with state and federal regulations.[1] Whether a consumer must use an IDM in such states is tricky, because there is no definitive advance ruling on whether the IDM complies or not. By skipping the IDM, your are gambling that a court will later agree with you that the IDM failed to comply with regulations.

Probably the easiest and best basis for claiming an IDM does not comply is if the IDM delays the proceeding. The federal regulations have several strict timing requirements designed for consumer protection. For example, Fannie Harrison submitted a warranty claim to Nissan's IDM, a program administered by the Better Business Bureau called "AUTOLINE." After the maximum forty days had passed without a hearing, she filed suit. The court held she did not have to resort first to the IDM because of the delay.[2] This happens with surprising frequency.[3]

Any consumer should therefore consult the following checklist to decide whether or not to submit to an IDM before going to court:
- Does the applicable state lemon law require prior resort to IDM?
- Does the applicable state lemon law require the IDM to comply with federal regulations or other state standards like certification?
- Does the manufacturer have an IDM?
- Is there a state-sponsored IDM?
- Does the IDM comply with state and federal regulations?

If the answers to these questions are unclear, you need the advice of a lawyer experienced in consumer protection. Never rely on the manufacturer's or dealer's interpretation of the law.

SHOULD YOU UTILIZE AN IDM IF YOU HAVE A CHOICE?

There is widespread criticism that industry-sponsored IDMs are not a level playing field, although many consumers obtain some form of remedy from the IDM process. Even former arbitrators have become disillusioned.[4] In exchange for an "expeditious" process, the consumer gives up the opportunity to obtain the opponent's internal documents, the right in some cases to make an oral presentation or to present independent expert reports, and the full array of remedies which may be available under a state court proceeding. A fast result is not necessarily a fair result.

Chrysler and Ford have a sufficient volume of sales and lemon law claims to sponsor their own IDMs. These are the Chrysler Customer Arbitration Board and the Ford Dispute Settlement Board respectively. Both are administered by Jo Demars and Associates. Ltd. of Waukesha, Wisconsin. The Better Business Bureau administers programs for Acura, Alfa Romeo, Am General (Hummer), Audi, General Motors (Buick, Cadillac, Chevrolet, GMC Truck, Pontiac, Oldsmobile), Honda, Hyundai, Infiniti, Isuzu, Kia, Land Rover, Lexus, Nissan, Maserati, Peugeot, Porsche, Range Rover, Rolls-Royce, Saab, Saturn, Sterling, Suburu, Toyota and VW. Their phone number is 1-800-955-5100.

If a manufacturer is not giving you a fair deal, can you expect any better from the manufacturer's own IDM?

Perhaps the most significant problem with these industry-sponsored IDMs is that they are biased in favor of the auto industry. The IDM members are supposed to be independent. Yet the Ford Board for example is composed of four members, three of whom must be present to decide a matter. Of the four, one must be a Ford or Mercury-Lincoln dealer, and one is an automotive expert who may be paid by the manufacturer for inspection of the vehicle "but in all other respects . . . may be . . . independent of the manufacturer."[5] Consumer advocates argue that "paid by the manufacturer" is patently inconsistent with the concept "independent of the manufacturer." The potential for private communications between the supposedly independent IDM members and the sponsoring manufacturers is great, and compromises both the requirement for insulation and the appearance of impartiality.

Consumers are lucky if industry-sponsored mechanisms even meet federal minimum standards. But those federal standards lack the strength and true balance needed for meaningful enforcement of the lemon law. For example, the federal regulations do not require that IDM decision-makers and staff apply the lemon law; they do not even have to be familiar with consumers' rights and remedies under applicable law. They just have to be "fair and expeditious."[6] Thus a manufacturer need not even train the staff in objective requirements of the state lemon law.

Moreover, oral presentations are only allowed if both parties agree.[7] That is, the manufacturer may have a veto power over the consumer's efforts to present a case orally. Many consumers are at a disadvantage in presenting written documentation, or may be missing part of the service record necessary to support their written narrative.

Not all IDMs are equally biased against the consumer. Industry sponsored IDMs do vary, and state run programs have a better public profile for the most part. The Florida Attorney General's office runs a program where, when the consumer is awarded a dollar recovery (about 43% of the time), the average recovery was $32,000.[8] The problem with such state run programs though is that when the consumer prevails, the manufacturer is likely to appeal the result.

HOW TO PREPARE FOR IDM

Importance of Taking IDM Seriously

When you appear before an IDM, it is essential to put your best foot forward. The IDM's eventual decision will have a profound impact on your eventual recovery, even if you plan on taking your case to court. In some states, the IDM award is close to final, with you having only very limited grounds to appeal the size of the award. More commonly, you can go to court if you are dissatisfied, but the IDM's decision can be introduced in evidence at that court trial. This evidence is often very persuasive to a jury, even though the evidence presented at the IDM might have been very different from that presented at trial.

Should a Consumer Use
an Attorney for IDM?

Even if a consumer does not use an attorney to actually appear before an IDM hearing, legal advice will be of great assistance in preparing the initial claim form and counseling the consumer on what materials are most relevant and persuasive. An attorney can also help the consumer focus on the material points to raise when the consumer appears in person before the IDM panel. The manufacturer has vast legal resources to help train its presenters who oppose your claim. You are up to bat against the pros.

More difficult is the question whether your attorney should actually appear at the IDM proceeding. In some states, such as New York, attorneys routinely appear at the IDM. In other states, they are categorically excluded. An important factor about bringing your own attorney into an IDM proceeding is whether the manufacturer will pay for your attorney if you prevail. Your legal entitlement for such fees varies from state to state. But even in states that authorize such fees, the IDM panel may have a practice of never awarding consumers their attorneys fees. For example, the California Chrysler Customer Arbitration Board ("CAB") Operating Procedures expressly provides: "CAB members understand that nothing in this section requires that decisions must consider . . . attorney's fees. . . ."[9]

Preparation Tips

How well you do at IDM depends on good preparation and proper anticipation of the manufacturer's defenses. Make sure you also carefully read Chapter 6 on establishing the facts.

Do not let your argument be restricted by the standard forms provided to you by the IDM. The forms sometimes discourage thorough presentation by offering little space for explanation. Use the space you need, with attachments if necessary. The form should be neatly typed rather than handwritten, because one of the most common complaints of IDM panels is the illegibility of forms and supporting documentation.

The checklist at Chapter 2, above, should help you walk through what you must prove in your lemon law dispute. Answer each question with the specific facts of your case, and where state laws differ, refer to the language of your particular statute.

The Chrysler Operating Procedures manual states that the CAB members are to investigate any or all of the following issues raised by the consumer, manufacturer or dealer:

- Whether the program has jurisdiction to decide the dispute;
- Whether there is a nonconformity;
- Whether the nonconformity is a substantial nonconformity;
- Cause or causes of a nonconformity;
- Whether the causes include unreasonable use of the vehicle;
- The number of repair attempts;
- Time out of service for repair;
- Whether Chrysler has had a reasonable opportunity to repair;
- Factors affecting the reasonableness of the number of repair attempts;
- Facts giving rise to a presumption, or rebuttal thereof;
- Whether a further repair attempt is likely to remedy the nonconformity;
- Damages calculation issues.

Clearly, the panel may consider any of these items, even if you do not raise them, because the manufacturer may. Your own claim package should thus satisfy any possible concern with regard to any of these issues, whether or not the initial form asks for this information.

A key part of your presentation is the repair history — a clear and chronological history of the complaints presented to the dealership acting as the manufacturer's agent for repair. An example of a repair chronology is found at Chapter 5, above.

The repair orders ("ROs") themselves may not give the whole picture. Particularly in the case of multiple repairs for the same complaint, the service writer at the dealership may omit mention of the problem, while you will want to argue that a "no problem found" repair instance counts as a repair attempt. The repair chronology should show each date the vehicle went into the shop, the mileage reading at the time, what the consumer told the dealer was wrong with the car, what work the dealer performed, what parts the dealer replaced, and the number of days in the shop at each repair.

The primary source for all of this is the repair orders, but the ROs routinely fail to state the day the vehicle was returned to the customer. Your job is to remember and record the full time. You may find old calendars, phone records, business diaries and the like refresh your recollection of the ordeal.

The repair chronology should also provide a summary totalling the number of repair attempts for each defect, the number of repair attempts for all defects, and the number of days in the shop. The corresponding figures for any presumption period found in the state lemon law (e.g., first 12,000 miles and 12 months) should also be calculated and appear in the claim package for the IDM's reference. All supporting documentation, particularly the repair orders should accompany the claim.

Let the manufacturer know about other damage to the vehicle caused by the defect — that way, the manufacturer cannot complain about the damage when you turn the car in.

You should be very clear in your application before the IDM as to the extent of any other damage the defect has caused to the car. When you turn the car into the manufacturer for a refund or replacement, the manufacturer cannot then complain about the car's condition. The manufacturer was fully informed that the defect caused the condition, and the manufacturer did not rebut this fact before the IDM.

You should request an in-person hearing if the IDM allows it. At the hearing the consumer should be prepared to demand pleasantly but firmly a full refund, and explain the anticipated futility of further repair attempts. You should be prepared to argue that the repair chronology shows the existence of a nonconformity which the manufacturer (through its dealer) has had a reasonable opportunity to repair already or you would not have come this far.

You should also be prepared to explain in an unemotional but concerned manner just how the nonconformity has affected the use, value or safety of the vehicle. Your own personal frustration at getting put on hold, shuttling back and forth to the dealer, annoyance, irritation and anger will probably not get you far with the IDM panel. Instead, provide specific details of the defect and its effect on you — be objective but present a sympathetic picture of the problem. You should also be prepared to describe any and all notice of the defect which you communicated directly or indirectly to the manufacturer.

ACCEPTING OR REJECTING THE IDM AWARD

Is the IDM Award Binding on Either Side?

As a general rule, IDM decisions do not bind the consumer, but the decision is admissible in evidence in a subsequent legal proceeding. The FTC standards under the Magnuson-Moss Warranty Act state this, and most state lemon laws follow this approach.

Some state lemon laws discourage rejection of the IDM decision by imposing penalties or the other side's attorney fees on a party who does not obtain a better result in court than provided by the IDM. A handful of lemon laws that provide state-run IDMs make the IDM decision more binding on the parties. For example, the New Hampshire lemon law only allows a court to overturn an IDM decision if there is clear and convincing evidence of corruption, fraud, prejudice or failure to follow the rules adopted by the board.

In most states, though, a consumer unhappy with an IDM ruling can proceed to trial. The award itself should specify a time-frame for the consumer to accept the IDM decision. In some states, your failure to reject the award within the designated time period may result in your waiver of your right to go to trial.

Deciding Whether to Accept the IDM Award

If the IDM grants you no relief, your choice is relatively simple. Walk away, or seek legal representation and proceed to court. In many instances, though, the issue is not so easy. The award may grant the manufacturer one more repair attempt when six previous efforts failed to fix the car. Or the award may grant you a refund which turns out to be insufficient to buy a new set of wheels in exchange for the vehicle. Or a refund which fails to satisfy the lien. Or a refund reduced by excessive offset for consumer use. Or a replacement vehicle of questionable comparable worth. There may be maintenance and repair issues if the vehicle must be returned. The IDM award language itself may be confusing, and you may not even know what it is saying. What's a consumer to do?

Unfortunately, there is no easy answer on whether to accept an award. Whether you do so may depend on a number of factors.

- Were you denied an oral presentation at the IDM and would that have helped your case?
- Were you denied the right to submit some evidence you could produce at trial which would help your case?
- Were you sandbagged by an in-house expert of the manufacturer?
- Did your case turn on a document, internal to the manufacturer, which you had been unable to get without civil discovery?
- Was there ambiguity in the IDM's written decision?
- Was there a significant unfair offset reducing the award?
- Do you have additional claims such as fraud or deceptive practices that you could not bring in the IDM?
- Do you have solid claims for damages that are unavailable through the IDM?
- What is your burden of proof if you proceed to trial?
- Will you be penalized if you do not achieve a higher award at trial, and what constitutes a higher award?
- Is the IDM result admissible at trial?
- What is the anticipated length of time from filing to trial in the court where you would bring your case?

While the IDM award may seem at first glance disappointing or facially unfair, the consumer must balance the actual difference in value achieved versus the cost of legal fees, likelihood of recovering a more favorable result, and the delay of the civil justice system. The time value of money is also an important concern.

If you are not certain whether you will do better at trial, it is wise to seek legal advice. The wisdom of an experienced litigator can help the consumer balance the pros and cons of further action or acceptance. The other thing a lawyer can do is balance the "fairness" of the award against what the consumer is entitled to under state law.

Thus, for example in a state which has a civil penalty, the lawyer reviewing the award will look to see, not just whether there is a nonconformity, but how the manufacturer's customer service department and dealer repair dealt directly with the consumer's complaints. Pertinent to this inquiry is whether the manufacturer had demonstrated any initiative in honoring its warranties, whether the manufacturer (through its authorized agent for repair) made serious and sincere attempts to discover the cause of the consumer's complaints, and whether the manufacturer had made a reasonable effort to gather the available information on repair history.

Negative Equity and the Refund Award

The consumer's decision to accept an IDM award is particularly difficult where the award offers the consumer a buyback of the car's purchase price, but that amount either is not specified or not enough to get the car owner out of the car loan on the defective vehicle and into a set of comparable wheels. There could be several reasons why the award will not be enough to return the consumer to the status quo — e.g. there could be a large offset for the consumer's use of the car or the award is just inadequate.

Another common reason for the insufficient size of an award, or of a manufacturer's payment pursuant to an award, is where the manufacturer re-writes the purchase price of the lemon car because the manufacturer claims there was undisclosed "negative equity" in the original purchase. (The issue of negative equity is also discussed at Chapter 4, above.)

Manufacturers may attempt to re-compute the original purchase price of the lemon vehicle where that purchase involved a trade-in, saying the original numbers were fictitious. For example, to purchase a new car, a consumer trades in her old car. While this may seem simple enough, the reality is often quite different. This situation can become complicated where the consumer still owes money for her old car. In order to facilitate the sale of the new car, dealers will frequently value her old car at the amount she still owes on it, despite the fact that the car is worth significantly less, giving rise to what is known as "negative equity." To maximize profits, the dealer will then add that amount to the purchase price of her new car.

Here's how it works: the consumer and the dealer sign a contract which says a trade-in was a wash after deducting the amount owed on its car loan, and specifies a car's purchase price as $24,000. The manufacturer may claim that the trade-in was actually worth $4,000 less than its loan pay-off. The dealer absorbed this $4,000 loss (negative equity) by increasing the new car's price from $20,000 to $24,000. At the time, none of this was disclosed to the consumer — the consumer was told the dealer was buying the trade-in for the amount outstanding on its debt and was selling the new car to the consumer for $24,000.

Faced with an IDM award to buy back the car, the manufacturer refuses to refund the full $24,000 amount. It claims it really sold the car for $20,000 and the dealer loaned the consumer $4,000 in cash to pay-off the old car loan. Ford Motor Company has been the most aggressive in this regard and the legality of the practice is in dispute.

Legal or not, Ford and other manufacturers may try to reduce lemon buy-back awards to amounts less than the car's cash price, as stated in the contract, where there appears to be negative trade-in financing embedded in the cash price. The manufacturer will make a unilateral decision concerning what it claims is the negative equity value, since that amount is usually not disclosed in the contract. This leaves the consumer with a loss.

Don't let the manufacturer unilaterally re-invent the car's original purchase price because of so-called "negative equity."

One alternative is to go back to the IDM and seek clarification as to what amount the IDM award requires the manufacturer to repay the consumer. If clarification is not provided, or if it is not to the consumer's liking, the consumer can reject the award as either ambiguous or inadequate.

Alternatively, you can treat the award as offering the full amount, and then charge the manufacturer with nonperformance of the terms of the award. Where the state lemon law requires refund of the "full purchase price," manufacturers unilaterally paying less than that amount are violating that state law. Consumers dealing with problems of negative equity should also get legal advice concerning the role of the dealer and lender in writing up a purchase agreement that was in effect fictitious. Has the lender or dealer violated federal or state law?

Steps to Take if You Accept the Award

If you decide to accept the IDM award, your next step is usually straight-forward. The IDM decision typically will instruct you on the deadline for accepting the award; otherwise it will be assumed you reject the award. Ford's Dispute Settlement Board form states: "If this form is not received by us within 14 days we will assume the decision has been *rejected* by you."

If you do send in the form, accepting the award, the manufacturer will then send you a release form for you to sign. You should review the release, because it will often ask you to settle not only the lemon law claim, but any other claim you have relating to the vehicle. Where there are fraud claims relating to the purchase of the vehicle (such as undisclosed pre-sale damage or false advertising), you may very well want to consult an attorney before signing off on the release. Nevertheless, in most cases, the manufacturer's overreaching in its release is immaterial and consumers will accept, signing off on the release in order to receive the payment check.

Often of more significance is the fact that most release forms expressly require return of the vehicle in undamaged condition. The Chrysler Customer Arbitration Board Release states that in exchange for the award, the consumer "will transfer the ownership of the vehicle to Chrysler with clear title and . . . return the vehicle with no original or substantial equipment missing and in an undamaged condition, except for normal wear and tear and any previously alleged defects."

Similarly the BBB AUTOLINE Program administering IDM for General Motors release form requires the consumer to "transfer title and possession of subject vehicle to [Chevrolet] unencumbered by any interest or lien, and undamaged by accident or any other manner including vandalism. . . ."

If the vehicle has been in an accident or has any defects not previously alleged, you should determine how these issues will be handled before accepting or rejecting the claim. There have been instances where the manufacturer refuses to accept return of the vehicle even where the consumer has explained that the damage to the vehicle is linked to the vehicle defect about which the consumer had appeared before the IDM.

One example might be where a nonconformity involving leaking windows caused water damage to the interior. More serious would be the instance where a stalling condition caused a rear-end collision. The consumer says the damage is related to the reason for the board's decision and the manufacturer attributes the condition to excess wear and tear. The consumer can avoid this thorny problem by describing in detail in the *initial* IDM application how the nonconformity caused other damage.

How to Reject the Award

The consumer who decides to reject an IDM award should promptly seek legal advice if that has not been done before. The clock resumes ticking on the time to file a civil action once the award is made, and a well-pleaded legal complaint is best not left to the last minute. Moreover, some state laws require that a court action be filed almost immediately after the award. Florida provides that an application for a court proceeding must be filed with the circuit court within thirty days of receipt of the written arbitration decision.

You should also strictly comply with any requirement of the IDM concerning how you are to notify it as to whether you are accepting or rejecting the award. The Chrysler Customer Arbitration Board, for example, requires the consumer to accept or reject the decision within thirty days, and failure to accept will be deemed rejection.[10] Even if there are no specific notice requirements for rejection, the consumer who plans to proceed to court is well advised to notify the manufacturer promptly. Even if the award states it is rejected if not accepted in writing, it is still safest to promptly reject the award in writing. That way you foreclose any manufacturer argument later in court that you had accepted the IDM award.

---

[1] Federal Trade Commission regulations pursuant to the Magnuson-Moss Warranty Act, 16 C.F.R. §703; *see* Motor Vehicle Manufacturers' Association of U.S., Inc. v. Abrams (S.D.N.Y. 1988) 697 F. Supp. 726, *rev'd on other grounds*, Motor Vehicle Mfgrs. Assn. v. Abrams 899 F.2d 1315.

[2] Harrison v. Nissan Motor Corp. 111 F.3d 343 (3d Cir. 1997).

[3] In one survey 79% of cases reviewed indicate that the BBB AUTOLINE was exceeding allowable decision timetables. Memo from California Arbitration Review Program to BBB dated October 20, 1997, author's files, obtained through Freedom of Information Act request.

[4] Interview with former IDM panelist Phil Nowicki (Dec. 28, 1997).

[5] Ford Dispute Settlement Board Operating procedures (1990, rev. 1994).

[6] 16 C.F.R. §703.3(a).

[7] 16 C.F.R. §703.5(f).

[8] New Motor Vehicle Arbitration Program, 1995 Annual Report, Office of Attorney General Bob Butterworth, Tallahassee, Florida 32399-1050.

[9] California Chrysler Customer Arbitration Board Operating Procedures §3398.10a

[10] California Chrysler Customer Arbitration Board Operating Procedures §3398.12a.

8

Going to Court
on a Lemon Law Claim

It is startling how many consumers balk at the thought of suing an American icon like General Motors. But when you have tried every other means to get your catalytic converter fixed or your money back, access to the civil justice system may be the only means of relief. The Big Three are not alone in sometimes taking a "see you in court" attitude. The automotive case law is replete with examples of Japanese, German, and other import companies thumbing their noses at consumer concerns.

Every state lemon law provides for a consumer to bring an action in court to enforce lemon law rights. The typical time a consumer seeks such enforcement in court is where multiple repair attempts have failed to correct a defect, and the manufacturer has met your demand for refund/replacement with silence or derision. You may have gone through an informal dispute mechanism, but rejected the IDM decision. Your only alternative now is to go to court.

This chapter walks you through the court process. Since a claim to enforce the lemon law is based on the specific language of a statute, you must dot the I's and cross the T's at every stage to avoid loopholes for which industry has heavily lobbied at the legislative level. While IDM proceedings are intended for self-represented consumers, the court system is not a level playing field for the layman. Once you get to this point, you really need a legal professional. If you are the lawyer, now is the time to explain to the consumer what to expect from the court system. What follows is an overview of a lemon law lawsuit.

WHAT THE CONSUMER MUST DO
BEFORE FILING SUIT

Industry's battle to keep lemon law claims out of court has resulted in your state lemon law most likely requiring one or both of the following before filing suit:
- that you provide notice to the manufacturer;
- that you go through an IDM.

Notice

The manufacturer in most states must be made aware of the car's nonconformity before you can go to court to enforce your lemon law rights. Follow the lemon law's notice requirements precisely to avoid much needless litigation later. But if suit is initiated without proper notice, all may not be lost. The notice need not always be direct; after all, the manufacturer's authorized dealers have been building the warranty history of the vehicle since its first repair.[1]

There is considerable state variation as to how, when and to whom the consumer must send the notice. The South Carolina lemon law specifies that notice must be given by registered, certified, or express mail.[2] Some states specify only that the notice must be in writing, and states vary whether notice must be to the manufacturer, or whether an authorized dealer can receive the notice. The lemon law will usually specify the content of the notice — typically listing the vehicle defects at issue. But a formal rejection or revocation of acceptance of the vehicle may not be required in the notice.

Whatever other notice a statute may require, prudent consumer lawyers make it standard practice to serve a notice of rescission prior to filing a complaint. A written election of the refund or replacement remedy, along with a specific demand for money damages should accompany or promptly follow this rescission notice. Samples of the two notices discussed above are provided at the end of this chapter.

Prior Resort to
Informal Dispute Mechanisms (IDM)

While the original intent behind IDM was to encourage warrantors to establish procedures whereby consumer disputes could be fairly and expeditiously settled, the process can in fact be just one more hurdle and delay. As described in Chapter 7, above, most state lemon laws require prior resort to an informal dispute mechanism, as long as the mechanism complies with applicable FTC regulations.

However, even where a particular IDM program purports to comply with the federal regulations, or is certified as being generally in compliance, you are free to proceed without it if delays render it noncomplying in a particular case. Federal law requires the mechanism to render a decision within forty days of notification of an action. Thus, the United States Court of Appeals for the Third Circuit has held that where Nissan had contracted with the BBB Autoline to provide an informal dispute mechanism, but the BBB did not respond to Fannie Harrison's complaint within forty days, nothing more was required before Ms. Harrison could file her complaint in district court.[3]

If prior resort to IDM is an express prerequisite to a civil action, be sure to plead that this requirement has been exhausted before filing suit. If recourse to the mechanism is excused because it fails to comply with the federal rules in general, or as applied in the particular instance, plead the facts excusing your client's failure of prior resort to avoid a motion to dismiss.

MOST LEMON LAW CLAIMS
ARE FILED IN STATE,
NOT FEDERAL COURT

Most individual suits to enforce lemon law rights will have to be brought in state court. A state lemon law claim provides no federal jurisdiction. In unusual cases, it will be possible to add on a federal claim to the lemon law claim, and then bring the claim in federal court. The best candidate for such a claim is under the federal Magnuson-Moss Warranty Act, which provides a cause of action for breach of a written warranty or an implied warranty. But that statute grants federal court jurisdiction only where the amount in controversy is $50,000 or more.

Under the Magnuson-Moss Act Warranty, a number of individuals' claims may be joined, and damages aggregated to reach $50,000. Whether punitive damages may support federal jurisdiction depends on their availability under applicable state law. On the other hand, your attorneys fee claim may not be used to satisfy the $50,000 jurisdictional amount because the Act requires that the amount in controversy be calculated "exclusive of interests and costs," and attorneys fees have been held to be "costs" under the Act. The amount in controversy is important even if the case is brought in state court because this amount will determine which of your available state courts have competent jurisdiction.

WHO SHOULD BRING A LEMON LAW CLAIM

Chapter 1 examines when a transaction is covered by a lemon law claim. If a transaction is covered by the lemon law, the consumer typically has the right to go to court to enforce that law.

You want a vehicle's principal driver to be a named plaintiff wherever possible. The actual driver is the best witness to prove the element of "substantial impairment" as well as the applicable items of damages. But the vehicle's principal driver may not be the person whose signature appears on the car's paperwork. Spouses will arrive together at the dealership, agree on the model, agree on the color, agree on the options, and agree on the price. Then one will leave to pick up the kids or race off to the office, while the other remains to "finish up the paperwork." Or well-meaning parents may use their own established credit to buy a car for their college-bound child to drive away to school.

In these contexts, the issue is whether the principal driver can sue under the lemon law where that driver is not the title owner. Where you name a plaintiff other than the party stated in the contract, it is wise to allege specific facts stating a third party beneficiary claim or other theory of equitable ownership.

A related question is this: do co-signers have the right to bring a lemon law claim? Yes. Certainly they accepted all the obligations of the contract; they should be entitled to the reciprocal bundle of rights as well.

The dangers of co-signing are too seldom considered by the consumer public. People may use their hard-earned credit to help out a relative, a friend, or business colleague. Co-signers are not in control of the goods, have no direct control over the mileage placed on the vehicle, no knowledge or control of use and abuse, merely remote control over whether required maintenance is performed, and only secondhand knowledge of the repair history.

Despite these practical drawbacks, the co-signer is a proper party to a lemon law claim. The co-signer is a purchaser damaged by the defective character of the goods and the failure of the manufacturer to conform those goods to warranty. Every actual purchaser named in the retail installment sales contract (or lease where applicable) should be made a party plaintiff.

WHO SHOULD BE SUED?

The Manufacturer

Typically, a lemon law case will name as a defendant either the manufacturer or the U.S. importer/distributor of a foreign manufacturer. The importer or distributor is an agent of the foreign manufacturer for purposes of warranty compliance; you do not have to translate the complaint into German under the Hague convention and fly off to Munich to serve BMW with a lemon law claim.

Where you are dealing with General Motors or Chrysler, the matter is pretty straightforward. However, in the case of obscure models like the now defunct Pininfarina sportster, the corporate trail can be challenging indeed. There are still a few lemon lawyers around who ruefully remember the Yugo, that sputtering Serbo-Croatian creation, which was briefly exported from the former Yugoslavia.

You may have multiple manufacturers and multiple warranties. In a motor home case you should look for the chassis manufacturer and the coach manufacturer separately. Study the terms and conditions of each company's express warranties. In states which allow lemon law protection for boats you may very well encounter multiple manufacturers of engine and hull components. These complications require patience and precision, but you should sort out the relationships as early as possible in the proceedings and protect yourself further by including DOE defendant allegations.

Privity is not a problem in a lemon law claim. It is irrelevant that the consumer did not purchase the vehicle directly from the manufacturer. The lemon law itself will provide the statutory basis to sue the manufacturer despite the lack of privity.

When Should You Name a Dealer as a Defendant?

Although the manufacturer, as principal warrantor, is the primary target defendant in a lemon law claim, you should always scrutinize the role and conduct of the authorized selling and servicing dealers. The selling dealer may well have breached an implied warranty of merchantability or fitness. If the selling dealer issued its own separate warranty in connection with the sale, that dealer is the express warrantor vis a vis its own warranty. This circumstance is relatively rare in the sale of a new motor vehicle, but may arise with respect to demonstrators or other vehicles whose prior use has triggered the in-service date on the manufacturer's warranty before its first retail sale. Selling dealer warranties are sometimes referred to as "adjustment warranties" which supposedly cover items such as squeaks and rattles, air leaks, alignment, and other minor annoyances.[4]

A critical tactical decision is deciding whether to bring the dealer and/or lender into the lawsuit.

If a selling dealer installed after-factory equipment such as a lift kit, cruise control, or rustproofing which actually operated to void the manufacturer's warranty, you should examine potential tort claims against the dealer whose acts or omissions the manufacturer will use as a defense against your lemon law claim. You should also examine all separate warranties which accompany the later installed options.

If the servicing dealer failed to perform warranty repairs in a sound and workmanlike manner, or otherwise acted negligently in its role as the manufacturer's agent for purposes of repair, you will want to name the dealer in a separately included tort cause of action. It is not unheard of for the servicing dealer to further damage the vehicle in the repair process during a technician's test drive or employee joy ride.

A large minority of state lemon laws include an express statutory exemption for dealers. Montana, for example provides "Nothing in this part imposes any liability on a dealer or creates a cause of action by a consumer against a dealer under [the refund/replacement section]."[5] This does not however prohibit claims against the dealer for common law torts such as negligence, fraud, and misrepresentation, or for a claim under a state deceptive practices statute. Even the dealer exemption clause must be reconciled with the uniform provision in state lemon laws which provides, for example, "The provisions of this part do not limit the rights or remedies available to a consumer under any other law."[6]

The advantage of naming the dealer in litigation is three-fold. First, you can obtain the complete service file in discovery, without having to use the subpoena power. Courts will generally allow you greater scope in two party discovery than in discovery from nonparties, should there be resistance to production. The complete service file can be the difference between success and failure in proving your lemon law claim.

Secondly, you do not want to be in the unfortunate position at trial of having the defendant manufacturer point the finger of blame at an empty chair. Although the dealer is the manufacturer's agent for purposes of repair, the merchant may try to argue that the dealer committed acts or omissions that were unauthorized and beyond the scope of the agency created by the warranty. These technical defense arguments are designed to confuse the jury and cause even a meritorious claim to fall through the cracks. At the outset of a case, you may not even know which repairs were authorized and which were denied in the repair history of your particular vehicle, despite all the pre-litigation investigation you can do.

The third reason is that the dealer usually originated the car loan, and a meritorious claim against the dealer raises defenses to loan repayment, either directly against the lender if the lender still has the paper or against the lender's assignee. In the several years it takes to resolve a lemon law claim, the lender will not agree to waive payment, but may damage the consumer's credit rating, repossess the lemon vehicle, or take other detrimental action. Bringing the dealer and lender into the case protects the consumer to some extent from these problems.

Lender Liability

Most consumers have one major blockade to bringing a lemon law claim. They don't own the whole vehicle; the bank holds a title lien. Yet the lemon law requires that the consumer return the vehicle in exchange for replacement or refund. The holder of title cannot be ignored. The lawyer who fails to recognize this problem at the outset does a gross disservice to the client. The bank may not cooperate at the settlement stage, or a confused jury may award the consumer less than the consumer still owes to the bank.

The lender or lessor is generally liable for all claims and defenses you have against the dealer.

The source of funds in a retail installment sale falls into one of two categories, which play very different roles in the litigation — dealer and independent financing. Independent financing is arranged directly by the consumers through their own bank or credit union.

Dealer financing includes either dealer paper or motor vehicle loans arranged or assisted by the dealer at the time of sale. Dealers will place the paper with local banks sometimes as a favor to benefit their own flooring relationship, with loan sharks which scavenge for higher risk credit customers, or with the captive finance companies which are subsidiaries of the manufacturer, such as Ford Motor Credit Corporation, General Motors Acceptance Corporation, Chrysler Credit, and Toyota Motor Credit Corporation.

Where the dealer has arranged the financing in a retail sale, the FTC "Holder Rule" places the lender directly in the shoes of the selling dealer.[7] The loan documents contain the following notice:

NOTICE

ANY HOLDER OF THIS CONSUMER CREDIT CONTRACT IS SUBJECT TO ALL CLAIMS AND DEFENSES WHICH THE DEBTOR COULD ASSERT AGAINST THE SELLER OF GOODS OR SERVICES OBTAINED PURSUANT HERETO OR WITH THE PROCEEDS HEREOF. RECOVERY HEREUNDER BY THE DEBTOR SHALL NOT EXCEED AMOUNTS PAID BY THE DEBTOR HEREUNDER.

Consequently, the holder of the consumer's car loan can be brought in as a defendant in the case.

For leases the analysis is a little different. The dealer is usually the originating lessor and assigns the lease to a finance company or bank. In that case, the assignee finance company or bank is subject to all of the consumer's defenses that could be raised against the assignor (i.e. the dealer).

In either the case of dealer-arranged financing or dealer-originated leasing, bringing in the lender as a party in the action simplifies the lawsuit. The consumer can force the lender to turn over title to the manufacturer if the court orders return of the vehicle to the manufacturer. It also allows for precise adjustment of the proper amount for the consumer's monetary recovery, so that the consumer comes out not owing anything to the lender. Bringing the lender into the case can also prevent repossession of the vehicle pending resolution of the case and prevents damage to the consumer's credit rating.

If, however, your client obtained independent financing, the Holder Rule will not apply. Where the consumer did not submit a credit application to the dealer, the FTC notice need not be given and the independent bank may demand payment. Payments should continue, unless you are able to negotiate a separate written forbearance agreement from the lender pending litigation. Sometimes the bank will agree to accept interest-only payments until the outcome of the case is resolved. If clients obtained the financing on their own, the bank may be convinced to cooperate in order to protect that relationship. In any event, you should maintain close communication with the bank to obtain accurate payoff figures as settlement or other dispute resolution nears.

DRAFTING THE COMPLAINT

By this time you are convinced your lemon law claim has merit. The client makes a credible witness; the documents are in order; the defendants appear solvent; your expert confirms this vehicle is a lemon. Just to be sure, you have checked off the elements of the lemon law claim discussed in Chapter 2 and evaluated the manufacturer's defenses described in Chapter 3.

Now is the time to pause and exercise some lateral thinking. You may have other statutory and common law claims which will strengthen your basic lemon law case, widen discovery, expand the available remedies, and guard against certain defenses. The relative impact of these secondary causes of action must await discovery. But at the outset, your client interview, investigation, careful analysis of documents, and some healthy skepticism will direct you toward the full range of possibilities.

On the other hand, drafting a complaint is not like writing a law school exam. You don't get extra points just for stating sixteen causes of action where three or four solid claims provide the full range of remedies and demolish the same defenses. A patchwork pleading loses persuasive effect and invites dismissal. You want to consider all the options with their various burdens of proof, elements, and available remedies. You should then focus on nailing down every element of the strongest claims in clear plain language without hot air or self-serving hyperbole. An example of a lemon law complaint with two other related claims is found at National Consumer Law Center, *Consumer Law Pleadings With Disk Number Two* (1995).

Identifying Parties to the Action and Other General Allegations

Your standard introductory paragraphs will include grounds for jurisdiction and venue, the identity of the parties, a provision for fictitious defendants, and agency allegations. Be sure to plead the agency relationship between the manufacturer and the dealer for purposes of repair or notice. If you have a foreign manufacturer whose domestic distributor is your warrantor, plead an agency relationship between the named defendant and any other entity whose acts and omissions will bear on the conduct of the named party.

If the lender is a named party defendant, you must allege the fact of dealer paper and the basis for a claim against the seller which will allow you to plead your case within the Holder Rule. If you have a party plaintiff who is not named in the contract, remember to plead your third party beneficiary relationship at the outset. If you are naming a dealer defendant, identify it as the sales or selling dealer and describe in agency language the fact that it is the authorized dealer of the manufacturer or warrantor.

Manufacturers routinely take the indefensible position that their authorized agents are independent contractors. To be on the safe side, in addition to pleading specific facts supporting actual agency, you should plead ostensible agency in terms like this:

> At all times relevant herein FITZPATRICK CHEVROLET held itself out to be an authorized GENERAL MOTORS/CHEVROLET DIVISION dealership and agent of the manufacturer and warrantor GENERAL MOTORS CORPORATION. The dealership bears the manufacturer's brand name, uses its logo in advertising and on its warranty repair orders, posts its sign for the public to see, and enjoys an exclusive regional franchise to sell the manufacturer's products including the subject vehicle.

If you are naming a corporate dealer defendant which is wholly owned by an individual, it is prudent to plead alter ego to protect against future dealer insolvency and to allow the dealer to avail itself of possible insurance coverage for the claim. For example: "Plaintiff is informed and believes and on that basis alleges, that SWIFT MOTORS is the alter ego of its owner JOHN D. SWIFT, and that there is insufficient separation of identity between the owner and the corporate entity, such that injustice would result to plaintiff in this matter if the corporate veil were to remain intact."

Pleading the Elements of a Lemon Law Violation

Before drafting you complaint, review the elements of your lemon law claim discussed in Chapters 2 and 3, above. Your statutory claim should be clear, concise, and accurate. Begin your narrative with a description of the sales transaction, identifying the vehicle by VIN number which appears on the contract and door panel. Attach the purchase contract as Exhibit 1. The retail installment sales contract itself is supposed to have boxes for "new" vehicle and "personal use" which should satisfy the threshold coverage requirements; however if the boxes are checked "used" vehicle or "business" use, you must allege facts which will bring you within the scope of your particular statute.

You must next allege terms of the applicable warranty or warranties. Some jurisdictions require you to quote the exact warranty language, which you can do by making pertinent portions of the warranty or warranties additional exhibits. If you do not in fact know which of the various warranties (each having different time periods and terms) will ultimately allow you to prevail, cover your bases with alternative allegations to avoid being caught in left field without a glove at the time of trial.

If you are even close to a statute of limitations problem, only careful and accurate pleading may avoid dismissal. One effective way to address the problem of a time-barred action is to point out by factual allegations that the warrantor's authorized repair dealer falsely represented that the vehicle was fixed after each repair thus triggering the doctrine of equitable tolling which estops the time-bar defense. The rationale is that the aggrieved consumer delayed asserting warranty rights only because the dealer repeatedly misrepresented that the car was fixed, thereby unlawfully lulling your client into inaction.

You will next want to describe the nonconformities by listing the conditions complained of or the history of work performed and plead substantial impairment. Set forth the specific conditions and components straight from the repair chronology which you initially prepared. You must also plead facts satisfying any notice requirements and prior resort to IDM.

Requested Relief

You should set forth in your pleading your request for replacement or refund, damages and attorney fees. Most lemon law statutes add some provision for incidental or collateral damages. You should be aware that courts tend not to allow compensation for emotional distress in lemon law cases, although there may be state variations. All but about five states provide for legal fees to the consumer who ultimately prevails in court on the lemon law claim.

About ten states provide for mandatory or discretionary multiple or statutory damages in the event manufacturers willfully or intentionally violate the lemon law. In some instances the penalty is assessed for a manufacturer's frivolous or bad faith appeal from an IDM award. In others, the statute speaks in terms of bad faith, unreasonable, or willful violation of the lemon law. If your lemon law provides for multiple or other special damages for willful or bad faith violation of lemon law rights, you will want, where applicable, to plead this willfulness or bad faith, and request such enhanced damages.

California cases have struggled with the wording of an appropriate jury instruction on the issue of when a violation is willful. A violation of the act is not willful "if the defendant's failure to replace or refund was the result of a good faith and reasonable belief the facts imposing the statutory obligation were not present." On the other hand, a "decision made without the use of reasonably available information germane to that decision is not a reasonable, good faith decision."[8]

The plaintiff should be prepared to prove that the particular manufacturer either had no policies in place to comply with the act, or failed to follow and implement such policies in the given instance. Discovery of policies and procedures manuals, internal memoranda, customer complaint handling, lapse of time between notice of defects and response are all relevant to proving the necessary corporate state of mind. The deposition of the zone representative involved in the decision not to buy back the vehicle may be crucial to obtaining multiple damages.

In states which provide for multiple damages, it is well worth the extra effort to establish willful, unreasonable, or bad faith behavior. This is not just to increase the recovery in a particular individual case, but because within the enhanced award lies the true enforcement value of this remedial legislation.

This chapter below provides a damage calculation sheet, which should be used only with the caveat that all items are not allowed in every state, and some items are applied differently in the case of replacement rather than refund. You must look at the specific language of your state statute in calculating damages in every case. The author advises constructing your own checklist.

DAMAGE CALCULATION SHEET

Contract Purchase Price

Purchase Price down payment including trade-in value $

Payments as of [current date] $
[Multiply the number times amount of actual payments made.
If you have made additional, partial, or non-payments, please
indicate the amounts separately.]

Loan payoff/Lease Buyout as of [current date] $
[The payoff amount should be after your most recent payment.]

Incidental & Consequential Damages

Loan Fee: $
[Processing fee for the loan. This is not the interest
due on the financed principle.]

Subsequent year registration: $
[Do not include the DMV registration fees that are listed on
your purchase contract, only DMV fees incurred later.]

Insurance from date of delivery to present: $

Unreimbursed alternative transportation: $

Unreimbursed repairs: [Include regular maintenance and oil changes.] $

Additional equipment: $
[Any items claimed in this section must be returned with the vehicle]

Inspection of vehicle: $

[Expenses for returning goods for repair, i.e.,
mileage ___ round trips to the dealer x ___ /mile;
cost of independent inspection to verify defects.] $

Telephone, postage, mileage, etc.: $

Loss of use for intended purposes: [minority rule] $

Inconvenience, annoyance $
[may not be available in most states]

                                                                         subtotal: $

Civil Penalty

2x actual damages $
[see statute to see multiplier and if available]

Attorneys Fees $

                                                                            total: $

Do You Plead a Magnuson-Moss Warranty Act Claim or UCC Article 2 Claim in Addition to Your Lemon Law Claim?

Lemon lawyers often disagree whether you should add to your lemon law complaint a claim under the federal Magnuson-Moss Warranty Act. This author feels that if you have a solid state law claim which provides for attorneys fees to the prevailing consumer, and you want to be in state court, there is no reason to plead an alternative claim under the federal act. The Magnuson-Moss Act looks to state law for remedies, and therefore if the state remedies are adequate, and state court is preferable, the federal claim is superfluous.

On the other hand, if you are in one of the six or so states whose lemon law does not provide for attorneys fees, the Magnuson-Moss Act does so. The Magnuson-Moss Act also uses an objective test for vehicles it covers — any vehicle whose common use is for consumer purposes even if a particular individual's use is for business purposes. If your state lemon law has a subjective test as to whether a vehicle is covered by the statute, and your client used her Ford Explorer partly for business, the objective test of Magnuson-Moss will be a preferable basis for the claim. Magnuson-Moss also provides the availability of a federal forum if you meet the amount in controversy and other jurisdictional requirements.

Do not forget that you can also bring a simple breach of warranty claim under UCC Article 2. This claim will not provide for attorney fees or enhanced damages, but it may provide a safe addition if there is some doubt about the viability of the lemon law claim. For example, if a consumer ignores a requirement for IDM and goes right to court, the lemon law claim may be dismissed, but the claim under Article 2 will still go forward.

Dealer Fraud, Deception at the Time of Repair, and/or Negligent Repair

In addition to claims against the manufacturer for failing to comply with the lemon law, you can also, based on the same facts, add claims for the dealer's failure to repair. Your client is prepared to testify that each time the repair dealer returned the car, the service manager said it was fixed and ready for pick-up. In most lemon law cases, this representation is false or your client wouldn't be in your office now.

Other times, the service department reports "no problem found" to frustrated consumers who have repeatedly attempted to repair a problem. Those whom the dealers perceive to be mechanically incompetent are made to feel they have imagined the abnormal engine noise, steering vibration, brake shudder, hard start, transmission whine. "Could not duplicate complaint" appears on the repair order which the customer receives.

It may be possible to establish that the servicing dealer intentionally and knowingly lied when it stated that the problem had been fixed or that there was no problem. Internal documents such as service advisories and Technical Service Bulletins may indicate that the manufacturer admits there is no fix currently available,[9] and the servicing dealer's possession of such bulletin indicates that it knew this as well.

The *backside* of the hard copy of the repair orders containing the technician's notes may in fact show the dealer and manufacturer know of the problem, but have no fix available at that time. The documents contain other clues. The repair order should give the mileage at the time delivered and returned; this data may reveal the car was not even test driven. Although many defects can be simulated up on the rack, many intermittent problems will go undetected unless the vehicle is driven under actual road conditions. Many such intermittent nonconformities involve steering, brakes or stalling — all of which may be safety problems rendering the vehicle unsafe to drive. It is thus either gross negligence or intentional fraud where the dealer does not even bother to test drive the car.

An allegation of servicing dealer fraud may be useful in tolling the statute of limitations, as discussed above, or extending warranty coverage past the designated period. It may also amount to a separate cause of action — fraud or deceit, and certainly a violation of a state unfair and deceptive trade practice statute. The fraud claim can lead to punitive damages, and the unfair and deceptive trade practice claim can lead in some states to multiple, minimum, or punitive damages and/or attorney fees. Both claims may also lead to recovery of damages based on emotional distress.

You may also be able to use your deceptive practices claim as a basis to seek injunctive relief — a remedy that may be particularly effective against a large manufacturer. If, for example, your investigation uncovers a Technical Service Bulletin stating that there is no fix currently available for fuel leaks in a particular duel tank system, you might recover damages for your own client under a lemon law claim and enjoin the manufacturer from asserting in other court or IDM cases that the nonconformity has been fixed. Your client goes away happy, and you have done a great deal of good for the consumer public.

The deceptive practices act claim has other advantages. You may bring it not against the dealer for deceptive repair practices, but against the manufacturer for failing to disclose vehicle defects, for selling a defective car, for engaging in a secret warranty program, or for false advertising as to vehicle quality.

Even if a dealer is not deceptive or fraudulent in its repair practices, it still can be negligent in failing to repair the vehicle. Some lemon law statutes expressly provide that manufacturers have the duty to maintain sufficient service and repair facilities to carry out the terms of their written warranties. Indeed, such a duty is implied under every lemon law.

Thus where such a facility fails to use due care in making repairs or fails to perform service in a workmanlike manner, and the plaintiff is thereby damaged, a claim in tort for negligence will lie against both the agent and its principal. The written warranty itself creates the duty. Even in those states which expressly exempt dealers from statutory lemon law claims, the dealer should be subject to this separate tort claim, because a consumer protection statute should not be read to reduce otherwise available common law claims.

Other Automobile Claims Not Related to Warranty Defects

Consumers can have a whole array of claims against a dealer or manufacturer relating to a car purchase that are in addition to the lemon law claim — undisclosed damage in a new vehicle, deceptive financing or leasing practices, high pressure sales tactics, treatment of trade-ins or rebates, service contracts, and much more. These other claims are listed in some detail in Chapter 10, below. Their inclusion in a lemon law case can significantly enhance the consumer's recovery and settlement position with the manufacturer, dealer, and lender.

SAMPLE RESCISSION NOTICE

NOTICE OF RESCISSION OF CONTRACT, REJECTION AND/OR REVOCATION OF ACCEPTANCE OF VEHICLE

I.

Notice is hereby given that Brian Jones rescinds that certain contract signed by him on February 2, 1999 at Thurston Toyota, an authorized Toyota dealership in Birmingham, Alabama, by the terms of which Brian Jones entered into the purchase of a 1999 Toyota 4-Runner, Vehicle Identification Number (VIN) JT4UD10D2S0009610. The total purchase price with financing was $47,965. A copy of the Purchase Contract is attached hereto as Exhibit A.

II.

Brian Jones hereby exercises his rights to revoke acceptance of this vehicle because the vehicle was sold to him under fraud and mistake, and further because it fails to conform to the applicable warranties.

III.

The grounds for rescission of the contract and revocation of acceptance of the vehicle are as follows:

a. Violation of the Repurchase/Replacement Provisions of the Lemon Law

Since the date of purchase, the vehicle has been in for repair an unreasonable number of times due to defective conditions in the vehicle. Such conditions substantially impair the use, safety and value of the vehicle. Toyota and its representatives have been unable to repair the defects and have refused to replace the vehicle or refund to Brian Jones the money paid for the vehicle pursuant to [the applicable state lemon law]. As a result the consideration received by Brian Jones under the contract has failed in whole or material part though the fault of the manufacturer and its representatives.

Brian Jones entered into the contract under the mistaken belief that the vehicle was free from defects and was in a fit and merchantable condition. In fact, the vehicle was defective, unfit for use as safe and reliable transportation, and in an unmerchantable condition at the time of sale. Had Brian Jones known the true condition of the vehicle, he would not have entered into the contract and would not have taken delivery of the vehicle.

b. Intentional Misrepresentation or Concealment [if applicable]

At the time of sale to Brian Jones, Toyota Motor Company and Thurston Toyota misrepresented that the vehicle was a new vehicle in new vehicle condition, when in fact it [had been previously damaged and improperly repaired/or other applicable facts].

IV.

Based on the above facts and circumstances, the vehicle has failed in material respect to comply with the representations and warranties made by Toyota Motor Company and its authorized representative Thurston Toyota, and justifies Brian Jones' revoking acceptance of the contract (Exhibit A). The public interest would be prejudiced in permitting this contract to stand, insofar as it was obtained by mistake of fact or fraud and breach of warranty, [and insofar as it would permit the maintenance of an unsafe or unreliable vehicle on our public highways if applicable], and therefore the contract should be rescinded.

V.

Brian Jones with this Notice of Rescission, Rejection and/or Revocation of Acceptance, hereby tenders to Toyota Motor Company, [and Thurston Toyota if dealer fraud is alleged in paragraph III(b) above] that certain 1999 Toyota 4-Runner, VIN JT4UD10D2S0009610. Demand is hereby made for refund of the full purchase price, finance charges, and all other consequential and incidental damages, along with legal fees and costs, as allowed by law.

Dated:

Signed:

DEMAND LETTER TO MANUFACTURER

[Date]

[Manufacturer]
[Manufacturer's Address]
   RE: Jane Jones v. Manufacturer

Dear Sir or Madam:

   This letter is to inform you that we have been retained by Jane Jones to represent her in her case against [Manufacturer] arising out of her purchase of a defective [year][make/model] from [dealership] on [date of purchase].

   With this letter I enclose a copy of the notice of Rescission of Contract, Rejection and/or Revocation of Acceptance of the vehicle. Pursuant to her rights under the Commercial Code, Jane Jones will be holding the vehicle to protect her secured interest in the vehicle until the [manufacturer] returns all money and consideration paid by her and compensates her for incidental and consequential damages, attorneys fees, costs and expenses arising out of this matter.

   At the present time we are prepared to settle this case for [specify dollar amount], based upon the damage calculation enclosed herewith. This is an offer to compromise this claim.

   You are specifically instructed not to contact our client, Mrs. Jones, and I suggest that you present this letter along with the enclosures to your legal counsel for review. Please have him or her contact me so that we can determine whether or not we can resolve this matter or whether it will be necessary to file a complaint. I look forward to hearing from you.

Very Truly Yours,

[Attorney]
enc
cc: Jane Jones

---

[1] Krotin v. Porsche Cars North America, 38 Cal. App. 3d 294 (1995) (direct formal notice to the manufacturer is not required where the warranty history itself has put the manufacturer on notice of the nonconformity).

[2] S.C. Code Ann. §56-28-50(E).

[3] Harrison v. Nissan Motor Corporation in U.S.A., 111 F.3d 343 (3d Cir. 1997).

[4] Sutton, R., *Don't Get Taken Every Time* (rev. ed. 1991).

[5] Montana Code Annot. §§61-4-505, -506.

[6] Gillis, J., *The CAR Book* (16th Ed. 1996).

[7] 16 C.F.R. §433.

[8] Kwan v. Mercedes Benz of North America 23 Cal. App. 4th 174(1994).

[9] A significant number of TSBs are available through NHTSA. Access these records via the Internet at www.NHTSA.dot.gov and see also Chapter 6, "Establishing the Facts," above.

– 9 –

Pretrial Discovery

When a consumer brings a lemon law claim before an informal dispute resolution mechanism (IDM), there is little or no opportunity to obtain information from the automobile manufacturer or dealer. Taking the case to court dramatically alters this imbalance. The consumer can compel the manufacturer and dealer to supply much valuable information. The complexities of this process of compelling the other side to provide information, called "discovery," is one of the reasons that legal representation is so important when a lemon law claim goes to court.

This chapter provides detailed pointers on what information to seek through discovery for a claim under a state's lemon law. As such, the chapter is primarily geared to lawyers, but it presented in plain language for laymen because consumers may find the information of interest.

The next chapter lists a number of other legal claims the consumer may have against the manufacturer or dealer that you may want to join in the same lawsuit. The discovery tips here may help you uncover these additional claims, but they are not designed to flesh out in detail information about these other causes of action. The focus here is on obtaining information relevant to the lemon law claim, including information that demonstrates that the manufacturer and/or dealer behaved with willful disregard for the consumer's rights.

There are three basic forms of discovery: interrogatories, requests for production of documents and depositions. This chapter deals with each in order. Interrogatories are written questions that call for a written response. Requests for production of documents require the other side to provide documents that exist in that party's control. Depositions require a particular individual to come forward well before the actual trial begins and be questioned under oath.

Each of these forms of discovery must be tailored differently depending on whether you are sending the request to the manufacturer, the selling dealer, the servicing dealer, or the lender. Often one or more of these parties will not comply voluntarily, and this chapter also discusses how to force that party to give you the information you want.

INTERROGATORIES TO SEND TO THE MANUFACTURER, DEALER, AND LENDER

Interrogatories are most useful to identify witnesses in lemon law cases, with the main sources of discovery being requests for documents and depositions. There is incredible turnover of personnel in the automotive industry. In asking for the identity of witnesses, take care to get the last known address of any employee who is no longer employed.

What follows is a list of interrogatory subjects to ask the manufacturer, dealer, and lender. You must break down these categories to avoid objections as to compound questions. These are not specific sample requests. (For an actual example of such interrogatories in print and on a floppy disk, see National Consumer Law Center, *Consumer Law Pleadings With Disk, Number Two* Ch. 5 (1995). In your interrogatories, start by defining the subject vehicle by the VIN number which you used in the complaint. Then you can ask questions in the following areas.

Interrogatories to the Manufacturer

You will want to ask the manufacturer to provide the identity of the following:
  • Employees who communicated with the plaintiff, as
    well as the date, nature and general substance of these
    communications.
  • Employees who inspected or repaired the subject vehicle,
    along with the date and nature of the inspection or repair.
  • Employees who communicated with any authorized dealership
    concerning the subject vehicle, as well as the date, nature and
    general substance of these communications.
  • Employees who communicated or submitted a report to any
    informal dispute mechanism concerning the vehicle.
  • The zone representative(s) responsible for warranty and service

matters in plaintiff's region from the purchase date and the person who had authority to offer a refund or replacement vehicle in accordance with the lemon law.

In addition you will want to ask contention interrogatories as to the basis for selected affirmative defenses, and those paragraphs of the complaint alleging that the defective conditions were not repaired within a reasonable time. You also want to know whether the manufacturer contends the dealer is at fault for not performing repairs in a workmanlike manner, and the precise basis for that contention.

Interrogatories to the Dealers

If the dealer is not a defendant, you should serve a subpoena duces tecum to the service manager for original repair orders, service file and warranty reimbursement claims history. If the dealer is a defendant, you need to ask the dealer to identity the following:

- Employees who communicated with plaintiff at any time, as well as the date, nature and general substance of these communications.
- Employees who inspected or repaired the vehicle, along with the date and nature of the inspection or repair. Examine repair orders for technician employees numbers; add these numbers to your request.
- Employees who communicated with the manufacturer or any other authorized dealership concerning the subject vehicle, as well as the date, nature and general substance of these communications.
- Employees who communicated or submitted a report to any informal dispute mechanism concerning vehicle.
- All service manager(s) from date of purchase to the present, with the dates they held such title.
- Employee most knowledgeable regarding warranty policies of that dealer and the subject manufacturer.

In addition, you will want to ask contention interrogatories as to the basis for selected affirmative defenses and those paragraphs of the complaint alleging the defective conditions were not repaired within a reasonable time. You also want to know whether the dealer contends that the manufacturer failed to make available sufficient service literature or replacement parts to effect repairs during the express warranty period, or denied warranty claims at any time, and the basis for these contentions.

Interrogatories to the Lender

From the lender you want the identity of employees who communicated with plaintiff, the manufacturer and the dealer concerning the loan or lease of the vehicle. Attach the purchase or lease contract to the discovery request to avoid overbreadth or ambiguity objections and to support good cause.

REQUESTS FOR PRODUCTION OF DOCUMENTS

As with interrogatories, define the subject vehicle by the VIN number used in the complaint. Include also in your definitions a statement that the term "document" includes computerized information. Communications between dealers and manufacturers are highly computerized these days and you must tap into that ephemeral material to prove your breach of warranty case.

Document Requests to Send to the Manufacturer

From the manufacturer, you want to ask for the complete file on the subject vehicle held in national, regional, district, or zone files, *and* all documents relating to the subject vehicle in the following categories:
- Pre-sale inspections, transit/transport bills of lading and invoices, pre-delivery inspection (PDI) reports, insurance claims and accounts of pre-sale damage.
- Repair orders, including dealer "hard copies" showing mechanics' notes.
- Warranty and repair history, warranty claims and payments or denials.
- Pre-litigation inspections, field service reports, universal data reports and technical inspections, and any evaluation as to whether the vehicle meets state or federal lemon laws.

- All communications with plaintiff, customer assistance requests, written correspondence, telephone records, notes of personal meetings, notices, complaints, and manufacturer response to each, and all internal notes or comments relating to such communication.
- Technical service bulletins (TSBs) relating to each condition or defect alleged in the complaint, as well as the most current TSB index relating to the make and model of the vehicle, OASIS/CAMS/DIAL printout coded for allege nonconforming conditions and components.
- Recall and service campaign notices relating to the make and model of the subject vehicle.
- Each express warranty accompanying sale of the vehicle.
- Warranty policy and procedure manuals, customer relations manuals, field operations manuals.
- Complete informal dispute preparation and hearing files.
- All documents relating to the performance of each of the servicing dealers during the time the first dealer took possession of the vehicle to the present.

Document Requests
to Send to the Dealers

From the dealers, you want to ask for all documents relating to the subject vehicle in the following categories:

- Pre-delivery inspections (PDI), insurance claims for pre-sale damage, transit documents, dealer trade invoices, records relating to use as a demonstrator or loaner, and all repair orders pre-dating sale to plaintiff, body shop invoices, and any after-factory equipment installations.
- The complete sales file or sales jacket, including the sales or lease contract, all other documents given to plaintiff at the time of sale or after delivery, the "4 square," the trade-in appraisal, notes on negotiations, credit application, "deal recap" sheets, commission vouchers, sales summaries involving the subject transaction, DMV record of sale, odometer disclosure statement, due bills.

- The complete service file or service jacket, including due bills, repair orders (front and back), "hard copies" of repair orders showing mechanics' notes and time flags, inspections, customer assistance requests, warranty claims for reimbursement submitted to the manufacturer, warranty reimbursements, warranty claim denials, manufacturer authorizations to proceed with service work, parts orders.
- All other communications concerning the subject vehicle between the responding dealer and
  — any other dealer;
  — the plaintiff;
  — the manufacturer.
- Technical service bulletins, service campaigns, and recalls relating to the conditions, components and defects alleged in the complaint.
- Warranty policy and procedure manuals, customer relations policy and procedure manuals.
- Each evaluation concerning whether the vehicle falls within the scope of any federal or state lemon law.
- Communications with plaintiff, customer assistance requests, written correspondence, telephone records, notes of personal meetings, notices, complaints, and dealer response to each.
- Complete file concerning any independent dispute mechanism as to the vehicle.

DEPOSITIONS

Deposition of the
Manufacturer Zone Representative

Notice of deposition should be phrased *duces tecum*, designating original documents which you demand to have produced at the time of the deposition. This should track your manufacturer document request. Add the individual's own file, if not otherwise produced. Demand to see the originals even if copies have been produced in prior discovery. The *backside* of the original documents (especially repair orders) often produces surprising material helpful to the consumer's case.

The depositions need not be longwinded or rambling; yet don't be afraid to use the opportunity to educate yourself. You want to walk away knowing this manufacturer's general policies concerning compliance with the lemon law and whether those general policies were applied in practice in your particular case. For example, did the manufacturer have a reasonable basis to deny the lemon law claim, or did it just stonewall the consumer? The absence of compliance procedures may show willful disregard for the consumer's rights.

The main deposition you need from the manufacturer is that of the person who had the authority to refund or replace the vehicle. (The individual with authority to offer a replacement is not always the same person with authority to offer a refund.) Zone representatives can be evasive and cagey, particularly if "prepped" by opposing counsel to be non-responsive. Stick with your lines of questioning. In reviewing the history of consumer contacts, for example, you may feel like your client felt when placed on "hold" in the perpetually revolving door of the customer relations system. Remember: The deponent cannot hang up on you. Follow up the "I don't know" response with inquiry as to whether that knowledge would be within his job description, who would know, what reports are filled out, or should have been filled out relating the issue of questioning, and what inferences can be drawn from the absence of internal memoranda.

Establish accountability or else the absence of corporate policy assuring accountability for compliance with the lemon law in general and compliance with the lemon law in this particular case. In preparing for the deposition, study the policy and procedures manual, so that you can discuss company practice and the paper trail, and trace coherently the complete triangle of contacts between the dealer, the consumer and that particular person within the manufacturer's vast hierarchy who was ultimately authorized to say "no" or "yes." If you don't understand a technical term, make sure you ask the deponent to define it in context.

In a nutshell, you want to establish:
- That the zone had notice of the nonconformity;
- That the dealer had ample opportunity to repair;
- That the zone did not adequately investigate the claim;
- That the refusal to refund/replace was unjustified;
- That the manufacturer omitted facts or lied at IDM;
- That the nonconformity complained of affects the use, value or safety of the vehicle.

If the manufacturer has asserted by way of affirmative defense that its warranty does not apply to the facts of the case, you must also use this deposition to ascertain all facts which support such a contention. If the zone representative verified written discovery responses, you also want to interrogate about the diligence — or lack thereof — in responding to discovery and actually obtaining the documents sought, as well as the document retention and destruction policies.

Finally, you want to interpret all documents produced by the manufacturer, including detailed examination of computerized documents so that you and your expert know exactly what codes, abbreviations, and evaluations mean. You particularly want to determine which documents were made available to dealers and which were made available to the consumer at what time.

Deposition of the Dealer Service Manager

If the dealer is not a party to the lawsuit, you may want to subpoena the service manager. Sometimes this person will discuss the matter informally, but off the record remarks have a funny way of evaporating at the time of trial. Make a record with a declaration or a deposition.

The dealer service manager very often strengthens a lemon law claim. Unless your client was an obnoxious whiner (which you should have detected in the initial client interview), the service manager may be sympathetic. After all, they have spent a lot of time together. The service department tried its best to fix the vehicle to the consumer's satisfaction.

He may share some of the consumers' frustration that the factory authorized fixes just did not work. He may have seen other vehicles with similar components malfunctioning. And when you show him the manufacturer's affirmative defense or discovery responses alleging that the service department he proudly heads failed to perform repairs in a good and workmanlike manner, he may be furious enough to divulge that the manufacturer failed to provide adequate technical assistance.

In a nutshell, you want to establish:
- The evidentiary foundation for all of the repair orders and the complete warranty history;
- That the conditions and components complained of in fact existed;
- That the nonconformity has not been repaired;

- The number of times in the shop for each nonconformity (and how the various complaints relate to one another);
- The total number of days in the shop;
- The basis for any warranty claim denials;
- That the manufacturer had notice of the nonconformity and the zone did inadequate investigation of the claim (what tests were performed/what equipment used);
- That the servicing dealer is an authorized agent of the manufacturer for purposes of repair;
- That the refusal to refund/replace was unjustified;
- That the basis for what the manufacturer argued to IDM was flawed.

If the service manager verified written discovery responses, you also want to interrogate about the diligence — or lack thereof — in responding to discovery and actually obtaining the documents sought, as well as the document retention policies. Somewhere along the line you want to throw in this no-lose question: "Now, you wouldn't replace something that didn't need repair, would you?" If he says "yes," he may have violated a state unfair trade practice regulation against unnecessary automotive repairs. If he says, "no," he is admitting the part was defective.

Finally, you want to interpret all documents produced by any party, including detailed examination of computerized documents so that you and your expert know exactly what codes, abbreviations, and evaluations mean. The service manager will also be able to describe what information *that may have been omitted in production* is in fact accessible to the dealer by computer. You particularly want to determine which documents came from the manufacturer and which were made available to the consumer at what time.

It is absolutely essential that you obtain the *original* hard copy of the dealer repair orders. On the backside is a wealth of information which rarely finds its way into document productions.

Deposition of Defense Experts

As trial approaches, depose every defense expert. The notice should be phrased *duces tecum* for the expert's reports, and all materials reviewed or relied upon in forming an opinion. In a nutshell, you want to establish the expert's opinions and the basis for those opinions, and as far as possible the following:

- That the manufacturer had notice of the nonconformity;
- That the manufacturer's agent had the opportunity to repair the nonconformity and failed to do so at all, or at least within a reasonable time;
- That the nonconformity either still exists or the expert failed to do adequate testing to render that opinion;
- That, even if the nonconformity could now be fixed, the manufacturer failed to provide literature or instructions to the servicing dealer during the relevant time to make the fix;
- That the nonconformity complained of could affect the use, value or safety of the vehicle.

FIGHTING FOR DISCOVERY

Once pre-litigation IDM and settlement efforts have failed, prepare for a battle. It is quite common for the dealer or manufacturer to fail to respond to your discovery requests, and you will have to seek from the judge an order to compel discovery responses. If a motion seems inevitable, the best strategy is simply to address your meet and confer obligations promptly and thoroughly, setting out your statements of relevance and good cause in the very correspondence which you will later attach as Exhibit A to the motion.

When automakers really have something to hide, the process of discovering it can get ugly. Although not lemon law cases, the notorious Suzuki rollover litigation demonstrates how far the industry will go in bad faith discovery tactics. In that litigation, the court ordered the doomsday sanction of default against Suzuki for discovery abuse, as well as a monetary sanction of $5,000 against Suzuki and $500 personally against each defense lawyer.[1]

Ford, General Motors and other manufacturers have also been penalized for discovery abuses. In one such case, the court reversed a jury verdict in Ford's favor because, "through its misconduct in this case, Ford completely sabotaged the federal trial machinery, precluding the 'fair contest' which the Federal Rules of Civil Procedure are intended to serve."[2] Up against such tactics, consumer counsel must be clear and methodical in discovery requests, suspicious of evasive and incomplete responses, persistent in discovery motion practice, and thorough in all aspects of independent investigation.

The Client's Deposition

The manufacturer will want to take your client's deposition. Just as you will set out to develop the plaintiff's case through discovery, defense counsel will want to blow holes in that case by pinning down your client's version of the facts. It is all, as the casebooks say, in the search for truth. It is also a time when the opposing side sizes up your client's appearance, demeanor, and credibility — in short, the potential effect upon the jury.

When it comes time for your client's own deposition, it is advisable to prepare the client for the experience of being under oath, of listening, and of responding to the questions. Also important, it is a time for you and your client to build trust and rapport, essential in the course of the litigation. The fact that you and your client have met prior to the deposition is discoverable, but the subject matter and substance of the communication is protected by the attorney-client privilege. You should discuss the scope and limitations of this privilege at the time of the meeting, because the client can waive the privilege by opening the door to describe your conversation.

This is a good time to tell the client that the process appears informal, but the answers, taken under oath, will be transcribed into a booklet. Those answers may be used at trial, so despite the apparent informality of the proceeding, it is a serious business. You may want to show the client a sample transcript to demonstrate the basic format. The client should appear in clean but comfortable clothes, without pretense. It is important to determine that the client will not be under any medication, drug, alcohol or other substance which would impair listening, thinking or judgment. Be aware that this includes things many people take quite normally, like antihistamines, heart or blood pressure medication, and prescription painkillers which may cause drowsiness.

Experienced litigators advise their clients of four basic things to prepare for in the deposition: (1) Listen to the question. (2) Wait for the question. (3) Answer the question. (4) Tell the truth. What could be simpler? Still, it helps to explain these phrases in more detail.

"*Listen to the question.*" There is hardly anyone among us who could not improve listening skills. Whole shelves of books have been written on just this problem. Men don't listen to women. Women don't listen to men. Children don't listen to teachers or parents. Parents don't listen to toddlers or teens. Psychologists lament the fact that much of human misunderstanding is due to the failure to listen. This can be a real detriment for the average consumer facing a corporate lawyer who considers herself the con-summate wordsmith. The problem for the consumer lawyer is that the client has in mind his story and just can't wait to spill his guts. Implied in the word "listen" is the concept "wait."

"Wait for the question." The court reporter cannot take down two voices at the same time and interruptions lead to a messy record. It might not be the question expected. It might not even make sense. Or it might be com-pound and the first half is straightforward, but the second half is confusing. Fairness, and the discovery rules, require that the deposing attorney frame a question that is clear and intelligible. The party being deposed may request that it be rephrased or restated. If the client will just pause to listen to and absorb the question, his or her own attorney has an opportunity to listen, too, and may pose any objection or even order the client not to answer at all.

"Answer the question." Just the question. Not some other question. As with listening, this instruction is not as easy as it sounds. We are all accus-tomed to certain knee-jerk responses. A classic and everyday example of this tendency is the common query from strangers: "Got a watch?" You check your wrist and respond: "Yeah, 10:25." Wait a minute. No one asked what time it was. Maybe the stranger just wanted to steal the watch. The proper answer was either "yes," or "no." In a deposition the party being deposed should avoid irrelevant narrative. This is particularly true when the client is angry, nervous, anxious, impatient or irritated, which consumers often are by the time they have gotten this far. The opportunity to tell the whole story will come at trial, if need be. The deposition is merely the time to answer the questions presented.

"Tell the truth." The client should be advised that she will be under oath. Her credibility is being assessed, as well as the facts. You cannot tell the truth if you have not listened to the question and prepared to answer that particular question. You cannot tell the truth if you don't understand that question. The duty to tell the truth requires focus on the specific question posed at the moment. Having said that, the answers "I don't know," or "I don't remember," are perfectly acceptable if that is the truth. Documents may be used to refresh recollection in most instances.

Thereafter, the place to begin the privileged attorney-client discussion in preparation for the deposition is with the Notice of Deposition itself. You have probably sent it to the client by mail in advance of the meeting, but in any case, it is wise to go over it together. If it is duces tecum, you should determine which categories of documents will be produced and which are objectionable or unavailable. Discuss the documents which will be produced or have been produced. The notice defines the extent of the obligation to produce anything at the deposition and the client should bring nothing else on the designated day. Even if there is some other document which you intend to use to prove your case, if it is not requested, it is not to be brought.

The subject matter of each case, as framed by the complaint and other pleadings, will dictate the remaining preparation. Surely the purchase transaction and vehicle repair history, communications with the dealer, and correspondence or other contact with the manufacturer are all areas touching on the claim. Likewise, it is the time to discuss facts which may bear on the merits of opposing counsel's contentions and any defenses which have been raised.

---

[1] Malautea v. Suzuki Motor Corp., 148 F.R.D. 362 (S.D. Ga. 1991), *aff'd* 987 F.2d 1536 (11th Cir. 1992), *cert. den.* 114 S. Ct. 181 (1993).

[2] *See* Rozier v. Ford Motor Co. 573 F.2d 1332 at 1347 (5th Cir. 1978).

10

Flim-Flam, Fraud and Forgery — Alternative Claims in Lemon Law Cases

If you have to go to court to enforce your lemon law rights, you may add on any other claims you have that can enhance your court award. In most cases, there are a number of other claims to consider. Chapter 9 described other claims closed related to your lemon law claim and repair of the vehicle's defects under warranty. This chapter examines other types of claims relating to your vehicle purchase and vehicle performance.

The auto business presents the modern analog of horse trading,[1] with all of its unsavory connotations. Not all car dealers are dishonest by any means, but it is naive to think the reputation unearned. Dealer fraud is rampant and as varied as all the means of deceit human ingenuity can devise.

Sometimes the deceptive practices begin at the factory. Recall Ford's fiasco, the notorious Pinto. In 1968, Ford began designing a new subcompact. Lee Iacocca, then a Ford vice president, conceived and promoted the project. Crash tests revealed that the Pinto's fuel system could not meet the 20-mile-per-hour proposed standard, exposing vehicle occupants to serious injury or death. This could have been remedied with a fix of less than $20, but top management chose to produce the vehicle without the fix. Then in one accident Lilly Gray died, and her passenger, 13 year old Richard Grimshaw, "managed to survive but only through heroic medical measures [including] . . . extensive surgeries and skin grafts. . . ," all as a result of burns suffered in a crash fire.

The Grimshaw and the Gray families filed suit and, after a six-month trial, the jury awarded $125 million in punitive damages in addition to a substantial compensatory award. The appellate court held Ford's management had acted reprehensibly by "engaging in a cost-benefit analysis balancing human lives and limbs against corporate profits. Ford's institutional mentality was shown to be one of callous indifference to public safety."[2]

Ford is by no means alone. NHTSA safety recall records and the Center for Auto Safety investigations reveal a history of profit-motivated corporate indifference to human tragedy. One type of claim thus involves the tangible package of wheels, paint, chrome and engine which forms the vehicle itself.

It is just as important to examine the intangible means by which the consumer pays for the car. Finance companies and dealers can be as avaricious as manufacturers. Most auto makers now have wholly-owned "captive" finance companies, such as General Motors Acceptance Corporation, Ford Motor Credit Company, and Toyota Motor Credit Corporation. The annual reports of the major manufacturers frequently reveal that earnings of the financial captives exceed the profit from vehicle sales themselves. Not only that, but the typical dealership will make far more from arranging financing or leasing and the sale of credit insurance or service contracts than it will make from the sale of new cars.

Lenders increasingly use form agreements whose incomprehensible terms constitute what Todd Rakoff coined "the invisible language of contract," onerous provisions which are not understood by the consumer at the time of purchase or lease. The small print has been carefully crafted by corporate attorneys to shift the level of risk away from their clients, the finance companies, and onto the consumer. Many instances of this form of cheating are nothing less than institutionalized flim-flam by money lenders. In plain and simple English, it's a swindle.

As you begin to juggle these claims, the challenge is to keep your eye on the ball. The focus on defendants may shift. The focus on remedies may shift. Patterns of practice invite class action treatment. Rather than throw out all theories in a diffuse and confusing complaint, carefully plan a strategy of selecting a few best options to present the most persuasive case at the outset.

The message is this: what looks at the outset like a lemon law case may in fact have all the elements of a much broader claim. And a case which fails to present the fact pattern of a winning lemon law claim may actually cry out for remedies based on physical injury or fraud. What follows are a dozen of the most common legal claims that consumers have concerning their car transactions, in addition to the lemon law and related claims already discussed in Chapter 9:

1. PRODUCTS LIABILITY

Injury to the person transforms many a garden variety lemon law case into a products liability claim. A product may be defective in either of two ways: design or manufacture. In theory, motor vehicles may fall into either category, but, because of mass production, the vast majority of auto cases falls under the rubric of design defect. An examination of the case law is a grim stroll through the annals of human tragedy: decapitation, death by fire, rollovers, crashes, crushes. The law of products liability, as applied and articulated nationwide, is too complex for full treatment here, but the nature of injury and expert inspection will help to recognize the claim.

Consider the plight of poor Gertrude Troensgaard, an 82 year old widow who purchased a motorhome. The defendant knew one thing that she did not, namely that the coach interior was constructed with urea-formaldehyde resin-infused plywood known by industry to be a toxic compound causing odors and serious illness. Suffering from headaches, nausea, and ear, nose and throat irritation, Mrs. Troensgaard returned the vehicle several times for repair and gave notice under the lemon law.

Eventually she sued and the jury awarded $90,000 compensatory damages, $90,000 statutory damages under the state lemon law and an additional $55,000 punitive damages under a products claim. On appeal, the court ruled that in California you could not recover both punitive and statutory damages, but allowed her to keep the greater of the two, in this case providing her with a $180,000 judgment.[3]

2. PRE-SALE DAMAGE TO *NEW* CARS

Suppose a consumer brings a lemon law problem to an attorney, who sends the subject vehicle to an independent expert for confirmation of a persistent pulling toward the left. A history of unresolved alignment problems has raised the attorney's antennae. Fingering some paint overspray on the inside of the hood, the expert asks bluntly, "When was the accident?" The consumer responds, "The car has never been in any accident."

It turns out that all of the defects in alignment, dashboard adjustments and electrical problems the potential client complains of are related to a bent frame caused in a pre-sale collision during a dealer demo drive with some other consumer. The manufacturer's arbitration board had refused to award a buyback without explanation. And now you know why.

Your garden variety lemon law case just ripened into a juicy hybrid. The contract on its face, as well as the factory-authorized sales dealer, represented this car to be "new." It was not sold in new-car condition. This shocking practice is actually quite common and can be proven as a pattern of practice on the part of some unscrupulous sales agencies. An appalling number of cars sold as new are in fact seriously damaged prior to sale. Accidents will happen at the factory, en route to the dealer, or while at the dealer's lot, and when they do, dealers are not going to get stuck with the loss if they can help it. Sometimes, dealers even accept the insurance proceeds and still sell the damaged vehicle for full price as "new."

One industry defense to such a charge is not denial but a callous "who cares?" Generally the buyer does in fact care. Intentional fraud is of course hard to prove, so you are wise to frame the pleading in terms of negligent misrepresentation, concealment and deception as well.

The other industry defense to such a charge is that it is exempted by state legislation that specifies that such pre-existing damage need not be disclosed if it is under a certain threshold amount. These provisions generally allow damage up to 3% or 5% of the car's value to go unreported to the consumer. And, at least in some states, not even counted toward the 3% or 5% threshold are repairs bumpers, window glass, lights, and other items that can be replaced with newly manufactured replacement parts. These laws regulating disclosure of damage to new cars are listed in National Consumer Law Center, *Automobile Fraud,* Appendix C (1998).

These statutes protect the dealer and manufacturer from having to disclose relatively minor damage that has been repaired. On the other hand, if the damage to the car costs more than the 3% or 5% threshold amount, then the dealer has a statutory duty to disclose the damage. Its failure to do so is a serious form of misconduct.

A fraud claim gives you the benefit of a tort measure of damages, including the possibility of punitive damages, which surely enhances the value of your case. The non-disclosure is also certainly a deceptive practice in violation of state deceptive practices laws. In some states, a claim for rescission is not inconsistent with a claim for punitive damages. In *Horn v. Guaranty*

Chevrolet Motors, the car dealer defendants sold as "new" a vehicle which had been stolen from a Southern California lot, driven through an orange orchard, and damaged. The purchasers rescinded and recovered restitution plus punitive damages.[4]

You must decide whether to name just the fraudulent dealer, or include the manufacturer whose actual *or ostensible* agent it is. Typically, the manufacturer takes toward dealer fraud the attitude of the three little monkeys: see no evil, hear no evil, speak no evil. "Fraud is outside the scope of our agency," it argues; "our dealers are independent contractors," it cries. This feigned ignorance is a front; the manufacturer quite happily profits from the flow of its goods to the marketplace. You can pierce the three monkey defense if you can prove that the manufacturer denied a pre-sale warranty claim based on the accident, and thus had actual notice of the dealer misconduct.

BMW found this out the hard way when it faced a $2,000,000 punitive damages verdict for concealing pre-sale damage by repainting and selling a defective car as "new." Although the U.S. Supreme Court found the punitive damages award of $2 million as grossly excessive based on the facts of that one vehicle sale, it upheld the trial court verdict on liability. "We accept," the court said, "the jury's finding that BMW suppressed a material fact which Alabama law obligated it to communicate to prospective purchasers of repainted cars in that state."[5]

3. LEMON LAUNDERING

Whenever a consumer faces a lemon law problem with a car that was not purchased as brand new (that is whenever the odometer reading had some significant mileage on it when purchased), you should at least consider whether it might be a recycled lemon. That is, the manufacturer bought the car back from some other consumer because of a persistent defect, and then turned around and re-introduced it into the automotive marketplace, where it was then resold to the present owner. This practice is examined in detail in Chapter 13, *infra*.

4. ODOMETER TAMPERING, NON-DISCLOSURE OF A PRIOR WRECK OR OTHER SUSPECT TITLE HISTORY

When examining a vehicle that was purchased used, be on the look out for a number of other possible frauds that may actually help explain the vehicle's persistent problems. These frauds also will result in the consumer recovering additional damages and potentially even punitive damages.

Odometer Tampering

One common problem is that the odometer has been tampered with and that the car's mileage was actually significantly higher when purchased. Mileage is the most important thing a used car buyer looks at, next to price. So significantly does high mileage impair the resale price that cadres of criminals engage in the lucrative practice of odometer rollback. The rollback practice is fueled by record new car prices and resulting sticker shock, causing a sharp shift in market demand for used cars and trucks with low mileage.

Odometer tampering

costs consumers

billions of dollars a year.

Anti-tampering devices make this practice a little more challenging than it once was, but there are plenty of professionals still in business. Federal investigators say they are swamped with odometer fraud cases. The National Highway Traffic Safety Administration (NHTSA) has numerous odometer tampering investigations underway at any one time. These are not instances of individuals tinkering with a pair of screwdrivers in a local garage. The biggest cases involve odometer fraud rings alleged to have turned back odometers on 2,000 to 4,000 cars. NHTSA estimates that odometer tampering costs U.S. consumers at least three to four billion dollars annually.

Meanwhile the victim has been overcharged for the vehicle and is probably paying finance fees on the overcharge; he or she is faced with unexpected repair and maintenance costs on a vehicle which has reduced engine longevity. In some cases, the vehicle might be out of warranty based on the true mileage history.

Yet consumers do have some remedies available. A private right of action is found in the Federal Odometer Act. Under federal law, rollback victims are entitled to recover three times their actual damages or $1,500, whichever is greater, plus attorneys fees. Bear in mind that odometer rollbacks are not individual accidents. They involve intentional fraudulent conduct that may also be part of a widespread pattern. So also consider fraud claims seeking punitive damages and/or a class action on behalf of all those with odometer rollbacks who purchased cars from a particular dealer. A thorough analysis of consumer remedies for odometer fraud is found in National Consumer Law Center, *Automobile Fraud* (1998).

The best way to detect odometer fraud is to run a title search on the vehicle. Each time a vehicle is sold, the seller must complete an odometer disclosure on the title. The titles are filed with the state department of motor vehicles. A search of a car's title history may uncover discrepancies. A vehicle history which shows a car or truck had a higher mileage at an earlier date than the mileage disclosed to the next buyer is probably a rollback. How to conduct a vehicle history is examined later in this chapter.

Attorney Andrew Ogilvie, who has handled numerous private odometer fraud cases, suggests that other ways to detect odometer fraud include your careful inspection of the service records. The repair orders must give the mileage at each repair attempt and that mileage, of course, should always go up. The oil change stickers on the inside door panel should also tell the mileage at maintenance. "Be suspicious of any car which looks like the mileage sticker has been removed. Unless someone has tampered with the odometer, there isn't any reason to remove the stickers."

The odometer itself may display evidence of tampering, but be careful not to damage the device in the course of the inspection. The odometer is located in the front dash area, usually near the speedometer. Most older cars have mechanical odometers with white numbers on a black background. An odometer which has been rolled back will often have scratches on the white numbers, misaligned digits, or fingerprints, smudges or scratches on the inside of the plexiglass odometer window. Furthermore, expert mechanics can find evidence of odometer rollbacks in tire wear or condition of the brake pedal covers.

Undisclosed Wreck History

This chapter has already described the common practice of selling brand new cars without disclosing wreck histories. Consider how much more common this practice is with cars purchased as "demonstrators," "executive cars" and other used vehicles. A wreck history can explain a car's mechanical defects, will cause the vehicle to be worth less than the consumer paid for the car, and will often result in a car being unsafe, because frame repairs have not returned the car to the same structural integrity as when it was manufactured.

**Millions of cars with a serious
wreck history are sold
to unsuspecting consumers.**

Sometimes this wreck history can be discovered by a title search where the car was branded as salvage. While the salvage brand may not appear on the title transferred to the consumer, it may appear on earlier titles, and was removed when the car was transferred between states or when a new title was applied for by a body shop. Another indicator of a problem is if an insurance company's name is on the title chain — odds are the car was once declared as salvage and transferred to the insurance company.

Many cars that were in serious wrecks were never declared salvage, and were never branded salvage on a title or transferred to an insurance company. In these cases, the best way to uncover the wreck history is for an expert to examine the car. Thus it is a good practice when an expert mechanic checks out the car's obvious defects to also look for any indication of a prior accident, such as paint overspray or remanufactured parts.

National Consumer Law Center, *Automobile Fraud* (1998) provides a detailed analysis of how to investigate and prove sale of vehicles with an undisclosed salvage or wreck history. It also analyzes various legal theories to challenge the practice and provides important litigation strategies.

Undisclosed Adverse Use

A car's title history may also provide other useful pieces of information. It will indicate how many prior owners a car has had, and often will indicate the nature of those prior owners, which in turn can lead to clues about a car's unusual prior use. Examples are cars used as rentals, fleet leases, taxicabs, and police cars. Some state laws expressly require disclosure of such use. Failure to disclose such use may be deceptive, as is any dealer representation about a vehicle that is contrary to its actual history.

How to Conduct a Title Search

There are two types of title search — a summary, computer search and a real examination of each title for a vehicle. With just a car's VIN (Vehicle Identification Number that is found on the car's registration, title, most other documents, and usually near the driver's side dashboard, near the windshield) you can obtain a summary of a car's title history over the Internet in seconds, and at minimal cost. The two most popular services are Carfax[6] and Vehicle History Report (VHR) (also known as Vinguard)[7] These services have huge databases of hundreds of millions of pieces of information provided from state DMVs and also from other sources, such as insurance companies, auto auctions, and body shops. The computer search identifies all information relating to a particular VIN, and retrieves that information in chronological order. The data that will be retrieved from a Carfax search is likely to be quite different than a VHR search, and it may even pay to run searches with both companies.

It is essential though *not* to rely solely on searches from either company, but instead to use these computer-based services in conjunction with a complete title search, as described below. If the shortcut service finds a problem, the complete title history may provide more compelling evidence of the problem, and it will certainly be more admissible in court. Conversely, even if the shortcut search shows no problem, a complete title history may still show up a serious problem.

The short-cut services do not provide a copy of the actual title or other documents, and thus cannot uncover forgeries, missing information, and alterations. They do not provide names and addresses of prior owners, which is often critical not only in providing witnesses, but also as an indicator of a car's history (e.g. the name of an insurance company as an owner of a vehicle may indicate a salvage history). A service which only provides title information when a new title is issued does not provide information about transfers to dealers and other merchants, which are recorded on the old title's assignment lines or on a separate reassignment document. The databases are not complete, even as to DMV titling information. Carfax still does not obtain title data from two states, and has only very recent data from a number of other states. VHR is also limited in this regard. Errors can occur in the recording of information from other sources, even if these other sources provide the information electronically. A Carfax or VHR report may appear clean, when a complete history report will uncover a fraud.

Complete title searches obtain copies of all titles and other records directly from state DMVs. If a vehicle has been titled in more than one state, one must obtain title information from each state. The title and accompanying reassignment documents will have the names, addresses, and signatures of all transferors and transferees taking possession through that title, the odometer reading at each transfer and a certification whether that reading is accurate, and any title brands, such as duplicate title, flood-damaged, salvage, lemon buyback, police car, taxi-cab, repossession, etc. Most DMVs can provide requesters with certified copies of the actual title documents, which can ease their introduction in court. Some states have enacted privacy legislation with prevents open access to DMV records. The requesting attorney may be required to verify that the VIN refers to a vehicle which is the subject of investigation or litigation.

For a more detailed discussion of both summary and detailed title searches, see National Consumer Law Center, *Automobile Fraud* (1998). That volume also lists telephone numbers, addresses, and other information about each state's department of motor vehicles that is essential to conducting a detailed title search.

5. PHANTOM AND ILLUSORY ADD-ONS

The last several topics examined problems with cars purchased as used. Also look for frauds concerning vehicles purchased as new. For example, the sale of vehicle options provide ample opportunity for fraud. There are two types of options, called "add-ons" or "adds" in the industry, which consumers are pressured to buy. "Hard adds" are roughly defined as items which add some actual resale value to the vehicle, such as a sun roof, spoke wheels, CD players, and even fake gold lettering trim.

"Soft adds" do not even arguably add residual value and include such ephemeral items as sealant packages, leather protection, service contracts and unnecessary insurance. Basically anything the "F&I guy" (finance and insurance manager) tries to sell after the purchase price has been agreed upon is suspect as a soft add.

Add-on scams are too numerous and diverse to detail here, but a few categories are particularly prevalent. The first involves the "phantom due bill." When the buyer or lessee is presented an array of documents to sign, sign, sign, after hours of tedious negotiating, the dealer may intentionally cover up the top portions of the stack of papers in a well-choreographed sales practice known as "fanning." Thus the unwitting consumer ends up signing some in blank. Among these may be short sheets entitled "due bills" which only later will list options never added to the car. In other cases, due bills are simply forged.

More than once this has come out in the course of depositions in a standard lemon law or leasing case. The CD player and sunroof listed on the due bill (which inflated the vehicle price) simply do not exist on the subject vehicle. When confronted, the dealer inevitably cries "mistake." In fact, this is theft, plain and simple. In the civil context these intentional tort theories of conversion and fraud can be proven by establishing frequency of such mistakes showing up in that dealer's sales jackets.

In addition to phantom add-ons you may find illusory add-ons. These are products which have no value to anyone. They are a fairy tale — like the invisible gold thread in the *Emperor's New Clothes*. The worthlessness of some are obvious, like an extended warranty sold for $1,100 with a 3-year lease on a vehicle which carried a 5-year factory warranty. Others are a little more subtle. Just what is leather protection, anyway? Does the consumer pay $350 for someone in the service department merely to press the nozzle of an aerosol can?

Certain add-ons do more harm than good. Dealer-installed options such as a lift kit, performance chip, and exhaust modifications may *void* the manufacturer's warranty. Manufacturers may claim after-factory cruise control and dealer-supplied rustproofing void the new car warranty.

6. MONRONEY STICKER ISSUES

The factory sticker, also known as the Monroney sticker, appears in the windshield of new motor vehicles. It sets forth standard equipment, factory installed options and pricing information to enable the consumer to make an informed purchase choice. But sometimes all of the equipment described on the sticker does not actually appear on the vehicle itself. The unwary buyer does not realize the omission until the brakes do not perform as expected of an ABS system in crisis mode. Or a truck buyer may not discover the absence of passenger air bags listed as standard until she looks for the PSIR suppression switch one day and finds it missing. These are serious misrepresentations. Yet cars and trucks are shipped in such volume, even a known mistake in the sticker may go unreported to avoid an expensive recall of thousands of vehicles. These cases involve fraud, false advertising and violation of express warranties.

Another deception is duplicate billing. For example, a consumer may pay more for a tire upgrade in the premium package without any credit for the standard tires which were removed, and then pay yet a third time for optional all-terrain tires added at the dealer. Similar double billing occurs where an option package replaces the radio with a cassette player and the whole thing is upgraded again with a dealer installed CD system. The buyer has not paid just the difference in value, but has in fact purchased three separate sound systems. Yet he only takes one home.

7. DECEPTIVE LEASING

Auto leasing is among the most controversial of today's consumer issues. An estimated one third of all new car transactions are now leases, and in luxury models, the figure is even higher. The popularity of leasing is not consumer-driven. Instead, it has come about through a calculated and carefully scripted sales program designed to increase profit to every level of the automobile business: manufacturing, dealerships and finance companies. The industry's increased profit all comes out of the consumer's pocket.

The reason for the big market push toward leasing is two-fold: first, manufacturers felt they had to respond to sticker shock in the recession of the early 1990s. Leases *appear* cheaper because you are not paying for the car, but only the use of the car, when in fact they could be more expensive for the consumer. At the end of a loan, the buyer owns the car and can trade it in for value toward the subsequent purchase. At the end of the lease, the lessee has nothing, except maybe a large charge for excess mileage or wear. The fact that the lessee has no trade-in often means that consumer is trapped in the leasing system.

The second reason the industry loves leases is that dealers and lenders learned they could increase their own profitability per automotive transaction by inflating the lease's monthly payments, because consumers had no understanding how much they were really paying for the lease. A consumer could negotiate a car price $1,000 under sticker and a trade-in worth $2,000. Then the dealer could switch the consumer to a lease and the consumer would never understand that the lease was actually now calculated on the car costing the consumer $2,000 *over* the sticker price and the dealer giving the consumer no credit for the trade-in at all!

"Leasing is a great thing for car sellers," says auto industry pundit Peter Levy, "They make more money on it, and the customer has to come back in two or three years, if only to give the car back. To sell something with a guarantee that you get to see the customer again when they need a replacement, that is heaven on earth for the seller."

Auto leasing is governed by provisions within the federal Consumer Leasing Act and its implementing regulation commonly known as Reg. M,[8] which set out disclosure requirements. These requirements have been made more consumer-friendly for all leases starting in 1998. Any violation leads to a claim for actual damages, $1,000 statutory damages, and attorney fees. This legislation is strengthened by additional state consumer protection laws.

**Dealers prefer leases because
they can steal thousands of dollars
from the consumer, who never
realizes what happened.**

The new Reg. M improves consumer awareness by requiring segregation of certain important disclosures in a box similar in format to the familiar Reg. Z statement for credit transactions. Areas of the lease to look at to see what is really going on are the gross and adjusted capitalized costs, the agreed upon value of the vehicle, any itemization of the gross capitalized cost provided to the consumer, and treatment of trade-ins, downpayments, and rebates. The disclosure does not include a lease rate that would be comparable to an annual percentage rate (APR) in a finance transaction that states how much the consumer is paying for use of the lender's money.

Besides claims under the federal Consumer Leasing Act and state leasing statutes, consumers will want to consider deceptive practices claims for any oral deceptions and for any failures to disclosure important information. In addition, in an egregious case, the consumer will want to bring a fraud claim seeking punitive damages. For a more detailed discussion of deceptive leasing practices, see National Consumer Law Center, *Unfair and Deceptive Acts and Practices* §5.4.6 (4th ed. 1997 and Supp.).

8. EATING REBATES AND SWALLOWING TRADE-INS

About twenty-five years ago, Chrysler made automotive history by offering price rebates during the Super Bowl half-time ads. That set off a frenzy of rebate competition which hasn't ended yet. This ongoing form of price war also has the potential for serious abuse as it presents dealerships with the choice of giving to consumers large chunks of money that belongs to the consumer or keeping it for themselves as profit, known as "eating the rebate."

One scam used by the unscrupulous is to have buyers sign a power of attorney in blank, sometimes billed by the salesman as a "convenience" to assist in transfer of registration documents. But in truth it enables the dealer to cash the rebate check from the manufacturer. The dealer who does so is no less a thief than the cat burglar who comes and goes in the night.

Another form of theft involves the disappearing trade-in, commonly called "swallowing the trade-in." Many a careful consumer has locked her car for years, parked under streetlights and avoided bad neighborhoods, only to hand over the keys to a dealer with no idea how much money, *if any*, is credited in the trade.

The value of the buyer's trade-in is highly negotiable. The buyer who does her homework will check the current range of trade-in value by checking a used car value guide or using the Internet to locate the information. Without this information, there is no way to know just how much of the trade-in value is being swallowed. But even if the consumer obtains a fair price for the trade-in, it is easy in the array of paperwork for the agreed-upon value of the trade-in just to disappear, and never be credited against the purchase price of the new car.

Leasing makes it particularly easy for trade-in fraud to occur. Consumers are not familiar with terms such as gross capitalized cost and capitalized cost reductions. Even if a lessor accurately discloses that no credit is given for the trade-in, the consumer may not understand this. A common ploy is to write "N/A" on the trade-in line. Or the lessor can provide a capitalized cost reduction reflecting the trade-in, but "bump" the gross capitalized cost enough to offset the trade-in credit. Comparable shenanigans are possible for cars sold on credit.

9. FINANCING ABUSES

"Never give a sucker an even break," quipped Groucho Marx. A great many car salesmen have taken his advice. The same consumers who are switched from the cars they test drove to a defective demo may very well be switched from a sale to a lease before leaving the lot.

Even though the lemon law client comes to you with mechanical problems in mind, scrutinize the entire transaction for related malfeasance that will strengthen your case. Consider the following:

- violation of disclosure provisions found for leases in state and federal leasing acts and for credit sales in the federal truth in lending act and state retail installment sales legislation;
- wrongful repossession, failure to provide rights to cure or reinstate defaults, unreasonable repossession sales, and faulty calculation of deficiencies;
- violation of laws providing special disclosures to co-signers;
- violation of Spanish language contract statutes;
- abuses connected with the forced placement of physical damage insurance where the consumer's own coverage lapses.

These violations of specific lending and leasing statutes generally lead to special statutory damages and attorney fees for a prevailing consumer. Because many of these violations are easy to prove — they are evident from just looking at the documents — they can improve your bargaining position vis a vis the dealer and lender. A good starting point in analyzing paperwork for credit or lease disclosure violations is National Consumer Law Center, *Truth in Lending* (3d ed. 1995 and Supp.).

10. NEGATIVE EQUITY

A trade-in value credited to a new car transaction may be positive or negative. The trade-in is negative if the car is assigned a value by the dealer that is less than the amount the consumer owes on the loan for that car. Then, when the dealer takes the car in trade and pays off the consumer's loan on that car, this increases the money the consumer owes the dealer for the new car, instead of lowering the new car's purchase price. When a consumer's trade-in has negative equity, the consumer is described as being "upsidedown," an apt phrase to describe the disoriented and vulnerable feeling of a car owner who is falling behind in finance obligations.

Many people are so relieved or bewildered to see a designation of "N/A" on the trade-in line as they hand over their keys they do not realize they are in fact paying real money for the privilege of refinancing that debt. The dealer will agree to dispose of the trade in order to close the deal. Warning: that offer has a price.

Even those who know that the manufacturer's suggested retail price ("MSRP") and positive trade-in value are negotiable lose their savvy when told a fixed negative trade value. The size of a negative trade-in is also negotiable, because the negative trade value is the difference between a negotiable price for the trade-in and the fixed amount of the debt.

Leasing increases the percent of the driving population which finds itself "upside-down." because a large number of leases terminate early, resulting in early termination charges of many thousands of dollars. This early termination charge when rolled into a new car transaction is treated the same as negative equity in a trade-in. Lease-to-lease transactions, a practice known as lease "churning," generate negative equity rolled over into the capitalized cost of the new lease. Lenders happily refinance this automotive debt and collect increased finance charges every step of the way.

Part of the deception with negative equity occurs when the dealer tries to hide the fact of the negative trade-in. The dealer wants to hide this not only from the consumer, but from the finance company or leasing company purchasing the paper, and from state regulators, because the dealer may not be permitted under state law to effectively re-finance earlier debt. What the dealer does instead is disclose the trade-in as having a net positive value, and then increase the car's cash price or capitalized cost to offset the amount by which the trade-in is inflated.

When the dealer has inflated the trade-in's value and the car's cash price, a special problem arrives with a lemon buyback. The manufacturer does not want to pay the consumer the full cash price of the car, because the dealer has inflated this amount beyond the car's M.S.R.P.

11. PACKING

Loan "packing" refers to the deceptive dealer practice of inflating the quoted monthly payment amount beyond an amount necessary to pay off a car at the agreed-upon price, based on financing at an agreed-upon rate. Having thus created "room" between the real monthly payment amount and an inflated quote, the dealer can then fill up this difference with whatever extra charges the dealer wants to use. Examples of such extra charges are credit insurance, a service contract sold at an inflated price, "soft" add-ons such as "leather protection" or paint sealant, or just a higher financing rate, with the increased amount going to the dealer.

> **Dealers regularly pack payments — an institutionalized form of theft.**

The practice works something like this: the lot salesman says, "How much do you want to pay per month?" or he may look at the credit application and insist a consumer can "afford" a certain monthly payment, whether or not she might have considered that amount within her means. Assume that figure is $350. But then the finance manager actually runs the figures based upon (1) the agreed upon price, (2) minus the trade-in, (3) minus the cash downpayment, (4) at the interest rate the bank quotes. Presto! The monthly figure shown on the manager's screen is just $310.

The dealer knows that consumer is willing to go up to $350 even though she keeps saying she want the best deal they will give. The store will not let that $40 per month allowance slip through its fingers. It thus "packs" the monthly payment with accessory items such as insurance she neither needs nor wants, or it may charge more for the extended service contract, or convince her to "go for" other add-ons.

She might be told, "for $350 per month, we can throw in rust protection at no extra charge." Is that a lie, or just a stretch? Let's face it, deception takes any form the creative and nefarious mind can devise. Generally, a dealer's commission structure for both the sales personnel, the sales manager, and the finance and insurance manager will encourage packing. A more thorough analysis of packing is found at National Consumer Law Center, *Unfair and Deceptive Acts and Practices* §5.4.4.6 (4th ed. 1997 and Supp.).

12. FORGERY

This chapter has descended into some of the more nefarious practices of autoland. The discussion would be incomplete without mention of one very old-fashioned crime which modern technology has brought back into popularity — forgery.

Sitting in the F & I booth to close the deal, the car buyer or lessee is required to sign multiple documents. These may include disclosures required by consumer protection laws, title or registration documents, a purchase or lease agreement, a rebate request or assignment, odometer statement, due bills, notice of used car transfer, credit application, warranties, service contracts, waivers, "as is" acknowledgment, notices, loan documents, payment checks, transfer documents relating to the trade-in, etc. etc. etc. Any one of these an be forged by cribbing the signature on the basic purchase or lease form.

The general rule is that documents pertinent to the vehicle transaction must be presented and signed at the time of delivery of the car. But disclosures and notice documents have a way of going missing. Such documents which fail to appear in the consumer's carefully kept files may arrive from the dealer or Department of Motor Vehicle files in the course of litigation. If this is the case, you may suspect the worst. If it is a disclosure document material to the case for fraud, hire a handwriting expert to confirm the forgery. Sometimes the counterfeit signature is crude, but use of modern copy machines can produce amazingly sophisticated duplicates making proof of forgery difficult indeed.

Demand the original, or use the best evidence rule to challenge the document. If multiple copies of a disclosure document exist, compare them to determine whether all signatures appear in proper sequence. This is a sleuthing task worth the effort, because neither judges nor juries like a cover-up. Fraud may sound and look bad, but forgery looks, feels, tastes and smells downright foul. Forgery is a crime.

---

[1] Indeed, Ford has favored the equine in naming its models e.g., the Mustang, the Pinto, the Maverick.

[2] Grimshaw v. Ford Motor Co., 119 Cal. App. 3d 757 (1981).

[3] Troensgaard v. Silvercrest Industries Inc., 175 Cal. App. 3d 218 (1985).

[4] Horn v. Guaranty Chevrolet Motors, 270 Cal. App. 2d 477 (1969).

[5] BMW of North America v. Gore, 116 S. Ct. 1589 (1996).

[6] *See* www.carfaxreport.com. This credit card transaction costs $12.50, reduced to $10 a report if an individual guarantees five requests a month. Or call 800-346-3846 from 8:30 AM to 6:00 PM EST, but the price is $20 for a history report ordered in this way.

[7] At www.vhronline.com. *See also* www.vehiclehistory.com. You can also order over the telephone at 800-348-1815. A VHR costs $19.95 plus tax, and payment is made by credit card. Offices running a number of searches a month can obtain a discount pricing plan by calling 800-887-9672.

[8] 15 U.S.C. §1667; 12 C.F.R. §213. *See generally* National Consumer Law Center, Truth in Lending Ch. 9 (3d ed. 1995 and Supp.).

11

Settlement, Jury Trial, and Attorney Fees

This chapter is primarily written for lawyers, but consumers may want to know what is in store for them as well — when to settle, what a jury trial is like, and who is going to pay your attorney.

SETTLEMENT

The first settlement opportunity is your pre-litigation demand letter. See examples of rescission and demand letters at Chapter 8, above. If these fail to produce a check in the mail, the service of your complaint acts like a snooze alarm. It is safe to say that more than 90% of lemon law cases settle before the jury comes in. However a case is more likely to settle favorably if the consumer and the consumer's lawyer are prepared to try the case, if necessary.

Keep the doors of communication open throughout the case. Discovery, meet and confer sessions, depositions, status conferences, all provide opportunities for face-to-face discussions on resolving your claims. An open mind, an easy debate style, and the ability to address corporate arrogance with a professionally intoned sense of humor all help.

Mediation through private judges can be successful, and definitely worth pursuing in jurisdictions where the civil court docket is hopelessly clogged. Discuss this possibility with your client when discovery and investigation have progressed far enough that you are on solid ground.

You will do well to remain open to creative solutions. If the automobile lender is the dealer's assignee or is related to the dealer, that lender may waive some or all of the obligation the consumer owes the lender, making the consumer's remaining damages more palatable to the manufacturer.

The settlement should address all aspects of the bargained for exchange. If the car is damaged, resolve this matter now, to avoid problems later when the consumer turns in the lemon car as part of a replacement or refund. If the lender has to be paid off to clear the title, demand that the manufacturer do that before or concurrently with the consumer's return of the vehicle.

If there are credit problems caused by the lemon vehicle, make sure these are cleared before signing the release. Particularly if the lender is a captive finance company of the manufacturer (e.g. GMAC, Ford Motor Credit), require the manufacturer to provide evidence that the car loan has been paid off and the date that occurred. Do not rely on defense counsel's common statement: "We'll take care of it." You don't want the consumer to find a bad credit report entry three months or even three years down the line. A good lawyer protects the client in all aspects of the transaction.

If the attorneys fee issue is causing difficulty, you might settle for a fixed recovery to the client, payable at once, while you submit a fee petition to the court. If you choose this latter path, be sure to explicitly provide in the release document that the consumer is the prevailing party. The court will then merely determine what amount is reasonable.

TRIAL

If you have done everything described in prior chapters, trial will not be the most difficult part of a lemon law case. You are prepared. The mechanics of trial preparation and presentation are the subject of extensive treatment in other publications. The following comments are intended to emphasize some particular applications of trial tactics to lemon law cases.

Length

You can explain the facts of your case over lunch, you think. Nevertheless, by the time you argue motions in limine, pick a jury, lay the foundation for the documentary evidence admitted, call your witnesses, argue instructions, and sum up, you probably will be in court a week.

Pre-trial Motions: Motions in Limine

In a jury trial, the attorneys may attempt to resolve, before the trial and out of the hearing of the jury, whether certain testimony can be presented to the jury. These are often called motions "in limine." Some cases are effectively won or lost in limine, and issues for appeal established, before the first juror is sworn.

Think about such motions. Draft them with care and precision. Begin each one with a clear and simple statement of what you want, before plunging into the facts and law. Deftly delivered, they are your opportunity to make a good impression with the trial judge. They can remove stressful issues of uncertainty from many aspects of the trial. Each time you resolve evidentiary issues in advance, you avoid distracting objections of the opposition and those bench conferences which so annoy the jury.

You should prepare motions to allow you to use the word "lemon." Defendants often try to prevent use of this term because of its pejorative nature, but the term in fact tells the jury what your case is really about in layman's terms. You also want to be able to argue that the dealer is the manufacturer's agent for purposes of repair and/or notice of the nonconformity. You also want to exclude any irrelevant but damaging personal facts about the plaintiffs which the defense counsel may try to introduce just to make your clients look bad.

If any of your evidence — such as videotapes or media reports — might be open to objection, deal with it now. If the defendant has refused to produce certain original documents harmful to your case, you may want to invoke the "best evidence rule;" this should be handled in limine at the outset of trial because of the conventional wisdom that you can't unring the bell. This is also the time to challenge opposing experts outside the presence of the jury.

The more you can streamline the case in advance, the better prepared you will appear before the jury. One caveat: the outcome of motions in limine are often grounds for appeal; if you are concerned about a ruling, make sure you have a court reporter present to build the necessary record.

Your Client

Your client should be present and presentable throughout the trial. Emphasize punctuality and attentiveness. If the case is not important enough to them, why should the judge or jury care?

Selecting the Jury: Voir Dire

The procedure for selecting juries differs from state to state and between federal and state courts. Jurors are always questioned before they are accepted onto the panel — a process called voir dire. In some courts, the attorneys conduct the voir dire; in other courts, the judge does the questioning, and may or may not accept suggested questions from the attorneys. This section will assume that the consumer's attorney can participate in the voir dire, although this is not always the case.

Without sounding like a used car salesman yourself, you must begin to sell your case to the jury the very first time you stand up. Use voir dire to interest the potential jurors in your client's cause and show your appreciation that they are there.

You should use voir dire to capture the interest of the jury.

Start this process by conveying interest in them as individuals; this will be your only opportunity to do so. Using open questions, you must ferret out any juror bias toward you, your client, your experts, or consumers in general. Is your client rich, poor, young, old, black, white, Spanish-speaking, highly educated, uneducated, a celebrity, gay, disabled, a welfare recipient, unemployed, cross-eyed, or blonde? Is your mechanical expert female? Would a juror be able to give the same weight to an American expert as to the Mercedes expert whose accent is German?

You must decide if any personal prejudice may affect the outcome and confront this without blame or shame at the outset. Trial lawyers themselves are not popular these days. Some citizens are so disgusted with the process that they cannot be trusted to be a fair part of it. Consumers themselves — and plaintiffs' trial lawyers — may have been portrayed poorly in the media, particularly around election time when industry pours money into advertising campaigns against consumer causes.

You want to ascertain potential jurors' attitudes toward various categories of damages, including punitive damages or civil penalties. You should carefully, but gently scrutinize mechanics, autoworkers, industry employees and shareholders. Finally, you want to find out attitudes toward authority. There are otherwise intelligent people out there who think that if a big corporation does something, it must be okay, or that if an expert works for Ford, well he must know what he's doing. Be wary of these subtle, subsurface biases which can create havoc in jury deliberation rooms.

Presentation of the Consumer's Case at Trial

Faced with a theater director's task, you suddenly realize there are some things they don't teach in law school. With narrative, witnesses, dialogue and audio visual effects, you must make your case. You must make it interesting and in some small way important. You must educate and entertain without appearing to do either.

Your job is to persuade a jury or judge that your client has been robbed — robbed of the quality she was lead to expect, robbed of the right to a decent repair, robbed of her remedies of refund or replacement, and now robbed of her dignity as the defense tries to make out her perfectly valid claims as trivial or nonexistent. You must convince the jurors — who to a man and woman do not really want to be sitting in that courtroom — that if the manufacturer had only done what it was supposed to do under the law, none of them would have to be sitting there today.

Your client and your expert will tell the story in a logical, preferably chronological manner. Consider the relative strengths of your witnesses in determining their order of presentation. Depending on strategy in an individual case, and whether the dealer is a defendant, you may want to examine the service manager in your case in chief; if so, remember to subpoena him. You must, of course, be equally prepared to cross-examine defense experts, and your own expert is your best asset in preparing for this task.

Demonstrative evidence will greatly enhance your chances of success. Color charts, with legible print and graphics, can guide the jury through your repair chronology or warranty history, present a diagram of principal defects, and itemize your damages claim. Michigan trial lawyer Dani Liblang attributes her success in handling lemon law cases in part to the use of exhibits in the courtroom. In one recent case involving brake defects in a 1995 Ford Econoline, she used a chart comparing normal brake service with the lemon vehicle's actual brake service history. Black dots representing Ford's recommended maintenance schedule every 15,000 miles up to 120,000 miles (taken from the maintenance schedule in the Ford owner's manual) stood out in stark contrast to red dots representing the four brake repairs before 15,000 miles, three repairs before 30,000 miles, and the eighth repair before 45,000 miles, as well as the inspection showing need for yet another repair at 48,000 miles.

To really drive her point home, attorney Liblang displayed a second chart, a blow-up of the Ford Owner's Guide stating, "Front Brakes: Front disc brakes are self-adjusting. The only service needed is periodic inspection for pad wear." This is a good example of how to use evidence to marshall the facts creatively and compellingly, riveting the jury's attention to your theory of the case. The jury returned a verdict of $38,000 and Ms. Liblang filed a separate petition for attorneys fees.

Your display of actual auto parts can educate the jury in an entertaining rather than condescending way. If alignment problems have caused uneven tire wear, bring in the tire to explain the nuances of camber and toe.

Videotapes of the defects can really be useful. That flame coming out of the rear wheel well will not be forgotten in the jury room. Noises such as dash rattle or engine whine can be trivialized by testifying service managers — until you turn on the audio portion of your authenticated videotape presentation.

THE CONSUMER'S ATTORNEY FEES

Statutory Basis for Manufacturer to Pay the Consumer's Attorney Fees

Let's assume you won at trial or obtain a favorable settlement. Now you want to get paid, or you want your client reimbursed for what she's paid you for all your good hard work.

The Magnuson-Moss Warranty Act and all but a handful of state lemon laws allow the court to assess the manufacturer for the consumer's attorneys fees if the consumer prevails in the case.[1] Some statutes make fees mandatory if the consumer prevails, others make the fees discretionary; all require the fee be reasonable. The fee-shifting statutes are part of the overall remedial scheme and should be construed broadly toward their goal of protecting consumers.[2] Senator Magnuson made his purpose clear in urging an attorney fee provision in the federal law:

> Because enforcement of the warranty through the courts is prohibitively expensive . . . there is a need to insure warrantor performance by monetarily [sic] penalizing the warrantor for non-performance and awarding the penalty to the consumer as compensation for his loss. One way to effectively meet this need is by providing for reasonable attorney's fees and court costs to the successful litigants, thus making consumer resort to the courts feasible.[3]

Size of Fee Award Not Limited by Size of Consumer's Recovery

State lemon laws and the federal Magnuson-Moss Warranty Act authorize the consumer's attorney fee award be *based on actual time expended* by the attorney, not some arbitrary figure based on a percentage of recovery. The fee may easily exceed the consumer's monetary damages.

This result is clarified where a statute states that fees will be "based on actual time expended." But even when that language does not appear in the statute, limiting fees based on the size of a potential recovery would defeat the very purpose of the statute. Manufacturers with unlimited legal resources could drag a case out until the consumer's legal fees far exceeded the actual damages. If the fees were then limited by the size of the award, the manufacturer could easily make lemon law litigation impractical to pursue. The consumer's attorney would have to ask prospective clients, "How much justice can you afford?" Fortunately, lemon law attorney fees are not so limited.

Calculating Fees and Costs

Different states use different procedures for computing the size of a consumer's attorney fee. But attorneys in all states should be prepared to specify with contemporaneous records the actual number of hours spent on the case, that all the time was reasonably necessary to pursue the case, and what the attorney's hourly rate would be in that community.

Some courts will also consider the novelty and difficulty of the case, the skill required, whether the attorney's fee is contingent on the consumer prevailing (higher awards allowed in contingent fee cases due to risk), and the attorney's experience, reputation and ability. Be sure to include the time and hourly rate not just for attorneys, but also paralegals or other assistants.

The burden of proving the size of the fee will be on the consumer's attorney. You should support the fee petition with an affidavit establishing each factor, starting with the actual time expended documented by *timeslips* or some other recognized legal timekeeping system. Attach the actual descriptive billing statement. You should not rely on judicial notice to determine market rate structure in their geographical area of practice, but provide a declaration from another attorney who has no interest in the outcome. You should state whether you accepted this case on a contingent fee basis and the hourly rate in your fee agreement. You should summarize your own resume to demonstrate your experience and you should justify the reasonableness of time spent on tasks and hearings.

Recovery of costs depends on state law. All those out-of-pocket expenses of litigation which are normally billed to the client and not included in the overhead component of the attorney's hourly rate are costs, unless the statute lists specific charges allowed. Expert witness fees are recoverable as costs under the federal Magnuson-Moss Warrant Act and under many state lemon laws.

The procedure for obtaining an award of fees and costs is usually very strict. Check local rules for filing fee petitions and cost bills, so that you can make your application in a timely fashion. You are asking the court to assess your worth. The petition should impress the court both in content and in form.

---

[1] Idaho, Illinois, Kansas, North Dakota, Ohio, Oklahoma, and Texas have no provision in the state lemon law for attorneys fees to the prevailing consumer, but may provide them under other statutory claims.

[2] Ford Dealers Assoc. v. DMV, 32 Cal. 3d 347, 356 (1982).

[3] S. Rep. No. 93-151, 1st Sess. pp. 7-8 (1973).

12

Lemon Laundering — Whatever Happened to All Those Lemons Returned to the Manufacturer?

Have you ever wondered what happened to the tens of thousands of lemon vehicles returned to the manufacturer? Unfortunately for anyone driving the public highways, these defective cars and trucks were not sent to the junkyard. They are back on the street, often being driven by consumers unaware of their lemon history. This insidious practice affects everyone, because every defective car which re-enters the stream of commerce also re-enters the stream of traffic.

The recycling of lemons is examined in this book for two main reasons. First, consumers and their attorneys should realize what happens to lemon vehicles they succeed in returning to the manufacturer, and what it means to the manufacturer to be able to take the car back as part of a "good will" settlement, compared with being forced to take the car back by a court or IDM panel. (One consumer, for the benefit of subsequent purchasers, hid throughout the car about a hundred tiny notices about the car's lemon history and the name of his attorney before he returned the car to the manufacturer.) Second, buyers of late model used cars still protected by a new or used car lemon law may gain new insights as to why their car is a lemon, and what the manufacturer knows about the car's defects, if they discover that it was previously bought back by the manufacturer.

HOW MANUFACTURERS LAUNDER LEMONS

When the manufacturer buys back the vehicle, who exactly returns what to whom? The manufacturer may reside in Detroit or Tokyo, Munich or Milan. And what, by the way, does the consumer have to return? Whether or not the buyer physically hands over the "pink slip," she usually has to physically hand over the car. In the simplest scenario, the manufacturer designates its nearest authorized sales or service dealer to accept the goods. The consumer returns the vehicle in person to the selling dealer or some other designated agent authorized by the manufacturer to accept the returned goods. Concurrently the manufacturer cuts a check either to the consumer or to the lender as pay-off on the automotive loan, or to both for full restitution. If the consumer has chosen a replacement vehicle, she takes delivery at the dealership and leaves — not necessarily a happy customer, but relieved to be rid of her detested lemon at last.

What happens at this point to the defective vehicle? Most states have passed laws dealing with lemon laundering, so the manufacturer must comply with the laws of the state in question. As of the present time, thirty eight (38) states, plus the District of Columbia have some form of law addressing lemon laundering. But apart from their common remedial intent, there is little uniformity in this legislation. A listing of state lemon laundering laws follows.

STATE LEMON LAUNDERING STATUTES

Alabama Statutes §8-20A-4

Alaska Statutes §45.45.335

Arizona Revised Statutes Annotated §44-1266

Arkansas Code Annotated §4-90-412

California Civil Code §§1793.23, 1793.24

Colorado Revised Statutes §6-1-105(1)(hh)

District of Columbia Code Annotated §40-1302(g)(3)

Florida Statutes Annotated §6861.114(2)

Georgia Code Annotated §10-1-785

Hawaii Revised Statutes §§481I-3(k), 481J-4

Idaho Code §48-901

Illinois Compiled Statutes §5/5-104.2

Indiana Code §§24-5-13.5-10, 24-5-13.5-11, 24-5-13.5-13

Iowa Code Annotated §322G.12

Kansas Statutes Annotated §50-659

Louisiana Revised Statutes Annotated §51-1945.1

Maine Revised Statutes Annotated tit. 10 §1163(7)

Maryland Commercial Law Code Annotated §14-1502

Massachusetts General Laws Ch. 90 §7N1/2(5)

Minnesota Statutes Annotated §§325F.655(5)(a), 325F.665(5)

Montana Code Annotated §61-4-525

New Jersey Statutes Annotated §56:12-35

New Mexico Statutes Annotated §57-16A-7

New York Vehicle & Traffic Law §417-a-2

North Carolina General Statutes §20-351.3(d)

North Dakota Cent. Code §51-07-22

Ohio Rev. Code Annotated §1345.76(l)

Pennsylvania Statutes Annotated tit. 73 §§1960(a) and (b)

Rhode Island Gen. Laws §§31-5.2-9, 31.5.2-10, 31-5.2-11

South Carolina Code Annotated §§56-28-100, 56-28-110

South Dakota Codified Laws Annotated §32-6D-9

Texas Revised Civil Statutes Annotated §4413(36)

Utah Code Annotated §§41-3-408, 409

Vermont Statutes Annotated tit. 9 §4181

Virginia Code §59.1-207.16:1

Washington Revised Code Annotated §19.118.061

West Virginia Code §46A-6A-7

Wisconsin Statutes Annotated §218.015(2)(d).

In general, these laws specify which buybacks trigger the Act's duties, require for those buybacks that the manufacturer fix the car, and disclose the car's lemon history. The manufacturer usually must also offer an extended warranty. What follows is a more detailed description of what these laws require, how manufacturers try to sideslip these requirements, and what manufacturers really do with lemon buybacks.

When Is a Lemon Not a Lemon
(According to Manufacturers)?

The major way that manufacturers attempt to evade state lemon laundering law requirements is to claim a defective vehicle is not a lemon — even if it has undergone numerous unsuccessful repair attempts and the manufacturer has purchased the car back. By doing so, the manufacturer not only avoids various legal requirements, but also increases the vehicle's resale value.

If a repurchase decision is compelled by jury verdict or a judge, or an IDM award binding on the manufacturer, then the manufacturer has little wiggle room — the buyback will be covered by the lemon laundering statute. But what if the buyback is part of a settlement of litigation after plaintiff's expert gives damaging testimony for which there is no rebuttal? Or the buyback may come after threat of litigation or while an IDM decision is pending. Or the repurchase decision may come even before the consumer takes any affirmative action, as a result of inside industry knowledge of a safety defect the manufacturer wants to conceal. A dealer may accept return of the vehicle in exchange for a coupon toward purchase of a later model vehicle, without any written documents explaining the reason for the return. Or, in a lease situation, the lemon may be returned for an undisclosed amount of credit simply churned into the terms of a new lease.

Manufacturers will often label any of these latter type of buybacks as "good will" buybacks, and claim they are not covered by the lemon laundering statute. It is not empty cynicism to assert that true "good will" gestures are infinitely rare. The real nature of these buybacks may be best explained by introducing testimony of the vehicle's previous owner. By the time a lemon owner has gotten the manufacturer to agree to replace or refund in exchange for the car, there is very often very little "good will" left. When she learns that a subsequent purchaser has been defrauded by nondisclosure, the original owner is usually so incensed she is happy to testify to the true facts, namely that the repurchase was compelled by her lemon law rights. "Good will? Hah! Those !@$%#&*!" is a pretty common response from a former lemon owner.

But manufacturers may point to the statutory language as stating that a "good will" buyback is not covered by the statute, and that the manufacturer does not have to disclose the car as a lemon to subsequent purchasers. Whether this defense will go anywhere of course will depend on the language of a particular state statute. Some lemon laundering statutes explicitly apply also to such voluntary agreements to take the car back. Others only apply to buybacks ordered by a court or IDM. Most laws are somewhere in between.

A manufacturer's "good will" in buying back a lemon doesn't change its real reason for the repurchase — that the car is a lemon.

Where the language is not clear, courts should look through the fiction of a "good will" buyback to effect the remedial intent of the legislation. Moreover, no matter what legalistic argument a manufacturer wants to make, it is still deceptive under a state deceptive practices statute to fail to disclose defects so serious that it actually took back the car. Manufacturers should not be able to hide a warranty history three, thirteen or thirty full pages long.

Sometimes the manufacturer will trip itself up in trying to avoid the lemon laundering statute. In some states, the sales tax authority (e.g., Board of Equalization), allows the manufacturer to recover a certain portion of sales tax previously paid if the repurchase is under the lemon law. In such states, the manufacturer's own zone representative may request such a refund in writing and such a written request offers good proof of the reason for repurchase, if the manufacturer later tries to contend the return was merely a "goodwill" gesture.

Another way manufacturers hide a lemon buyback is through the captive finance arm of the manufacturer (e.g., GMAC, Chrysler Credit, FMCC,

Toyota Motor Credit Corporation). In the situation where the payoff of the loan amount in the buyback transaction merely involves a paper trail (or, indeed, an electronic transfer) between the manufacturer and its wholly owned subsidiary lender, the manufacturer itself never takes title and may attempt to argue the vehicle was not "transferred" back to it at all. Where a captive finance company is the lienholder, General Motors Acceptance Corporation may say it never "transferred" the vehicle back to the manufacturer when General Motors paid off the loan balance. This ruse is fraudulent where a court or IDM panel in fact ordered the buyback.

How Do Manufacturers
Repair Lemons for Resale Where They
Could Not Repair Them Before?

How can a manufacturer buy back a vehicle it had failed in repairing and then re-sell it as if it is repaired? Many state lemon laundering statutes require that the manufacturer correct the nonconformity before it can be resold. It would seem that a minimum duty of care would be to do so in any event, even if state law does not so require.

What happens in practice is that the manufacturer either instructs its dealer to make specified repairs or takes the vehicle to another authorized service depot or dealer for reconditioning. What it should do is determine that *all* complaints which contributed to the repurchase are repaired. What instead often transpires is that the zone identifies a single "reason" for repurchase, and attempts to fix that one defect. The repaired defect is the one which is disclosed to a subsequent purchaser, leaving the other problems hidden and woefully unresolved. The limited disclosure of the defect will also conflict with the manufacturer's internal documents summarizing the repurchase and repair history.

The common practice of repairing a single defect should be addressed as a clear violation of the law in the many cases where the original owner in fact had numerous complaints. Lemon laws which provide a presumption of reasonable repair do so in the conjunctive, designating a reasonable number of repair attempts for a single defect or a cumulative number of days in the shop for a litany of complaints. In the latter case it is clearly deceptive to repair a single problem raised by the original purchaser when in fact the nonconformity was general poor quality.

Laundering Made Simple

After the manufacturer has accepted return of the defective vehicle and its title documents, the vehicle is either shipped out of state to a jurisdiction with no resale disclosure law, purchased and resold by the dealer which took re-delivery (in which case the dealer has *actual* knowledge of the fraudulent concealment), sold by the repairing dealer (in which case it has *actual* knowledge of the repair history), or sent to auction.

Automotive auction seems to be the laundry of choice for resale of repurchased lemons. The manufacturer submits a "memorandum of sale" which typically has a two-inch box for full explanation of the reason for repurchase. Its very size says, "We don't know and we don't want to know." Thus even where some disclosure is made, it is often only partial and misleading. Moreover, this disclosure statement is the first *funnel* of information; the disclosure will never improve after this first statement.

This is hardly adequate if the reason for the buyback is in fact a cumulative number of 30 days in the repair shop for a variety of reasons. This might include transmission failure, five minor electrical defects, *and* a seat belt retraction problem. The manufacturer cannot just select which of several defects it chooses to disclose, just as it cannot just select which defects to correct.

The auction procedure also facilitates deceptive nondisclosure practices. Typically auto auctions are not public, but exclusive to dealers, and may even be exclusive to only that manufacturer's dealers. Thus on Mondays, an auction may be open only to Chrysler dealers; Tuesdays accessible to authorized Toyota franchisees; and Wednesdays limited to Ford dealers. The vehicles may be held on a crowded "inspection" lot prior to sale, where they are parked too closely to encourage or allow thorough engine inspection and no test drive. Buyers view the vehicles as they roll through on a conveyor belt. A flashing light system identifies car categories known to affect resale value: salvage, frame damage, rental fleet, title defects (red light), good condition (green light).

Retail buybacks are supposed to get a red light, but since some repurchased vehicles are not lemons and only some states require title branding, the process is somewhat subjective and enforcement is nil. Among the milling professional auction crowd, the volume is heavy, the pace is swift, the dealing is slick. Indeed, the wholesale auto auction is like the Coin Automat of lemon laundering.

In this commercial circus, there is a lot of opportunity — and a lot of incentive — for disclosure to get lost. First, the manufacturer may disclose only one or some of the defects for which it was returned; or it may disclose the symptom complained of rather than the mechanical defect found; or it may disclose a problem without revealing the vehicle was actually repurchased for that reason, thereby minimizing the severity of the defect. The dealer which buys at auction may then sell it directly to the used car market, or it may change dealer hands several times.

When the car is eventually sold at retail, the retail seller will disavow all knowledge of the lemon history, and sell the car with no disclosure. This, despite the fact that in most instances the complete computerized warranty repair history is available to dealer management. Dealers get around this by saying that their sales personnel does not have access to this information, which resides in the service department. Since a typical returned lemon has relatively low mileage, a favorite ploy is to describe the buybacks as "executive trade-ins," connoting high class status and white glove care attractive to used car buyers. Nothing could be further from the truth.

How Dealers Avoid the "Lemon" Brand on the Title

Under many state lemon laundering statutes, the manufacturer is required to brand the vehicle's title when it buys the car back. The wording of the actual "brand" is specified in the statute, or by implementing regulation. Several states require some variation of the words "manufacturer buyback," others, like California, use the readily recognizable "lemon law buyback." Other states' brands use a phrase such as "did not conform to its warranty."

Dealers show remarkable ingenuity in removing lemon buyback brands from vehicle titles.

This would seem a dead give-away to a subsequent purchaser. But there are ways the brand is laundered just as written disclosure of the car's history is evaded. One way to do so is to move the lemon buyback to a state that does not require title branding, or that does not recognize a prior state's brand, so the title in the new state is unmarked. A perusal of the chain of title for many lemon buybacks shows a significant interstate movement, movement that would not be explained by the economics of the marketplace.

Moreover, even if the brand stays on the title, the buyer may not actually get the title documents until weeks later. In a financed transaction, the buyer may never see the title at all. Nevertheless, a lender may not fund a loan when it scrutinizes the brand, and the deal could unravel for lack of approved funding.

Consumers May Acknowledge the Lemon History While Being Oblivious to That History

Lemon laundering statutes vary as to the disclosure requirement. Some specify only that the manufacturer disclose the lemon history to the buying dealer, and not to the eventual consumer. Some require that a disclosure be attached to the vehicle or be made directly to the retail buyer.

A growing practice today, that is required in a number of states, is for the consumer to sign a written statement acknowledging that the car being purchased has a lemon buyback history. Dealers avoid the impact of this disclosure by use of the deceptive practice known as "fanning." Many people who have experienced the process of car buying as an exhausting and irritating process recall being presented with an array of documents. The standard set is known by the industry as "the six pack," but in fact there may be even more than six separate papers to sign. Dealership personnel are trained to present these papers in a stack which is then fanned out before the confused buyer. The signature lines are visible while the top half of the document is obscured by the stack itself. No wonder buyers are surprised and dismayed to later find they signed something they swear they have never seen.

> Most dealerships are very smart when it comes to the moment of signing. They seem to invariably pick the very second your heart is beating wildly, your lips are smacking in anticipation, and your common sense is visiting in a neighboring state; *then*, and only they, will your salesman or finance

> manager stealthily slide a large mound of papers under your quivering hand and say, "Sign here, and here, and here."[1]

It is not unheard of for the dealer to have obtained signatures on all documents, only to slide a disclosure notice into the stack after the deal is consummated.

Even when consumers realize that they are acknowledging a car had defects, they may not realize the extent of the defects. If the manufacturer is given any leeway at all to designate the "reason" for reacquisition, the tendency will be to minimize the prior owners' complaints. The disclosure of replaced tires would not necessarily deter purchase whereas disclosure that frame damage or steering problems caused the tire wear would make the buyer balk.

HOW TO UNCOVER A LAUNDERED LEMON

A consumer can take several investigative steps to determine whether a car was previously returned as a lemon. A car returned to the manufacturer prior to 12,000-miles on the odometer always raises a red flag. On the other hand, a car with more than 12,000 miles may still be a lemon, since the lemon law warranty period often exceeds this mileage, and the warranty dispute may have been resolved only after years of delay.

An independent repair dealer or body shop may be the first to clue the owner into the ugly reality. Lemon laundering is often first noticed when something else goes wrong and the scars of prior repair work catch the attention of a skilled auto technician. Good independent technicians have computer-assisted tools so sophisticated they can measure paint depth in millimeters to ferret out evidence of replacement parts and repeat repairs. The repair shop may have access to technical service bulletins, in which the manufacturer instructs its dealers on known defects and suggested repairs. (You too, can obtain these bulletins on the Internet (see Chapter 6, Establishing the Facts.))

The consumer can also contact the previous owner. At least five states require a dealer to provide the name of the previous owner to prospective buyers, and a title search will also uncover this information. Tracing the title will also provide other indications of a laundered lemon, such as the manufacturer listed as a prior owner. The title may have to be traced back several sales if the car has been moved around to obscure its history.

The consumer can also demand the vehicle title and repair history from the manufacturer who maintains records of all cars in order to issue recall notices. Other good sources of information on a retail buyback are testimony of dealer personnel and records of the service department of the previous repair dealers; previous independent expert reports; correspondence between the dealer or manufacturer and the prior owner; the prior owner's application for IDM and the manufacturer's response papers, whether or not a decision was rendered; pleadings on file if there was previous litigation; customer inquiry history of the prior owner; and settlement and release documents between the manufacturer and the previous owner. Some of these require formal discovery requests. Finally, in states which allow the manufacturer who offers a buyback the right to recoup fees and registration paid to the state, the manufacturer's request for reimbursement from the state is direct evidence that the vehicle was in fact repurchased pursuant to the lemon law.

Of all these factors, statements of the previous owner or owners are perhaps most persuasive. Owning a lemon is an experience few consumers forget. The fact that the prior owner has no technical knowledge is immaterial.

LEGAL THEORIES TO PURSUE

If a consumer uncovers a hidden sale of a laundered lemon, the consumer has a number of legal claims available to challenge the sale — a state deceptive practices act claim (that may provide attorney fees and multiple, minimum, or punitive damages), common law fraud, and negligent misrepresentation.

The consumer may also have warranty claims based either on the manufacturer's original warranty or on a warranty provided by the state's lemon laundering statute. For example, certain lemon laundering statutes provide a warranty for 12 months or 12,000 miles, pertaining either to the specific non-conformities which formed the basis of the repurchase, or for the entire vehicle.

There may be additional recourse in the state vehicle code for those classes of vehicles involving safety defects. To cite one example, the California Vehicle Code states "No dealer or person holding a retail seller's permit shall sell a new or used vehicle which is not in compliance with this code and departmental regulations adopted pursuant to this code. . . ." The legislative scheme then sets out numerous requirements for the safety of automotive equipment from turn signals to brake systems, from windshields to windshield wipers, which should be viewed as the applicable baseline standard for automotive safety. Similar federal vehicle safety regulations may be of use in this regard.

Last, but not least, the state lemon laundering statute may provide a valid claim for the consumer. Despite language which clearly places the responsibility for disclosure on the manufacturer, and legislative intent that clearly seeks to place the true facts in the hands of the subsequent consumer, manufacturers frequently try escape liability by claiming there is "no privity" — that the consumer never dealt with the manufacturer and only the dealer should be liable. Courts should give short shrift to this lack of privity argument, for, to accept the privity argument, is to ignore the letter of the lemon laundering law and emasculate its intent.

Another favorite manufacturer defense is to claim that it provided full disclosure to the dealer to whom it sold the lemon vehicle, and it cannot be responsible if that dealer did not pass on the information. Passing on material disclosures from original owner to manufacturer to auction to dealer to subsequent owner is unfortunately much like the children's game of "telephone." While it is true that the dealer *service* departments usually have access to the warranty repair history kept on the manufacturer's computer system, the dealer *sales* department is kept in the dark relying only on the one-inch disclosure in the auction memorandum of sale.

Where the manufacturer has a duty of disclosure to the consumer, but relies on the dealer to pass it on (or not to pass it on), the consumer has a strong argument that the dealer was the agent of the manufacturer for this purpose. Thus the manufacturer is not absolved of the omissions of the dealer.

LITIGATION POINTERS

The most effective way to prove the buyback case is to present a "trial within a trial," establishing the fact that the vehicle was a lemon buyback from the original owner and introducing detailed evidence of the reasons for the return. Sometimes expert testimony is necessary to sort out whether the subsequent complaints are related to the non-conformities previously alleged. For example, the symptom may be uneven tire wear while the defect is in fact somewhere in the steering or alignment. Pervasive water leaks to the passenger compartment may be evidence of frame damage. A clutch repair may relate to a faulty transmission. The dealer and manufacturer may know exactly what the real problem is because they have access to the technical service bulletins which the average consumer does not have.

Even in litigation, industry aggressively fights discovery requests. Motions to compel the prior history are more the norm than the exception. Without a lawyer, the consumer is simply not equipped either with the savvy nor the subpoena power to accomplish this task.

---

[1] Sutton, R. *Don't Get Taken Every Time* 288 (Penguin Books 2d rev. ed. 1991).

Appendix

STATE-BY-STATE ANALYSIS
OF NEW CAR LEMON LAWS

This appendix analyzes state *new* car lemon laws in all fifty states and the District of Columbia. Caution is advised because this analysis is a summary and should be used as a beginning to a thorough reading of the statute itself. Moreover, because lemon laws are frequently amended, make sure to use the most current version of a statute or the version in effect at the time of the lemon dispute. This appendix is derived from NCLC's *Consumer Warranty Law* Appx. F (1997 and Supp.). Refer to annual supplements to that volume for the most up-to-date summary of state lemon laws.

Ala. Stat. §8-20A-1

1. *Vehicles covered:* All vehicles, new or previously untitled, that are under 10,000 lbs., self-propelled, and intended primarily for operation on public highways. Excludes motor homes. §8-20A-1(2)

2. *Persons covered:* Purchasers or any persons entitled to enforce the warranty where vehicle used in substantial part for personal, family, or household purposes. §8-20A-1(1)

3. *Period covered:* Whichever is first: one year after date of original delivery or first 12,000 miles. §8-20A-1(8)

4. *Notice requirement:* (a) Manufacturer — none; (b) Consumer — written notification describing the vehicle and all previous attempts to correct the nonconformity. §8-20A-1(7)

5. *Repair requirements:* It is presumed that a reasonable number of attempts have been made if the same nonconformity has been subjected to three or more repairs, or the vehicle is out of service for a cumulative total of 30 or more calendar days. §8-20A-2(c)

6. *Affirmative defenses:* The nonconformity does not significantly impair the use, market value or safety of the vehicle, or is the result of abuse, neglect, or any unauthorized modification or alteration by the consumer; statute of limitations. §§8-20A-3(b), 8-20A-6.

7. *Replace/refund:* At the consumer's option, the manufacturer shall replace with a comparable vehicle, or refund the full purchase price less a reasonable allowance (defined). §8-20A-2(b)

8. *Other reimbursement:* Collateral charges, taxes, fees, finance charges and incidental costs. §8-20A-2(b)

9. *Other remedies:* There is no limit on other consumer remedies. Reasonable attorney fees. §8-20A-3

10. *Informal dispute mechanism:* For remedies under this section, a consumer must use the informal dispute procedure established by the manufacturer. §8-20A-3(a)

11. *Resale of lemon:* Full disclosure required. §8-20A-4

Alaska Stat. §45.45.300

1. *Vehicles covered:* Vehicles normally used for personal, family, or household purposes and registered under Alaska Stat. §28.10. Excludes tractors, farm vehicles, and off-road vehicles. §45.45.360(6)

2. *Persons covered:* Purchasers, other than for resale, of new motor vehicles, and transferees. §45.45.360(8)

3. *Period covered:* Whichever is first: term of express warranty or within one year from date of delivery. §45.45.305

4. *Notice requirement:* (a) Manufacturer — none; (b) Consumer — specific written notice by certified mail to the manufacturer and its dealer or repairing agent. §45.45.310

5. *Repair requirements:* It is presumed that a reasonable number of attempts have been made if the same nonconformity has been subjected to repair three or more times, or the vehicle has been out of service for 30 or more business days. §45.45.320

6. *Affirmative defenses:* The nonconformity does not substantially impair the use or market value of the vehicle, or is the result of the consumer's abuse or neglect; unauthorized modifications or alterations were made to the vehicle. §45.45.315

7. *Replace/refund:* At the consumer's option, the manufacturer shall replace with a new comparable vehicle, or refund the full purchase price less a reasonable use allowance. §45.45.305

8. *Other reimbursement:* Reimbursement for costs incurred in shipping the vehicle to the repair facility; refund to the lienholder and consumer. §§45.45.305; 45.45.350

9. *Other remedies:* There is no limit on other remedies that may be available. §45.45.340 Failure to refund or replace may be an unfair trade practice. §45.45.330

10. *Informal dispute mechanism:* For remedies under this section, a consumer must use an informal dispute settlement procedure established by the manufacturer provided the procedure complies with 16 C.F.R. 703. §45.45.355

11. *Resale of lemon:* Full disclosure required. §45.45.335

Ariz. Rev. Stat. Ann. §44-1261

1. *Vehicles covered:* Vehicles under 10,000 lbs. that are designed primarily for transportation of persons or property. Excludes living portions of motor homes. §§44-1261(A)(2), (B), (C)

2. *Persons covered:* Purchasers, transferees during express warranty period, or any person entitled to enforce the warranty. §44-1261(A)(1)

3. *Period covered:* Whichever is first: term of express warranty or within two years or 24,000 miles following the date of original delivery. §44-1262

4. *Notice requirement:* (a) Manufacturer — none; (b) Consumer — written notification to the manufacturer from or on behalf of the consumer; opportunity to cure. §§44-1262, 44-1264(C)

5. *Repair requirements:* It is presumed that a reasonable number of attempts have been made if the same nonconformity has been subjected to four or more repairs, or the vehicle is out of service for a cumulative total of 30 or more calendar days. §44-1264(A)

6. *Affirmative defenses:* The nonconformity does not substantially impair the use and market value of the vehicle, or is the result of the consumer's abuse, neglect, or unauthorized modifications or alterations; statute of limitations. §§44-1263(B), 44-1265(B)

7. *Replace/refund:* The manufacturer shall replace with a new motor vehicle, or refund the full purchase price less a reasonable use allowance. §44-1263(A)

8. *Other reimbursement:* Collateral charges; refunds to consumer and lienholder. §44-1263(A)

9. *Other remedies:* Reasonable costs and attorney fees. §44-1265(B)

10. *Informal dispute mechanism:* For remedies under this section, a consumer must use an informal dispute settlement procedure provided the procedure complies with 16 C.F.R. 703. §44-1265(A)

11. *Resale of Lemon:* Full written disclosure required of manufacturers ordered by judgment or decree to replace or repurchase motor vehicle. Applies to vehicles repurchased or replaced under Arizona or laws of another state. §44-1266

Ark. Code Ann. §4-90-401

1. *Vehicles covered:* Self-propelled vehicle under 10,000 lbs., licensed, purchased or leased in-state, and primarily designed for the transportation of persons or property. Excludes mopeds, motorcycles, and the living quarters of mobile homes. §4-90-403

2. *Persons covered:* Purchaser or lessee either for the purposes of lease or resale. §4-90-403(4)

3. *Period covered:* Ends two years (24 months) after the vehicle is delivered to the consumer or the first 24,000 miles attributable to the consumer, whichever is later. §4-90-403(12)

4. *Notice requirements:* (a) Manufacturer — must provide a written state-approved notice to the consumer explaining the consumer's rights at the time of lease or purchase; (b) Consumer — none if the manufacturer has failed to notify consumer of his/her rights at the time of the lease or purchase, otherwise the consumer must notify the manufacturer by mail of the need to repair the nonconformity. §4-90-404

5. *Repair requirements:* After three attempts to repair a nonconformity which "substantially impairs" the motor vehicle or one repair attempt for a nonconformity that is life threatening or which could cause bodily injury, plus one final opportunity to repair. §4-90-406(a)(1)

6. *Affirmative defenses:* Nonconformity does not impair use, value or safety of vehicles; the nonconformity is the result of an accident, abuse, neglect or unauthorized alteration; claim by consumer was not filed in good faith; other defenses allowed by law; statute of limitations. §§4-90-413, 416

7. *Replace/refund:* At the consumer's option, the manufacturer must replace with an identical or reasonably equivalent vehicle acceptable to the consumer, or refund the full purchase or lease price less a reasonable use and damage allowance (defined). §§4-90-406, 4-90-407

8. *Other reimbursement:* Collateral and reasonably incurred incidental charges, §4-90-406(b)(2) and (3), plus towing and rental costs, §§4-90-407, 4-90-408, attorney fees and costs. §4-90-415

9. *Other remedies:* Violation of the statute is a deceptive trade practice. §4-90-417 There is no limit on other consumer remedies. §4-90-415(b)

10. *Informal dispute mechanism:* Consumer must first submit to informal proceedings before commencing a civil action and collecting under §4-90-406(b)(2) and (3) unless the manufacturer allows otherwise. The dispute procedure must comply with 16 C.F.R. §703.1 *et seq.* §4-90-414

11. *Resale of lemon:* Full written disclosure signed by the consumer required; same express warranty offered to the original purchaser (with maximum of first 12,000 miles or one year required). §4-90-412

Cal. Civ. Code §1793.2 to 1793.4

1. *Vehicles covered:* New motor vehicles used or bought primarily for personal, family or household purposes, including dealer-owned vehicles and demonstrators. Excludes motorcycles, the portion of motor homes used primarily for habitation and off-road vehicles. "New vehicle" includes demonstrator or other motor vehicle sold with new car warranty. Includes up to five vehicles bought or used for business use by businesses. §1793.22(e)(2)

2. *Persons covered:* No definition; refers to buyer and lessee. §1793.22(e)(1)

3. *Period covered:* Whichever is first: 12,000 miles or one year. §1793.22(b)

4. *Notice requirements:* (a) Manufacturer — clear, conspicuous notice to the buyer in the warranty or owner's manual of statute, including the requirement that the buyer notify the manufacturer; (b) Consumer — direct notice to the manufacturer only if manufacturer made required disclosures. §1793.22(b)

5. *Repair requirements:* The same nonconformity is subjected to four or more repairs, or the vehicle is out of service for a cumulative total of 30 or more calendar days. §1793.22(b)

6. *Affirmative defenses:* None specifically set forth.

7. *Replace/refund:* Consumer may choose restitution instead of replacement. In the case of replacement, the manufacturer shall replace the buyer's vehicle with a new motor vehicle substantially identical to the vehicle replaced. The replacement vehicle shall be accompanied by all express and implied warranties that normally accompany new motor vehicles. The manufacturer shall also pay for sales or use tax, license fees, and registration fees, plus any incidental damages that the buyer is entitled to under §1974, including but not limited to reasonable repair, towing, and rental car costs actually incurred by the buyer. §1793.2(d)(2)

8. *Other reimbursement:* Taxes, fees, and incidental damages (explained). §§1793.25, 1793.2(d)(2)(B)

9. *Other remedies:* There is no limit on other consumer remedies; double damages and attorney fees. §1794

10. *Informal dispute mechanism:* For remedies under this section, a consumer must use an informal dispute settlement procedure established by the manufacturer provided the procedure complies with 16 C.F.R. 703. §1793.22(c), (d)

11. *Resale of lemon:* Manufacturer must reissue title with notation "Lemon Law Buyback" affixed thereon and affix a decal to the vehicle. Any person who resells such vehicle must give written notice to subsequent buyer, and must obtain buyer's written acknowledgment of the notice. Manufacturer must warrant for one year period that vehicle is free of problems reported by original owner. Statute bars gag clauses in reacquisition agreements. §§1793.23, 1793.24

Colo. Rev. Stat. §42-10-101

1. *Vehicles covered:* Passenger vehicles normally used for personal, family, or household use and sold in-state, including pick-up trucks and vans. Excludes vehicles that carry more than 10 persons, motor homes, and vehicles with three or fewer wheels. §42-10-101(2)

2. *Persons covered:* Purchasers, transferees during express warranty period, or any person entitled to enforce the warranty. §42-10-101(1)

3. *Period covered:* Whichever is first: term of warranty or within one year from date of delivery. §42-10-102

4. *Notice requirements:* (a) Manufacturer — form with name and address inserted in owner's manual; disclose requirements of consumer remedies, §42-10-103(2)(d); (b) Consumer — written notification by certified mail to manufacturer; opportunity to cure. §42-10-103(2)(c),(d)

5. *Repair requirements:* It is presumed that a reasonable number of attempts have been made if the same nonconformity is subjected to four or more repairs, or the vehicle is out of service for a cumulative total of 30 or more business days. §42-10-103(2)

6. *Affirmative defenses:* The nonconformity does not substantially impair the use and market value of the vehicle, or is the result of the consumer's abuse, neglect, or unauthorized modifications or alterations. §42-10-104 Statute of limitations. §42-10-107.

7. *Replace/refund:* At the manufacturer's option, the manufacturer shall replace with a comparable vehicle, or refund the full purchase price less a reasonable use allowance. §42-10-103(1)

8. *Other reimbursement:* Taxes, fees, and charges; refund to the consumer and lienholder. §42-10-103(1)

9. *Other remedies:* There is no limit on other consumer remedies. §42-10-105. Attorney fees recoverable. §42-10-103(3)

10. *Informal dispute mechanism:* For remedies under this action, a consumer must use the manufacturer's informal dispute settlement procedure provided it complies with 16 C.F.R. 703. §42-10-106

Conn. Gen. Stat. Ann. §42-179

1. *Vehicles covered:* Passenger motor vehicles or passenger and commercial vehicles, as defined in Conn. Gen. Stat. §14-1, sold or leased in-state. §42-179(a)(2)

2. *Persons covered:* Purchasers or lessees, transferees during express warranty period, or any person entitled to enforce the warranty. §42-179(a)(1)

3. *Period covered:* Whichever is first: two years following date of delivery or first 18,000 miles. §42-179(b)

4. *Notice requirements:* (a) Manufacturer — disclose in the warranty or owner's manual that written notice of nonconformity is required; include name and address, §42.179(c); (b) Consumer — written notification, if the manufacturer complied with notification requirements. §42-179(c)

5. *Repair requirements:* It is presumed that a reasonable number of attempts have been made if the same nonconformity is subjected to repair four times, or the vehicle is out of service for a cumulative total of 30 or more calendar days with at least one attempt to repair or refusal to repair, §42-179(e); if the nonconformity is likely to cause death or serious bodily injury, then subjected to repair two times during earlier of one-year period or within express warranty term. §42-179(f)

6. *Affirmative defense:* The nonconformity does not substantially impair the use, safety or value of the vehicle, or is a result of abuse, neglect, or unauthorized modifications or alterations. §42-179(d)

7. *Replace/refund:* The manufacturer shall replace with a new motor vehicle acceptable to the consumer, or refund the contract price minus a reasonable allowance for use (defined). §42-179(d)

8. *Other reimbursement:* Collateral charges, incidental damages, and other charges and fees (defined). §42-179(d)

9. *Other remedies:* There is no limit on other consumer remedies. §42-179(i) The consumer may recover costs and reasonable attorney fees. §42-180 Violation is unfair trade practice. §42-184

10. *Informal dispute mechanism:* For remedies under this section, a consumer must use an informal dispute settlement procedure certified by the attorney general if the manufacturer has established such a procedure. §42-179(j) Otherwise, state arbitration is available. §42-181

11. *Resale of lemon:* Full disclosure required. §42-179(g)

Del. Code Ann. tit. 6, §5001

1. *Vehicles covered:* Any passenger motor vehicle sold, leased or registered in-state. Excludes motorcycles and living facilities of motor homes. §5001(5)

2. *Persons covered:* Purchasers, transferees during express warranty period, or any person entitled to enforce the warranty. §5001(1)

3. *Period covered:* Whichever is first: term of warranty or within one year from date of delivery. §5002

4. *Notice requirement:* (a) Manufacturer — none; (b) Consumer — written notice to the manufacturer by or on behalf of the consumer; opportunity to cure. §5004(b)

5. *Repair requirements:* It is presumed that a reasonable number of attempts have been made if the same nonconformity has been subjected to four or more repairs, or the vehicle has been out of service for 30 or more calendar days. §5004(a)(1), (2)

6. *Affirmative defense:* The nonconformity does not substantially impair the use or value of the vehicle, or is the result of the consumer's abuse, neglect, or unauthorized modifications or alterations. §5006

7. *Replace/refund:* At the consumer's option, the manufacturer shall replace with a comparable new automobile acceptable to the consumer, or repurchase the automobile and give the consumer a full refund minus a reasonable allowance for use (defined §5003(c)(1)). §5003

8. *Other reimbursement:* Incidental costs (explained), other charges, and fees. §5003(b). Attorney fees. §5005

9. *Other remedies:* There is no limit on other consumer remedies. §5008 Violation is unlawful trade practice. §5009

10. *Informal dispute mechanism:* For remedies under this section, a consumer must use an informal settlement procedure if it is approved by the Division of Consumer Affairs. §5007

D.C. Code Ann. §40-1301

1. *Vehicles covered:* Passenger vehicles sold or registered in D.C. Excludes buses sold for public transportation, motorcycles, motor homes, and recreational vehicles. §40-1301(9)

2. *Persons covered:* Purchasers or lessees, transferees during express warranty period, or any person entitled to enforce the warranty. §40-1301(2)

3. *Period covered:* Whichever is first: 18,000 miles or two years. §40-1302(a)

4. *Notice requirements:* (a) Manufacturer — written notice to the prospective consumer of consumer rights, §40-1304; (b) Consumer — report the nonconformity to the manufacturer, its agent, or the authorized dealer by certified mail. §40-1302

5. *Repair requirements:* It is presumed that a reasonable number of attempts have been made if the same nonconformity is subjected to four or more repairs, or the vehicle is out of service for a cumulative total of 30 or more days; or if a safety-related defect is subjected to one or more repair attempts. §40-1302(d)

6. *Affirmative defenses:* The nonconformity does not substantially impair the vehicle, or is the result of the consumer's abuse, neglect, or unauthorized modifications or alterations. §40-1302(c) Statute of limitations. §40-1307(b)

7. *Replace/refund:* At consumer's option, the manufacturer shall replace with a comparable vehicle, or refund the full purchase price less a reasonable use allowance (defined). §40-1302(b)

8. *Other reimbursement:* Taxes, fees, and charges; refund to the consumer and lienholder. §40-1302(b)

9. *Other remedies:* There is no limit on other consumer remedies. §40-1307

10. *Informal dispute mechanism:* For remedies under this section, a consumer must use the government-run arbitration board informal dispute settlement procedure. §§40-1302(f), 40-1303

11. *Resale of lemon:* Dealer must disclose to prospective buyer. §40-1302(g)(3)

Fla. Stat. Ann. §681.102 (West)

1. *Vehicles covered:* Motor vehicles sold or leased in-state used primarily for personal, family or household purposes that transport persons or property, including demonstrators and lease-purchases with warranty. Excludes off-road vehicles, mopeds, trucks over 10,000 lbs., the living facilities of recreational vehicles, and motorcycles. §§681.102(4), (15)

2. *Persons covered:* Purchasers, transferees during express warranty period, or any person entitled to enforce the warranty. §681.102(4)

3. *Period covered:* Two years after original delivery date. §681.102(10)

4. *Notice requirements:* (a) Manufacturer — provide list of service offices, written notice of claim procedure and all consumer rights under lemon law; itemized statement of repair if vehicle returned for defect. §681.103; (b) Consumer — written notice to manufacturer by registered or express mail. §681.104(1)(b)

5. *Repair requirements:* It is presumed that a reasonable number of attempts have been made if the same nonconformity is subjected to three repairs plus a final attempt, or the vehicle is out of service for a cumulative total of 30 or more working days, exclusive of maintenance and final 10 day repair period. §§681.104(1)(a), (3)

6. *Affirmative defenses:* The nonconformity does not substantially impair the use, safety or market value of the vehicle, or is a result of an accident, abuse, neglect, or unauthorized modification or alteration by the consumer, or the claim is not filed in good faith. §681.104(4)

7. *Replace/refund:* At the consumer's option, the manufacturer shall replace with a comparable or replacement automobile acceptable to the consumer, or repurchase the automobile and give the consumer a full refund minus a reasonable allowance for use (defined). §681.104(2)(a)

8. *Other reimbursement:* Collateral and incidental charges; refund to the consumer and lienholder. §681.104(2)(a)

9. *Other remedies:* Misrepresentation by the manufacturer is an unfair and deceptive trade practice. §681.111 Damage action; attorney fees. §681.112(1) No limit to consumer remedies (§681.112).

10. *Informal dispute mechanism:* For remedies under this section, a consumer must use an informal dispute settlement procedure established by the manufacturer provided the procedure complies with 16 C.F.R. 703. §681.108 The consumer may also use the state arbitration board. §681.109

11. *Resale of lemon:* Full disclosure required. §681.114(2)

Title must be stamped: "manufacturer's buyback." Fla. Stat. Ann. §319.14, as amended by 1996 Fla. Laws ch. 96-227. Manufacturer must warrant defect for one year or first 12,000 miles. §681.114(2)

Ga. Code Ann. §10-1-780

1. *Vehicles covered:* New vehicles that are under 10,000 lbs. and purchased, leased or registered by the original buyer in-state. Excludes those portions of motor homes used for dwelling, or office or commercial space. §10-1-782(11)

2. *Persons covered:* Purchasers, transferees or lessees of new motor vehicles used primarily for personal, family or household purposes, and any sole proprietorship, partnership or corporation which owns or leases fewer than three motor vehicles, has ten or fewer employees and has a net income of $100,000 or less per annum. §10-1-782(3)

3. *Period covered:* Whichever is first: one year after date of original delivery or first 12,000 miles. §10-1-782(9)

4. *Notice requirements:* (a) Manufacturer — owner's manual published by the manufacturer must include a list of the addresses and phone numbers where consumers may, at no cost, contact the manufacturer's customer service personnel, §10-1-783(a); (b) Dealer — written statement of the consumer's rights under this article, §10-1-783(b); (c) Consumer — written notice to the manufacturer sent certified mail, return receipt requested. §10-1-784(a)(1)

5. *Repair requirements:* It is presumed that a reasonable number of attempts have been made if a serious safety defect in the brakes or steering system has been repaired once during the earlier of one year or 12,000 miles, any other serious defect has been repaired two or more times (one of those times within the earlier of one year or 12,000 miles), or, within the earlier of 24 months or 24,000 miles, either the same nonconformity has been subject to three or more repairs or the vehicle has been out of service for a cumulative total of 30 or more days (15 of them within the earlier of one year or 12,000 miles). §10-1-784(b)

6. *Affirmative defenses:* The nonconformity does not substantially impair the use, value or safety of the vehicle, or is the result of the consumer's abuse, neglect or unauthorized modification or alteration. §10-1-787(e)

7. *Replace/refund:* The manufacturer shall replace with a new identical or reasonably equivalent vehicle, or accept a return and refund the purchase price. In either case, the manufacturer is allowed a reasonable offset for use. §10-1-784(a)(2),(3),(4)

8. *Other reimbursement:* All collateral and incidental charges less a reasonable offset for use. §10-1-784(a)(4)

9. *Other remedies:* Any violation of this article is an unfair and deceptive act or practice. There is no limit on other consumer remedies. §§10-1-790, 792

10. *Informal dispute mechanism:* For remedies under this section, a consumer must use an i nformal dispute settlement procedure if available and Administrator-certified. §10-1-793 If no manufacturer settlement procedure is available, the consumer may apply to the new Motor Vehicle Arbitration Panel. §10-1-787

11. *Resale of lemon:* Full disclosure required in writing. §10-1-785

Haw. Rev. Stat. §481I-2

1. *Vehicles covered:* New motor vehicles bought or used primarily for personal, family or household purposes, including demonstrators and other vehicles sold with a warranty. Excludes mopeds, motorcycles, motor scooters, and vehicles over 10,000 lbs. §481I-2

2. *Persons covered:* Purchasers, lessees, transferees during express warranty period, or any person entitled to enforce the warranty. §481I-2

3. *Period covered:* Whichever is first: term of express warranty, within two years from date of delivery, or within 24,000 miles. §481I-2

4. *Notice requirements:* (a) Manufacturer — written notice of provisions to the consumer, §481I-3(g); (b) Consumer — in writing to the manufacturer, its agent, or its authorized dealer only if manufacturer has provided a written notice of terms of arbitration board and rights of consumer. §48lI-3(a), (h)

5. *Repair requirements:* It is presumed that a reasonable number of attempts have been made if the same nonconformity has been subjected to three or more repairs, or the vehicle has been out of service for 30 or more business days. §481I-3(d)

6. *Affirmative defenses:* The nonconformity does not substantially impair the use and market value of the vehicle or is a result of abuse, neglect, or unauthorized modifications or alteration. §481I-3(c)

7. *Replace/refund:* Manufacturers shall replace with a comparable motor vehicle, or accept a return and refund the full purchase price less a reasonable allowance for use. §481I-3(b)

8. *Other reimbursement:* Refund of the full purchase price including all collateral charges, excluding interest. §481I-3(b)

9. *Other remedies:* A violation is an unfair or deceptive act or practice. §481I-3(*l*)

10. *Informal dispute mechanism:* Consumer can use a state-funded arbitration procedure. §481I-4

11. *Resale of lemon:* Full disclosure required. Must provide one year or 12,000-mile warranty covering same defect or defects. Haw. Rev. Stat. §481I-3(3)(k)

Idaho Code §48-901

1. *Vehicles covered:* Vehicles as defined in §49-123, but not including motorcycles, farm tractors, house trailers, or vehicles over 12,000 lbs. §48-902(4)

2. *Persons covered:* Purchasers other than for resale, of vehicles used for personal, family or household purposes, and other transferees or individuals entitled to enforce the warranty. §48-902(1)

3. *Period covered:* Whichever is first: one year or 12,000 miles. §48-905(1)

4. *Notice requirement:* (a) Manufacturer — none; (b) Consumer — in writing to the manufacturer or dealer. §48-904

5. *Repair requirements:* It is presumed that a reasonable number of attempts have been undertaken where the same nonconformity has been subjected to four or more repair attempts, or the vehicle has been out of service 30 or more business days. §48-905(1)(a), (b)

6. *Affirmative defenses:* Buyer's abuse, neglect, or unauthorized modifications; buyer's claim in bad faith; other defenses allowed by law. §48-903

7. *Replace/refund:* Replacement with a comparable new motor vehicle or purchase price less the amount attributable to the buyer's use. §§48-903, 904

8. *Other reimbursement:* If buyer pursues civil action against manufacturer for refusal to refund or replace, treble the full purchase price, including all collateral charges, less a reasonable use allowance. §48-908

9. *Other remedies:* All other remedies provided by law. §48-909

10. *Informal dispute mechanism:* For remedies under this section, a consumer must utilize a dispute resolution mechanism complying with 16 C.F.R. 703, if such mechanism exists. §48-906

815 Ill. Comp. Stat. 380/1

1. *Vehicles covered:* Passenger cars as defined in Ill. Vehicle Code ch. 625 Ill. Comp. Stat. 5/1-157 and recreational vehicles as defined in 625 Ill. Comp. Stat. 5/1-216, except camping trailers or travel trailers. §380/2(c)

2. *Persons covered:* Individual consumers who purchase or lease new cars to transport themselves and others, and their personal property, for primarily personal, household or family purposes. §380/2(a)

3. *Period covered:* Whichever is first: one year or 12,000 miles. §380/2(f)

4. *Notice requirements:* (a) Manufacturer — must inform the consumer of consumer rights, §380/7; (b) Consumer — written notification to the manufacturer from or on behalf of the consumer; opportunity to cure. §380/3(h)

5. *Repair requirements:* It is presumed that a reasonable number of attempts have made if the same nonconformity has been subjected to four or more repairs, or the vehicle has been out of service for 30 or more business days. §380/3(b)

6. *Affirmative defenses:* Failure to conform is the result of abuse, neglect, or unauthorized modification or alterations. §380/3(d)

7. *Replace/refund:* Manufacturers shall provide a new car of a like model line, if available, or a comparable vehicle, or accept a return and refund the full purchase price less a reasonable allowance for use. §380/3(a)

8. *Other reimbursement:* Collateral charges. §390/3(a) Refunds to the consumer and lienholder. §380/3(f)

9. *Other remedies:* A consumer may bring a civil action if dissatisfied with arbitration decision. §380/4. Persons electing to proceed and settle under this act are barred from a separate cause of action under the UCC. §380/5

10. *Informal dispute mechanism*: For remedies under this section, a consumer must use an informal dispute settlement procedure established by the manufacturer provided the procedure complies with 16 C.F.R. 703. §380/4(a)

11. *Resale of Lemon*: Full written disclosure and warranty for defects required. 625 Ill. Comp. Stat. §5/5-104.2

Ind. Code §24-5-13-1

1. *Vehicles covered*: Vehicles that are sold, leased, transferred or replaced, and registered in-state, and are under 10,000 lbs. Excludes conversion vans, motorhomes, farm tractors and machines, road building equipment, truck and road tractors, motorcycles, mopeds, snowmobiles, and off-road vehicles. §24-5-13-5

2. *Persons covered*: Buyers who enters into a contract to transfer, lease or purchase motor vehicles. §24-5-13-3

3. *Period covered*: Whichever is first: 18 months or 18,000 miles. §24-5-13-7

4. *Notice requirements*: (a) Manufacturer — must describe in the warranty or buyer's manual that written notification is required for refund or replacement; disclose manufacturer's name and address, §24-5-13-9(b); (b) Consumer — notify the manufacturer if it has met notice requirements. §24-5-13-9(a)

5. *Repair requirements*: It is presumed that a reasonable number of attempts have been made if the same nonconformity is subjected to four or more repairs, or if the vehicle is out of service for a cumulative total of 30 or more business days (defined). §24-5-13-15

6. *Affirmative defenses*: The nonconformity does not substantially impair the use, value or safety of the vehicle, or is the result of the consumer's abuse, neglect, or unauthorized modifications or alterations. §24-5-13-18

7. *Replace/refund*: At the consumer's option, the manufacturer shall replace with a comparable vehicle, or refund the full purchase price less a reasonable use allowance (defined). §§24-5-13-10, 11

8. *Other reimbursement*: Incidental costs (defined). §24-5-13-11(c) For a leased vehicle, the lessee may recover all deposits, lease payments, and credits for allowances less a reasonable use allowance (defined). §24-5-13-11.5 If buyer accepts a replacement, manufacturer shall reimburse for transfer of registration and any sales tax. §24-5-13-12 Buyer also entitled to towing and storage fees. §24-5-13-13

9. *Other remedies*: There is no limit on other consumer remedies. §24-5-13-20

10. *Informal dispute mechanism*: For remedies under this section, a consumer must use an informal dispute settlement procedure provided the procedure complies with 16 C.F.R. 703 and the buyer has had notice. §24-5-13-19

11. *Resale of lemon*: Full disclosure required; must give 12 months or 12,000 mile warranty. §24-5-13.5-10

Iowa Code Ann. §322G.1

1. *Vehicles covered*: Vehicles purchased or leased in-state and primarily designed for transportation of persons or property. Excludes mopeds, motorcycles, motor homes, or vehicles over 10,000 lbs. §322G.2(13)

2. *Persons covered*: Purchasers, lessees, or any other person entitled to enforce the warranty. §322G.2(3)

3. *Period covered*: Whichever is first: term of express warranty, within two years from date of delivery, or within 24,000 miles of operation. §322G.2(8)

4. *Notice requirements*: (a) Manufacturer — written notice of warranty, §322G.3(1); (b) Consumer — report the nonconformity; notice to manufacturer via certified, registered, or overnight service mail. §322G.4(1)

5. *Repair requirements*: It is presumed that a reasonable number of attempts have been made if the same nonconformity is subjected to three or more repairs, or after one attempt to repair a nonconformity likely to cause death or serious bodily injury, or if the vehicle is out of service for a cumulative total of 30 or more calendar days. §322G.4(3)

6. *Affirmative defenses*: The nonconformity does not substantially impair the vehicle, or is the result of the consumer's abuse, neglect, or unauthorized modifications or alterations, or the claim was not raised in good faith; other defenses allowed by law. §322G.5

7. *Replace/refund*: The manufacturer shall replace with a comparable new vehicle, or accept a return and refund the purchase price less a reasonable offset for use. §322G.4(2)

8. *Other reimbursement*: Collateral charges; refunds to consumer and lienholder. §§322G.2(1), 322G.4(2). Attorney fees. §322G.8(3)

9. *Other remedies*: There is no limit on other consumer remedies. §322G.1

10. *Informal dispute mechanism*: For remedies under this section, a consumer must use an informal dispute settlement procedure established by the manufacturer provided the procedure complies with 16 C.F.R. 703. §322G.6

11. *Resale of lemon*: Full disclosure required. Title must indicate vehicle previously returned under lemon law. §322G.12

Kan. Code Ann. §50-645

1. *Vehicles covered*: New motor vehicles that are under 12,000 lbs. and sold or leased and registered in-state; vehicles not modified by second stage manufacturers. §50-645(a)(2)

2. *Persons covered*: Original purchasers or lessees. §50-645(a)(1)

3. *Period covered*: Whichever is first: term of all applicable warranties or one year from date of delivery. §50-645(b)

4. *Notice requirement*: (a) Manufacturer — none; (b) Consumer — report the nonconformity to the manufacturer, its agent or an authorized dealer. §50-645(b)

5. *Repair requirements*: It is presumed that a reasonable number of attempts have been made if the same nonconformity is subjected to four or more repairs, or the vehicle is out of service for a cumulative total of 30 or more calendar days, or there have been 10 or more attempts to repair any substantial nonconformities. §50-645(d)

6. *Affirmative defenses*: The nonconformity does not substantially impair the use and value of the vehicle, or is the result of the consumer's abuse, neglect, or unauthorized modifications or alterations. §50-645(c)

7. *Replace/refund*: The manufacturer shall replace with a comparable motor vehicle under warranty, or accept a return and refund the full purchase price less a reasonable use allowance (defined). §50-645(c)

8. *Other reimbursement*: Collateral charges; refund to the consumer and lienholder. §50-645(c)

9. *Other remedies*: There is no limit on other consumer remedies. §50-646

10. *Informal dispute mechanism*: For remedies under this section, a consumer must use an informal dispute settlement procedure established by the manufacturer provided the procedure complies with 16 C.F.R. 703. §50-645(e)

Ky. Rev. Stat. §367.840

1. *Vehicles covered*: Vehicles primarily for use on highways, required to be registered or licensed in-state prior to use. Excludes conversion vans, motor homes, motorcycles, mopeds, and farm machinery including tractors or vehicles with more than two axles. §367.841(3)

2. *Persons covered*: Residents who buy or contract to buy a new motor vehicle in-state. §367.841(1)

3. *Period covered:* Whichever is first: 12,000 miles or 12 months from date of delivery. §367.842(3)

4. *Notice requirements:* (a) Manufacturer — notify the buyer, at the time the dispute arises, of the arbitration system, §367.865(4); (b) Consumer — in writing to the manufacturer. §367.842(1)

5. *Repair requirements:* It is presumed that a reasonable number of attempts have been made if the same nonconformity is subjected to four or more repairs, or the vehicle is out of use/service for a cumulative total of 30 or more calendar days. §367.842(3)

6. *Affirmative defenses:* The nonconformity does not substantially impair the use, value or safety of the vehicle, or is the result of the consumer's abuse, neglect, or unauthorized modifications or alterations. §367.842(2)

7. *Replace/refund:* At the consumer's option, the manufacturer shall replace with a comparable motor vehicle, or accept a return and refund the full purchase price less a reasonable allowance for use. §367.842(2)

8. *Other reimbursement:* Full purchase price, including amount paid, finance charge, sales tax, license fee, registration fee, other government fee, and all collateral charges; refunds to the consumer and lienholder. §367.842(2). Attorney fees. §367.842(9)

9. *Other remedies:* There is no limit on other consumer remedies. §367.842(6)

10. *Informal dispute mechanism:* For remedies under this section, a consumer must use the manufacturer's informal dispute settlement procedure if the procedure complies with 16 C.F.R. 703. §367.842(4) The decision shall be binding on the manufacturer, but not binding on the buyer. §367.865(2)

La. Rev. Stat. Ann. §51-194 (West)

1. *Vehicles covered:* Passenger or passenger and commercial vehicles, as defined in La. Rev. Stat. Ann. §32:1252(1), sold in-state. Excludes vehicles over 10,000 lbs. vehicle weight and commercial vehicles. §1941(6)

2. *Persons covered:* Purchasers, transferees during express warranty period, any person entitled to enforce the warranty, and lessees, where vehicle normally used for personal, family, or household purposes. §1941(2)

3. *Period covered:* Whichever is first: the warranty term or one year from date of delivery. §1943(A)

4. *Notice requirement:* (a) Manufacturer — none; (b) Consumer — report the nonconformity to the manufacturer or any authorized dealer, and make the vehicle available for repair. §1942

5. *Repair requirements:* It is presumed that a reasonable number of attempts have been made if the same nonconformity is subjected to four or more repairs, or the vehicle is out of service for a cumulative total of 30 or more calendar days. §1943(A)

6. *Affirmative defenses:* None stated.

7. *Replace/refund:* At the manufacturer's option, the manufacturer shall replace with a comparable new vehicle, or accept a return and refund the full purchase price minus a reasonable use allowance (defined). §1944(A) For leases, see §1944(B).

8. *Other reimbursement:* Any amounts paid by the consumer at the time of sale and collateral costs. §1944(A)(2) Temporary replacement. §1948 Attorney fees. §1947 For leases, see §1944(B).

9. *Other remedies:* There is no limit on other consumer remedies. §1946

10. *Informal dispute mechanism:* For remedies under this section, a consumer must use an informal dispute settlement procedure established by the manufacturer provided the procedure complies with 16 C.F.R. 703. §1944(D)

11. *Resale of lemon:* Full disclosure required. Certificate of Title must include notice that car was returned because it did not conform to its warranty. §1945.1

Me. Rev. Stat. Ann. tit. 10, §1161

1. *Vehicles covered:* Vehicles sold or leased in-state to convey passengers or property. Excludes commercial vehicles over 8500 lbs. gross vehicle weight. §1161(3)

2. *Persons covered:* Purchasers or lessees, transferees during express warranty period, or any person entitled to enforce the warranty. Excludes government, business or commercial enterprises with three or more vehicles. §1161(1)

3. *Period covered:* Whichever is first: term of express warranty, within two years from date of delivery, or within 18,000 miles. §1163(1)

4. *Notice requirements:* Manufacturer — disclosure in the warranty or owner's manual that written notification of a nonconformity is required; include name and address, §1163(6); (b) Consumer — written notification to the manufacturer, its agent, or authorized dealer, if the manufacturer complied with above, §1163(1); final opportunity to cure within seven days of receipt. §1163(3-A)

5. *Repair requirements:* It is presumed that a reasonable number of attempts have been made if the same nonconformity is subjected to three or more repairs or is sent two times to the same agent, or if the vehicle is out of service for a cumulative total of 15 or more business days. §1163(3)

6. *Affirmative defenses:* (a) Lack of impairment — the nonconformity does not substantially impair the use, safety or value of the vehicle. §1164(1); (b) Abuse — the nonconformity is the result of the consumer's abuse, neglect, or unauthorized modifications or alterations. §1164(2)

7. *Replace/refund:* At the consumer's option, the manufacturer shall replace with a new, comparable vehicle, or refund the full purchase price less a reasonable use allowance (defined). §1163(2)

8. *Other reimbursement:* Refund of the purchase price, or if a lease, payments made to date, collateral charges (defined), and costs. §1163(2). Attorney fees. §1167

9. *Other remedies:* There is no limit on other consumer remedies. §1162(1). Violation considered unfair and deceptive trade practice under Title 5, §205-A. §1163

10. *Informal dispute mechanism:* For remedies under this section, a consumer must use an informal dispute settlement procedure established by the manufacturer provided the procedure complies with 16 C.F.R. 703, or state certified arbitration (defined in §1169). §1165

11. *Resale of lemon:* Full disclosure required. §1163(7)

Md. Code Ann. Com. Law §14-1501

1. *Vehicles covered:* Vehicles registered as passenger vehicles, trucks that are 3/4 ton or less, and multipurpose vehicles. Motorcycles are explicitly covered. Excludes motor homes. §14-1501(c)

2. *Persons covered:* Purchasers, transferees during express warranty period, or any person entitled to enforce the warranty. §14-1501(b)

3. *Period covered:* Whichever is first: 15,000 miles or 15 months from date of delivery. §14-501(g)(1)

4. *Notice requirements:* (a) Dealer — shall notify the manufacturer of the existence of a nonconformity, defect, or condition within seven days after the fourth attempt at the same repair, or when the vehicle is out of service for one or more nonconformities for a cumulative total of 20 days, §14-1502(f)(1)(i). Notice of procedure for reporting defect must be conspicuously disclosed to consumer in writing at time of sale or delivery of vehicle, §14-1502(b). (b) Consumer — written notice by certified mail to the manufacturer or factory branch; opportunity to cure. §14-1502(b)(1)

5. *Repair requirements:* It is presumed that a reasonable number of attempts have been made if the same nonconformity is subjected to four or more repairs, or the vehicle is out of service for a cumulative total of 30 or more calendar days, or a braking or steering system failure is subjected to at least one repair attempt which is not successful. §14-1502(d)

6. *Affirmative defense*: The nonconformity does not substantially impair the use and market value of the vehicle, or is the result of the consumer's abuse, neglect, or unauthorized modifications or alterations. §14-1502(c)(3)

7. *Replace/refund*: At the consumer's option, the manufacturer shall replace with a comparable vehicle acceptable to the consumer, or refund the full purchase price less a reasonable use allowance. §14-1502(c)(1), (2)

8. *Other reimbursement*: Refund of the purchase price including taxes and fees. §14-1502(c)(1)(ii)

9. *Other remedies*: There is no limit on other consumer remedies. §14-1502(h). Plaintiff may recover reasonable attorney fees. §14-1502(1) A violation is an unfair and deceptive trade practice. §14-1504

10. *Informal dispute mechanism*: For remedies under this section, a consumer may use an informal dispute settlement procedure established by the manufacturer provided the procedure complies with 16 C.F.R. 703. §14-1502(i)

11. *Resale of lemon*: Full disclosure required. §14-1502(g)

Mass. Gen. Ann. Laws ch. 90, §7N 1/2

1. *Vehicles covered*: Vehicle sold, leased, or replaced, including motorcycles. Excludes auto homes, off-road vehicles, and vehicles used for business purposes. §7N1/2(1)

2. *Persons covered*: Consumer buyers, lessees, transferees during express warranty period, or any person entitled to enforce the warranty. §7N1/2(1)

3. *Period covered*: Whichever comes first: one year or 15,000 miles from date of delivery. §7N1/2(1)

4. *Notice requirements*: (a) Manufacturer — notice of consumer's rights must be on the window sticker, and in the owner's manual, §7N 1/2(6A); (b) Consumer — notice to the manufacturer, its agent or an authorized dealer, §7N1/2(2); but the consumer does not need to provide notice prior to arbitration. §7N1/2(5)

5. *Repair requirements*: It is presumed that a reasonable number of attempts have been made if the same nonconformity is subjected to three or more repairs, or the vehicle is out of service for a cumulative total of 15 or more business days, plus a final cure attempt. §7N1/2(4)

6. *Affirmative defenses*: The nonconformity does not substantially impair the use, market value or safety of the vehicle, or is the result of the consumer's negligence, or is caused by an accident, vandalism, or unauthorized repair or modification. §7N1/2(3)

7. *Replace/refund*: At the consumer's option, the manufacturer shall replace the vehicle, or refund the full purchase price less a reasonable use allowance (defined). §7N1/2(3)

8. *Other reimbursement*: Incidental costs, fees, and charges; refund to the consumer and lien-holder. §7N1/2(3)

9. *Other remedies*: There is no limit on other consumer remedies. §7N1/2(5) The manufacturer's failure to comply with the statute is an unfair or deceptive act. §7N1/2(7)

10. *Informal dispute mechanism*: The manufacturer shall submit to state-certified arbitration if it is requested by the consumer. §7N1/2(6)

11. *Resale of lemon*: Full disclosure. §7N1/2(5)

Mich. Comp. Laws §257.1401

1. *Vehicles covered*: Passenger vehicles purchased in-state or by a resident of the state. Excludes motor homes, buses or trucks other than pick-ups or vans, and vehicles with less than four wheels. §§257.1401(d), (e)

2. *Persons covered*: Purchasers for personal, family or household use, or persons entitled to enforce the warranty, but not lessees. §257.1401(a)

3. *Period covered:* Whichever is first: term of express warranty or within one year from date of delivery. §257.1402

4. *Notice requirements:* (a) Secretary of State notice to accompany title to new car as specified in §257.1408; (b) Consumer — shall notify the manufacturer by return receipt service. §257.1403(3)

5. *Repair requirements:* It is presumed that a reasonable number of attempts have been made if the same nonconformity is subjected to four or more repairs, or the vehicle is out of service for a cumulative total of 30 or more days or parts of days. §257.1403(3)

6. *Affirmative defenses:* Defect is the result of unauthorized modification, abuse, neglect or damage due to an accident. §257.1406

7. *Replace/refund:* The manufacturer shall have the option to replace with a comparable vehicle in production, acceptable to the consumer, or accept the return and refund the full purchase price less a reasonable use allowance (defined). §257.1403(1)

8. *Other reimbursement:* Cost of options, modifications, manufacturer's charges, towing costs, and rental replacement; refund to the consumer and secured party. §257.1403(1)

9. *Other remedies:* No limit on other consumer remedies. §257.1404 Court costs, expenses, and reasonable attorney fees. § 257.1407 Rights and remedies may not be waived. §257.1407

10. *Informal dispute mechanism:* For remedies under this section, a consumer must use an informal dispute settlement procedure established by the manufacturer provided the procedure complies with 16 C.F.R. 703. §257.1405(5)

Minn. Stat. Ann. §325F.665

1. *Vehicles covered:* Passenger automobiles, including pickup trucks and vans, and motor or van portions of recreational equipment, that are sold or leased in-state. §325F.665(1)(e)

2. *Persons covered:* Purchasers or lessees for personal, family or household purposes for at least 40% of the time, transferees, or any other person entitled to enforce the warranty. §325F.665(1)(a)

3. *Period covered:* Whichever is first: term of express warranty or within two years from date of delivery. §325F.665(2)

4. *Notice requirements:* (a) Manufacturer — provide specific written statement to the consumer at the time of purchase, §325F.665(3)(g); (b) Consumer — written notice to the manufacturer, its agent or an authorized dealer; opportunity to cure. §325F.665(3)(e)

5. *Repair requirements:* It is presumed that a reasonable number of attempts have been made if the same nonconformity is subjected to four or more repairs, or the vehicle is out of service for a cumulative total of 30 or more business days; or a braking or steering system failure that is likely to cause death or serious injury is subjected to one or more repairs. §325F.665(3)(b),(c)

6. *Affirmative defenses:* The nonconformity does not substantially impair the use and market value of the vehicle, or is the result of consumer's abuse, neglect, or unauthorized modifications or alterations. §325F.665(3)(a)

7. *Replace/refund:* At the consumer's option, the manufacturer shall replace with a comparable vehicle, or refund the full purchase price less a reasonable use allowance (defined). §325F.665(3)(a) A lessee is not entitled to a replacement, but to a refund. §325F.665(4)

8. *Other reimbursement:* Costs of options or modifications, fees, costs of towing and rental expenses, and refunds to the consumer and lienholder. §325F.665(3)(a)

9. *Other remedies:* A consumer may bring a civil action to redress a violation of this section, and can recover costs and disbursements, including reasonable attorney fees. §325F.665(9) No limit on other consumer remedies. §325F.665(11)

10. *Informal dispute mechanism:* For remedies under this section, a consumer must use the manufacturer's informal dispute settlement procedure if it complies with 16 C.F.R. 703, unless the manufacturer allows the consumer to commence an action. §325F.665(6)(a)

11. *Resale of lemon:* Full disclosure required, 12 month/ 12,000 mile warranty. §325F.665(5)(a). No sale of a vehicle with serious defect pursuant to lemon law returned in this or any other state. §325F.665(5)(b)

12. *Dealer liability:* None except for written express warranties made by dealers apart from the manufacturer's warranties. §325F.665(13)

Miss. Code Ann. §63-17-151

1. *Vehicles covered:* Vehicles sold in-state, including lease-purchases and demonstrators, if warranty is issued. Excludes off-road vehicles, motorcycles, mopeds, and add-on parts of motor homes. §63-17-155(f)

2. *Persons covered:* Purchasers, transferees during express warranty period, or any person entitled to enforce the warranty, where vehicle primarily used for personal, family or household purposes. §63-17-155(c)

3. *Period covered:* Whichever is first: term of express warranty or within one year from date of delivery. §63-17-157

4. *Notice requirements:* (a) Manufacturer — provide list of service office addresses in the owner's manual; notice of informal dispute settlement procedure after consumer's notice, if not given prior to complaint; (b) Consumer — written notice of the nonconformity to the manufacturer who has ten days to cure after delivery of vehicle to designated dealer. §63-17-159(5)

5. *Repair requirements:* It is presumed that a reasonable number of attempts have been made if the substantively same nonconformity is subjected to three or more repairs, or the vehicle is out of service for a cumulative total of 15 or more working days. §63-17-159(3)

6. *Affirmative defenses:* The nonconformity does not substantially impair the use, market value or safety of the vehicle, or is the result of the consumer's abuse, neglect, or unauthorized modifications or alterations; a claim is not filed in good faith; any other defenses allowed by law. §63-17-159(2)

7. *Replace/refund:* At the consumer's option, the manufacturer shall replace with a comparable vehicle or refund the full purchase price less a reasonable use allowance, §63-17-159(1); "comparable" is defined as identical or reasonably equivalent. §63-17-155(b)

8. *Other reimbursement:* Collateral charges (defined at §63-17-155). §63-17-159(1)

9. *Other remedies:* There is no limit on other consumer remedies. §63-17-153 Costs, expenses, and attorney fees. §63-17-159(7)

10. *Informal dispute mechanism:* For remedies under this section, a consumer must use an informal dispute settlement procedure established by the manufacturer provided the procedure complies with 16 C.F.R. 703. §63-17-163

Mo. Ann. Stat. §407.560 (Vernon)

1. *Vehicles covered:* Vehicles, including lease-purchases and demonstrators, transferred for the first time from the manufacturer/dealer which have not been registered or titled. Excludes commercial and off-road vehicles, mopeds, motorcycles, and non-motor parts of recreational vehicles. §407.560(6)

2. *Persons covered:* Purchasers, transferees during express warranty period, or any person entitled to enforce the warranty, where vehicle primarily used for personal, family, or household purposes. §407.560(3)

3. *Period covered:* Whichever is first: term of express warranty or within one year from date of delivery. §407.565

4. *Notice requirements:* (a) Manufacturer — provide the consumer with complaint remedies; (b) Consumer — written notification to the manufacturer so it may cure within ten days after delivery of vehicle to authorized repair facility. §407.573(2)

5. *Repair requirements:* It is presumed that a reasonable number of attempts have been made if the same nonconformity is subjected to four or more repairs, or the vehicle is out of service for a cumulative total of 30 or more working days. §407.571

6. *Affirmative defenses:* The nonconformity does not substantially impair the use, market value or safety of the vehicle; or is the result of the consumer's abuse, neglect, or unauthorized modifications or alterations; a claim is not filed in good faith; any other defenses allowed by law. §407.569

7. *Replace/refund:* At the manufacturer's option, the manufacturer shall replace with a new comparable vehicle, acceptable to the consumer, or refund the full purchase price less a reasonable use allowance. §407.567

8. *Other reimbursement:* Collateral charges (defined in §407.560(1)). §407.567(1) Refunds to the consumer and lienholder. §407.567(2)

9. *Other remedies:* There is no limit on other consumer remedies. §407.579(1) Costs, expenses, attorney fees. §407.577(1)

10. *Informal dispute mechanism:* For remedies under this section, a consumer must use an informal dispute settlement procedure established by the manufacturer provided the procedure complies with 16 C.F.R. 703. §407.575

Mont. Code Ann. §61-4-501

1. *Vehicles covered:* Vehicles sold in-state to transport persons and property, including nonresidential portions of motor homes. Excludes trucks over 10,000 lbs. and motorcycles. §61-4-501(5)

2. *Persons covered:* Purchasers, transferees during express warranty period, or any person entitled to enforce the warranty. §61-4-501(2)

3. *Period covered:* Whichever is first: two years after date of delivery or 18,000 miles. §61-4-501(7)

4. *Notice requirements:* (a) Manufacturers — clear and conspicuous written notification of nonconformity is required in the warranty or owner's manual, §61-4-502(3); include name and address; (b) Consumer — written notification to the manufacturer. §61-4-502(1)

5. *Repair requirements:* It is presumed that a reasonable number of attempts have been made if the same nonconformity is subjected to four or more repairs, or the vehicle is out of service for a cumulative total of 30 or more business days. §61-4-504

6. *Affirmative defenses:* The nonconformity does not substantially impair the use, market value or safety of the vehicle, or is the result of the consumer's abuse, neglect, or unauthorized modifications or alterations. §61-4-506(3)

7. *Replace/refund:* Manufacturers shall replace with new motor vehicle of same model, style, and value, if available, or of comparable market value, §61-4-503(1); or the manufacturer shall accept return of a motor vehicle from the consumer and give a full refund of the purchase price less a reasonable use allowance (defined §61-4-501(6)). §61-4-503

8. *Other reimbursement:* Collateral and incidental charges; refunds to the consumer and lienholder. §61-4-503(2)

9. *Other remedies:* There is no limit on other consumer remedies. §61-4-506(1)

10. *Informal dispute mechanism:* For remedies under this section, a consumer must use an informal dispute settlement procedure established by the manufacturer provided the procedure complies with 16 C.F.R. 703. §61-4-507

11. *Resale of lemon:* Full disclosure required. §61-4-525

Neb. Rev. Stat. §60-2701

1. *Vehicles covered:* Vehicles, as defined in Neb. Rev. Stat. 60-1401.02(7), sold in-state. Excludes self-propelled mobile homes. §60-2701(2)

2. *Persons covered:* Purchasers, transferees during express warranty period, or any person entitled to enforce the warranty. §60-2701(1)

3. *Period covered:* Whichever is first: term of express warranty or within one year from date of delivery. §60-2702

4. *Notice requirement:* (a) Manufacturers — none; (b) Consumer — certified mail to the manufacturer from or on behalf of the consumer; opportunity to cure. §60-2704

5. *Repair requirements:* It is presumed that a reasonable number of attempts have been made if the same nonconformity is subjected to four or more repairs, or the vehicle is out of service for a cumulative total of 40 or more days. §60-2704

6. *Affirmative defenses:* The nonconformity does not substantially impair the use and market value of the vehicle, or is the result of the consumer's abuse, neglect, or unauthorized modifications or alterations. §60-2703

7. *Replace/refund:* The manufacturer shall replace with a comparable vehicle, or refund the full purchase price less a reasonable use allowance. §60-2703

8. *Other reimbursement:* Taxes, fees, and charges; refunds to the consumer and lienholder. §60-2703 Attorney fees. §60-2707

9. *Other remedies:* There is no limit on other consumer remedies. §60-2708

10. *Informal dispute mechanism:* For remedies under this section, a consumer must use an informal dispute settlement procedure established by the manufacturer provided the procedure complies with 16 C.F.R. 703. §60-2705

Nev. Rev. Stat. §597.600

1. *Vehicles covered:* Vehicles as defined in Nev. Rev. Stat. §482.075. Excludes motor homes and off-road vehicles. §597.600(2)

2. *Persons covered:* Purchasers, transferees during express warranty period, or any person entitled to enforce the warranty, where vehicle normally used for personal, family, or household purposes. §597.600(1)

3. *Period covered:* Whichever is first: term of express warranty or within one year from date of delivery. §597.610

4. *Notice requirement:* a) Manufacturer — none; (b) Consumer — in writing to the manufacturer. §597.610 Must notify manufacturer of any address change. §597.675

5. *Repair requirements:* It is presumed that a reasonable number of attempts have been made if the same nonconformity is subjected to four or more repairs, or the vehicle is out of service for a cumulative total of 30 or more calendar days. §597.630(2)

6. *Affirmative defenses:* The nonconformity does not substantially impair the use and value of the vehicle, or is the result of the consumer's abuse, neglect, or unauthorized modifications or alterations. §597.630(1)

7. *Replace/refund:* The manufacturer shall replace with a comparable motor vehicle of the same model with the same features; if unavailable, it shall replace with a comparable or substantially similar motor vehicle, or refund the full purchase price less a reasonable use allowance. §597.603(1)(a), (b)

8. *Other reimbursement:* Taxes, fees, and charges; refund to the consumer and lienholder. §597.630(1)(b)

9. *Other remedies:* There is no limit on other consumer remedies. §597.670

10. *Informal dispute mechanism:* For remedies under this section, a consumer must use an informal dispute settlement procedure established by the manufacturer provided the procedure complies with 16 C.F.R. 703. §597.620

N.H. Rev. Stat. Ann. §357-D

1. *Vehicles covered:* Vehicles as defined in N.H. Rev. Stat. Ann. §259.60, four-wheel vehicles under 9000 lbs., and motorcycles. Excludes tractors, OHRVs, and mopeds. §357-D:2(X)

2. *Persons covered:* Purchasers, lessees, transferees during express warranty period, or any person entitled to enforce the warranty. §357-D:2(III)

3. *Period covered:* Period of express warranty. §357-D:3(III)

4. *Notice requirements:* (a) Manufacturer — written notice of consumer's rights at time of delivery of vehicle along with form to report defects. §357-D:9 If vehicle is repaired, manufacturer must provide a written repair order and summary of all work performed. §357-D:3; (b) Consumer — report the nonconformity to the manufacturer, agent, or authorized dealer in writing on specific forms provided by the manufacturer. §§357-D:3(III); 357-D:4

5. *Repair requirements:* It is presumed that a reasonable number of attempts have been made if the same nonconformity is subjected to three or more repairs, or the vehicle is out of service for a cumulative total of 30 or more business days. §357-D:3(VII)

6. *Affirmative defenses:* The nonconformity does not substantially impair the use, market value or safety of the vehicle, or is the result of the consumer's abuse, neglect, or unauthorized modifications or alterations. §357-D:3(VI)

7. *Replace/refund:* At the consumer's option, the manufacturer shall replace with a new vehicle, or refund the full purchase price less a reasonable use allowance. §357-D:3(V)

8. *Other reimbursement:* Collateral charges (listed in §357-D:3(V)). Refunds to the consumer and lienholder. §357-D:3(V)

9. *Other remedies:* Legal fees and costs. §357-D:10 Violation is an unfair and deceptive act. §357-D:7

10. *Informal dispute mechanism:* Consumer must elect whether to use the dispute settlement mechanism or arbitration provisions established by the manufacturer. §357-D:4(I)

11. *Dealer liability:* None, except for written express warranties made by the dealer apart from the manufacturer's warranties. §357-D:8

12. *Sale of Defective Motor Vehicles:* Manufacturer or agent may not resell vehicle determined as having a defect that is life-threatening, that creates a risk of fire or explosion, or that impedes a consumer's ability to control or operate a motor vehicle for ordinary use or the reasonable or intended purposes. §357-D:12

N.J. Stat. Ann. §56:12-30

1. *Vehicles covered:* Passenger vehicles or motorcycles as defined in N.J. Stat. Ann. 39:1-1, purchased, leased or registered in-state. Excludes living facilities of motor homes. §56:12-30

2. *Persons covered:* Purchasers, lessees, transferees during express warranty period, or any person entitled to enforce the warranty. §56:12-30

3. *Period covered:* Whichever is first: 18,000 miles or within two years from date of delivery. §56:12-31 Consumer must pay for repairs made after 12,000 miles or one year after delivery unless covered by a manufacturer's warranty. §56:12-31

4. *Notice requirement:* (a) Manufacturer — specific written notice upon sale or lease and notice of applicability of lemon law statement of repair each time vehicle serviced within lemon law period. §56:12-34 (b) Consumer — written notice by certified mail, return receipt, to the manufacturer by or on behalf of the consumer; opportunity to cure within ten days of receipt of notice. §56:12-33(b)

5. *Repair requirements*: It is presumed that a reasonable number of attempts have been made if the same nonconformity is subjected to three or more repairs, or the vehicle is out of service for a cumulative total of 20 or more business days within the shorter of two years or 18,000 miles. §56:12-33(a)

6. *Affirmative defenses*: The nonconformity does not substantially impair the use, value or safety of the vehicle, or is the result of abuse, neglect, or unauthorized modifications or alterations. §56:12-40

7. *Replace/refund*: The manufacturer shall replace with a new comparable vehicle, or refund the full purchase price less a reasonable use allowance. Consumer may reject replacement §56:12-32(a)

8. *Other reimbursement*: Taxes, fees, and charges; refund to the consumer and lienholder. §56:12-32(a)

9. *Other remedies*: There is no limit on other consumer remedies. §56:12-39. Attorney fees, fees for expert witnesses and court costs recoverable. §56-12-42

10. *Informal dispute mechanism*: There is no requirement to arbitrate, but there is a right to an administrative hearing, §56:12-37, or an informal dispute settlement procedure. §56:12-36

11. *Resale of lemon*: Full disclosure required. §56:12-35

12. *Dealer liability*: None, except for express warranties made by the dealer apart from the manufacturer. §56:12-46

N.M. Stat. Ann. §57-16A-1

1. *Vehicles covered*: Passenger vehicles sold and registered in-state, whose gross vehicle weight is less than 10,000 lbs., including automobiles, pick-up trucks, motorcycles and vans. §57-16A-2(F)

2. *Persons covered*: Purchasers, transferees during express warranty period, or any person entitled to enforce the warranty, where vehicle normally used for personal, family, or household purposes. §57-16A-2(C)

3. *Period covered*: Whichever is first: term of express warranty or within one year from date of delivery. §57-16A-3(A)

4. *Notice requirements*: (a) Manufacturer — written notice and instruction, in the warranty or separate notice, of the consumer's obligation to file a written notice to the manufacturer; (b) Consumer — direct written notice from or on behalf of the consumer; opportunity to cure. §57-16A-3(C)(2)

5. *Repair requirements*: It is presumed that a reasonable number of attempts have been made if the same nonconformity is subjected to four or more repairs, or the vehicle is out of service for a cumulative total of 30 or more business days. §57-16A-3(C)

6. *Affirmative defenses*: The nonconformity does not substantially impair the use and market value of the vehicle, or is the result of the consumer's abuse, neglect, or unauthorized modifications or alterations; the claim is not filed in good faith; any other defenses allowed by law. §57-16A-4

7. *Replace/refund*: Less a reasonable use allowance (defined), the manufacturer shall replace with a comparable vehicle, or refund the full purchase price. §57-16A-3(B)

8. *Other reimbursement*: Collateral charges (defined in 57-16A-2(A)). Refund to the consumer and lienholder. §57-16A-3(B). Attorney fees. §57-16A-9

9. *Other remedies*: A consumer who seeks enforcement under this act is foreclosed from pursuing any UCC remedy. §57-16A-5

10. *Informal dispute mechanism*: For remedies under this section, a consumer must use an informal dispute settlement procedure established by the manufacturer provided the procedure complies with 16 C.F.R. 703. §57-16A-6

11. *Resale of lemon*: Full disclosure required. §57-16A-7

N.Y. Gen. Bus. Law §198-a; N.Y. Veh. & Traf. Law §417-a, 417-b

1. *Vehicles covered:* Vehicles sold or registered, and leases. Excludes motorcycles, living portions of motor homes, and off-road vehicles. §198-a(a)(2)

2. *Persons covered:* Purchasers or lessees, transferees during express warranty period, or any person entitled to enforce the warranty, where vehicle primarily used for personal, family, or household purposes. §198-a(a)(1), (5)

3. *Period covered:* Whichever is first: 18,000 miles or two years from date of delivery. §198-a(b)(1)

4. *Notice requirements:* (a) Manufacturer — specific notice requirements, §198-a(m)(2), (o); (b) Consumer — report the nonconformity to the manufacturer, its agent or dealer, §198-a(b); notice to the manufacturer must include a statement indicating whether any repairs have been undertaken. §198-a(b)(1)

5. *Repair requirements:* It is presumed that a reasonable number of attempts have been made if the same nonconformity is subjected to four or more repairs, or the vehicle is out of service for a cumulative total of 30 or more calendar days. §198-a(d)

6. *Affirmative defenses:* The nonconformity does not substantially impair the value of the vehicle, or is the result of the consumer's abuse, neglect, or unauthorized modifications or alterations. §198-a(c)(3)

7. *Replace/refund:* At the consumer's option, the manufacturer shall replace with a comparable vehicle, or refund the full purchase price less a reasonable use allowance (defined). §198-a(c)(1)

8. *Other reimbursement:* All fees and charges; sales tax refunds by a government agency. §198-a(c)(1)

9. *Other remedies:* There is no limit on other consumer remedies. §198-a(f) Refunds to the consumer and lienholder. §198-a(c)(2). Attorney fees. §198-a(k), (*l*)

10. *Informal dispute mechanism:* For remedies under this section, a consumer may use an informal dispute settlement procedure established by manufacturer provided the procedure complies with statutory requirements. §198-a(g) An alternative procedure is the N.Y. Lemon Law Arbitration Program. Attorney fees are available to prevailing consumers. Tit. 13 N.Y.C.R.R. Chap. VIII Part 300

11. *Resale of lemon:* Full disclosure required. N.Y. Veh. & Traf. Law §417-a(2)

N.C. Gen. Stat. §20-351

1. *Vehicles covered:* Vehicles, as defined in N.C. Gen. Stat. § 20-4.01, sold or leased in-state. Excludes house trailers and vehicles over 10,000 lbs. gross vehicle weight. §20-351.1(3)

2. *Persons covered:* Purchaser, transferees during express warranty period, or any person entitled to enforce the warranty. §20-351.1(1)

3. *Period covered:* Consumer entitled to repairs for defects reported within the first twelve months or 12,000 miles. Consumer may demand a replacement or refund of purchase price for defects occurring during the first twelve months or 12,000 miles. §20-351.2

4. *Notice requirements:* (a) Manufacturer — clear, conspicuous notice of arbitration process in the warranty, §20-351.7; (b) Consumer — report the nonconformity to the manufacturer, its agent or an authorized dealer, §20-351.2; if notice is to manufacturer, it has 15 calendar days to correct nonconformity, §20-351.5(a)(2); written notice 10 days prior to filing a civil suit. §20-351.7

5. *Repair requirements:* It is presumed that a reasonable number of attempts have been made if the same nonconformity is subjected to four or more repairs, or the vehicle is out of service for a cumulative total of 20 or more business days. §20-351.5(a)

6. *Affirmative defenses:* The nonconformity is the result of abuse, neglect, odometer tampering by the consumer, or unauthorized modifications or alterations. §20-351.4

7. *Replace/refund:* At the consumer's option, the manufacturer shall replace with a new comparable vehicle, or refund the full purchase price less a reasonable use allowance. §20-351.3(a)

8. *Other reimbursement:* Collateral charges (defined), finance charges, and incidental and consequential damages. §20-351.3(a) Refunds to the consumer and lienholder. §20-351.3(c)

9. *Other remedies:* There is no limit on other consumer remedies. §20-351.10 Injunctive relief, monetary damages (trebled), and attorney fees. §20-351.8

10. *Informal dispute mechanism:* For remedies under this section, a consumer must use an informal dispute settlement procedure established by the manufacturer provided the procedure complies with 15 U.S.C. §2301. §20-351.7

11. *Resale of lemon:* Full disclosure required. §20-351.3(d)

12. *Dealer liability:* None. §20-351.9

N.D. Cent. Code §51-07-16

1. *Vehicles covered:* Passenger motor vehicle as defined in §39-01-01, or trucks under 10,000 lbs. gross vehicle weight, sold or leased in-state. Excludes house cars. §51-07-16(2)

2. *Persons covered:* Purchasers, transferees and lessees during express warranty period, or any person entitled to enforce the warranty. §51-07-16(1)

3. *Period covered:* Whichever is first: term of express warranty or within one year from date of delivery. §51-07-17

4. *Notice requirement:* (a) Manufacturer — none; (b) Consumer — report of the nonconformity to the manufacturer from or on behalf of the consumer; opportunity to cure. §51-07-19(3)

5. *Repair requirements:* It is presumed that a reasonable number of attempts have been made if the same nonconformity is subjected to three or more repairs, or the vehicle is out of service for a cumulative total of 30 or more business days during one year. §51-07-19

6. *Affirmative defenses:* The nonconformity does not substantially impair the use and market value of the vehicle, or is the result of the consumer's abuse, neglect, or unauthorized modifications or alterations. §51-07-18(2)

7. *Replace/refund:* At the consumer's option, the manufacturer shall replace with a comparable vehicle, or refund the full purchase price less a reasonable use allowance. §51-07-18(1)

8. *Other reimbursement:* Collateral charges; refunds to the consumer and lienholder. §51-07-18(1)

9. *Other remedies:* Exclusive remedy; if proved under this section, a consumer may not pursue other remedies. §51-07-20

10. *Informal dispute mechanism:* For remedies under this section, a consumer must use the manufacturer's informal dispute settlement procedure if it complies with 16 C.F.R. 703. §51-07-18(3)

11. *Resale of lemon:* Must provide full disclosure and a twelve month or 12,000 mile warranty for vehicles sold in-state may not ship to another state unless full disclosure is made. §51-07-22

Ohio Rev. Code Ann. §1345.71

1. *Vehicles covered:* Passenger cars, noncommercial vehicles, and parts of motor homes not used for living. Excludes manufactured home or recreational vehicles (vehicles defined in Ohio Rev. Code §4501.01). §1345.71(D)

2. *Persons covered:* Purchasers and transferees, who lease automobiles during express warranty period, or any person entitled to enforce the warranty. §1345.71(A)

3. *Period covered:* Whichever is first: one year from the date of delivery or 18,000 miles. §1345.72(A)

4. *Notice requirements:* (a) Manufacturer — provide specific, separate notice at the time of purchase of right to replacement or compensation for nonconforming vehicle, §1345.74; (b) Consumer — notify the manufacturer, its agent or an authorized dealer. §1345.72(A)

5. *Repair requirements:* It is presumed that a reasonable number of attempts have been made if the substantially same nonconformity is subjected to three or more repairs, the vehicle is out of service for a cumulative total of 30 or more calendar days; there have been eight or more attempts to repair any nonconformity; or there has been at least one attempt to repair a condition likely to cause death or serious bodily injury if the vehicle is driven. §1345.73

6. *Affirmative defenses:* The nonconformity is the result of abuse, neglect, or unauthorized modification or alteration. §1345.75(D)

7. *Replace/refund:* At the consumer's option, the manufacturer shall replace with a new vehicle, or refund the full purchase price (defined). §1345.72(B)

8. *Other reimbursement:* Collateral charges (defined), finance charges, and incidental charges (defined). §1345.72(B) Refund to the consumer and lienholder. §1345.72(D)

9. *Other remedies:* There is no limit on other consumer remedies. §1345.75(B). A violation is an unfair and deceptive act or practice. 1345.77(C). If a civil suit is filed, attorney fees. §1345.75

10. *Informal dispute mechanism:* For remedies under this section, a consumer must use an informal dispute settlement procedure established by the attorney general. §1345.77

11. *Resale of lemon:* Full disclosure required. §1345.76(A) Twelve month or 12,000 mile warranty required on resale. §1345.76(A)(1). If the vehicle is returned under any state law for a nonconformity likely to cause death or serious bodily injury, it may not be sold in-state. §1345.76(B)

Okla. Stat. Ann. tit. 15, §901

1. *Vehicles covered:* Vehicles registered under tit. 47 §22. Excludes vehicles over 10,000 lbs. and living facilities of motor homes. §901(A)(2)

2. *Persons covered:* Purchasers, transferees during express warranty period, or any person entitled to enforce the warranty. §901(A)(1)

3. *Period covered:* Whichever is first: term of express warranty or within one year from date of delivery. §901(B)

4. *Notice requirement:* (a) Manufacturer — none; (b) Consumer — direct written notification from or on behalf of the consumer; opportunity to cure. §901(C)

5. *Repair requirement:* It is presumed that a reasonable number of attempts have been made if the same nonconformity is subjected to four or more repairs, or the vehicle is out of service for a cumulative total of 45 or more calendar days. §901(D)

6. *Affirmative defenses:* The nonconformity does not substantially impair the use and value of the vehicle, or is the result of the consumer's abuse, neglect, or unauthorized modifications or alterations. §901(C)(1), (2)

7. *Replace/refund:* The manufacturer shall replace with a new vehicle, or refund the full purchase price less a reasonable use allowance. §901(C)

8. *Other reimbursement:* Taxes and fees, excluding interest; refunds to the consumer and lienholder. §901(C)

9. *Other remedies:* There is no limit on other consumer remedies. §901(E)

10. *Informal dispute mechanism:* For remedies under this section, a consumer must use an informal dispute settlement procedure established by the manufacturer provided the procedure complies with 16 C.F.R. 703. §901(F)

Or. Rev. Stat. §646.315

1. *Vehicles covered:* Passenger motor vehicles, as defined in Or. Rev. Stat. §801.360, sold in-state, including leased vehicles and motorcycles. §646.315(2)

2. *Persons covered:* Purchasers or lessees, transferees during express warranty period, or any person entitled to enforce the warranty, where vehicles normally used for personal, family, or household purposes. §646.315(1)

3. *Period covered:* Whichever is earlier: one year from date of delivery or within 12,000 miles. §646.325(2)

4. *Notice requirements:* (a) Manufacturer — notify the consumer of the informal settlement procedure, §646.355; (b) Consumer — written notice to the manufacturer from or on behalf of the consumer; opportunity to cure. §646.325(3)

5. *Repair requirements:* It is presumed that a reasonable number of attempts have been made if the same nonconformity is subjected to four or more repairs, or the vehicle is out of service for a cumulative total of 30 or more business days. §646.345(1)

6. *Affirmative defenses:* The nonconformity does not substantially impair the use, market value or safety of the vehicle, or is the result of the consumer's abuse, neglect, or unauthorized modifications or alterations. §646.335(3)

7. *Replace/refund:* At the consumer's option, the manufacturer shall replace with a new motor vehicle, or refund the full purchase price less a reasonable use allowance. §646.335(1), (2)

8. *Other reimbursement:* Taxes, fees, and collateral charges, excluding interest; refunds to the consumer and lienholder. §646.335(1), (2)

9. *Other remedies:* There is no limit on other consumer remedies; treble damages, attorney fees, and costs. §§646.359, 646.375

10. *Informal dispute mechanism:* For remedies under this section, a consumer must use an informal dispute settlement procedure established by the manufacturer provided the procedure complies with 16 C.F.R. 703. §646.355

11. *Dealer liability:* None. §646.361

73 Pa. Stat. Ann. tit. 73, §1951 (Purdon)

1. *Vehicles covered:* New and unused vehicles purchased and registered in-state, including demonstrator or dealer cars which convey fewer than 15 persons. Excludes motorcycles, motor homes, off-road and commercial vehicles. §1952

2. *Persons covered:* Purchasers, persons, successors or assigns, who purchased or received by transfer a new motor vehicle, for primarily personal, family, or household use. §1952

3. *Period covered:* Whichever is first: one year from date of delivery or 12,000 miles. §1954(a)

4. *Notice requirements:* (a) Manufacturer — provide written statement of attorney general's bulletin explaining rights under this law, §1953; (b) Consumer — if delivery for repair is impossible, written notice to the manufacturer. §1954(b)

5. *Repair requirements:* It is presumed that a reasonable number of attempts have been made if the same nonconformity is subjected to three or more repairs, or the vehicle is out of service for a cumulative total of 30 or more calendar days. §1956

6. *Affirmative defenses:* The nonconformity does not substantially impair the use, value or safety of the vehicle, or is the result of the consumer's abuse, neglect, or unauthorized modifications or alterations. §1955

7. *Replace/refund:* At the purchaser's option, the manufacturer shall replace with a comparable vehicle of equal value, or refund the full purchase price less a reasonable use allowance (defined). §1955

8. *Other reimbursement:* Collateral charges and refunds to the consumer and lienholder. §1955

9. *Other remedies:* There is no limit on consumer remedies. §1962 Civil action for manufacturer's noncompliance, attorney fees and all court costs. §1958. Noncompliance is deemed a violation of the Unfair Trade Practices and Consumer Protection Act (P.L. 1224, No. 387). §1961

10. *Informal dispute mechanism:* For remedies under this section, a consumer must use an informal dispute settlement procedure if such procedure provided by manufacturer complies with 16 C.F.R. 703. §1959

11. *Resale of lemon:* Full disclosure required. §1960(a) If the vehicle is likely to cause death or serious bodily injury if driven, then it may not be resold. §1960(b). Manufacturer must provide an express warranty lasting for the first 12,000 miles, or the first 12 months after resale. §1960(a)

R.I. Gen. Laws §31-5.2-1

1. *Vehicles covered:* Automobiles, motorcycles, vans or trucks, under 10,000 lbs., sold or replaced. Excludes motorized campers. §31-5.2-1(8)

2. *Persons covered:* Purchasers, transferees during express warranty period, or any person entitled to enforce the warranty. §31-5.2-1(1)

3. *Period covered:* Whichever comes first: one year or 15,000 miles from date of delivery. §31-5.2-1(10)

4. *Notice requirements:* (a) Manufacturer — notice of arbitration proceeding to the buyer at the time of delivery, §31-5.2-7; (b) Consumer — report the nonconformity to the manufacturer, its agent or dealer §31-5.2-2; opportunity to cure of seven days. §31-5.2-5

5. *Repair requirements:* It is presumed that a reasonable number of attempts have been made if the same nonconformity is subjected to four or more repairs, or the vehicle is out of service for a cumulative total of 30 or more calendar days plus one additional attempt to cure. §31-5.2-5

6. *Affirmative defenses:* The nonconformity does not substantially impair the use, market value or safety of the vehicle, or is the result of the consumer's abuse, neglect, or substantial unauthorized modifications or alterations. §31-5.2-4

7. *Replace/refund:* At the consumer's option, the manufacturer shall replace with a new comparable vehicle or refund the full purchase price less a reasonable use allowance (defined). §31-5.2-3

8. *Other reimbursement:* Incidental costs, including sales tax, registration fees, finance charges, and towing and rental costs; refunds to the consumer and lienholder. §31-5.2-3

9. *Other remedies:* There is no limit on other consumer remedies. §31-5.2-6. Right to bring civil action. §31-5.2-10. Attorney fees. §31-5.2-11. The manufacturer's failure to comply with the statute is a deceptive trade practice. §31-5.2-13

10. *Informal dispute mechanism:* For remedies under this section, a consumer must use an informal dispute settlement procedure provided the procedure complies with 16 C.F.R. 703 or approved by FTC or by state. §31-5.2-7

11. *Resale of lemon:* Full disclosure required. §31-5.2-9

S.C. Code Ann. §56-28-10 (Law. Co-op.)

1. *Vehicles covered:* Passenger motor vehicles as classified by §56-3-630, including demonstrators. Excludes living portion of recreational vehicle and off-road vehicles sold and registered in state. §56-28-10(4), (5)

2. *Persons covered:* Purchasers or lessors, other than for resale, of vehicles normally used for personal, family or household purposes, and any other person entitled to enforce the warranty. §56-28-10(1)

3. *Period covered:* Whichever is first: one year or 12,000 miles. §56-28-30

4. *Notice requirements:* (a) Manufacturer — information about consumer complaint remedies and dispute resolution procedure, §56-28-50; Consumer — written notice to the manufacturer or agent; manufacturer has ten days to notify consumer of accessible repair facility and has ten days after delivery to cure. §56-28-50(B)

5. *Repair requirements:* It is presumed that there have been a reasonable number of attempts if there have been three or more repair attempts, or the vehicle is out of service for a cumulative total of 30 calendar days. §56-28-50(A)

6. *Affirmative defenses:* Three year limitations period. §56-28-70 The nonconformity does not substantially impair the use, value, or safety of vehicle, or it is result of abuse, neglect, modification, or alteration. §56-28-40.

7. *Replace/refund:* At the manufacturer's option, replacement or refund of the purchase price, including finance charges, sales taxes, license fees, and registration fees, less a use allowance; refunds to the consumer and lienholder. §56-28-40

8. *Other reimbursement:* Costs and expenses, including attorney fees, and all other costs attributed to the nonconformity. §56-28-50(D)

9. *Other remedies:* None specified.

10. *Informal dispute mechanism:* A consumer must first utilize an alternative dispute resolution established by the manufacturer provided that procedure complies with 16 C.F.R. 703. §56-28-60

11. *Resale of lemon:* May not be resold, with certain exceptions. §56-28-100. Full disclosure to the consumer is required. §56-28-110

12. *Dealer liability:* None, except for express warranties made by the dealer apart from those of the manufacturer. §56-28-80

S.D. Codified Laws Ann. §32-6D-1

1. *Vehicles covered:* Self-propelled vehicle under 10,000 lbs. intended primarily for use on public highways. Excludes motor homes. §32-6D-1(5)

2. *Persons covered:* Purchasers of new or untitled vehicles used in substantial part for personal, family or household purposes, or any person entitled to enforce the warranty. §32-6D-1(1)

3. *Period covered:* Two years from date of delivery or within one year, or first 12,000 miles, whichever occurs first. §§32-6D-1, 2. However, notice of the problem must have been given to the manufacturer within one year, or first 24,000 miles.

4. *Notice requirement:* (a) Manufacturer — none; (b) Consumer — must send a written statement to the manufacturer one year after delivery or within the first 12,000 miles. The notice must describe the vehicle. The nonconforming condition, all previous repair attempts and the identities of those who made repair attempts. §§32-6D-1(3), (8); 32-6D-2

5. *Repair requirements:* It is presumed that a reasonable number of attempts have been made if the same nonconformity has been subjected to four or more repair attempts, or the vehicle has been out of service for a cumulative total of 30 days during the first two years after delivery or first 24,000 miles. At least one such repair attempt, however, must have occurred during the first year or first 12,000 miles. §32-6D-5

6. *Affirmative defenses:* The nonconformity does not significantly impair the use, market value or safety of the vehicle, or is a result of neglect, abuse, or unauthorized modification or alteration. §32-6D-7

7. *Replace/refund:* At the option of the consumer, replace the vehicle with a comparable new vehicle, or refund the full contract price less a reasonable allowance for use (defined by statute). §§ 32-6D-3; 32-6D-4

8. *Other reimbursement:* Charges for undercoating, dealer preparation, and transportation, plus nonrefundable portions of extended warranties and service contracts, all collateral charges including excise tax, and license and registration fees, all finance charges incurred after consumer notice to the manufacturer, all incidental charges including reasonable cost of alternative transportation, attorney fees if the manufacturer has breached any of its obligations. §§32-6D-3; 32-6D-8

9. *Other remedies:* None specified.

10. *Informal dispute mechanism:* Consumer must use an informal dispute settlement procedure if such procedure established by the manufacturer complies with federal regulations before bringing civil suit. §32-6D-6

11. *Resale of lemon:* Full disclosure required; the manufacturer must return the vehicle title to the state motor vehicle department of revenue to be branded with a statutory notice. §32-6D-9

Tenn. Code Ann. §55-24-201

1. *Vehicles covered:* Vehicles, as defined in Tenn. Code Ann. §55-1-103, sold and registered. Excludes motorized bicycles, motor homes, lawn mowers or garden tractors, recreational vehicles, off-road vehicles and vehicles over 10,000 lbs. §55-24-201(3)

2. *Persons covered:* Purchasers, lessees, transferees during express warranty period, or any person entitled to enforce the warranty. Excludes government or business entity with three or more vehicles. §55-24-201(1)

3. *Period covered:* Whichever is first: term of express warranty or within one year from the date of delivery. §55-24-201(5)

4. *Notice requirements:* (a) Manufacturer — notify the consumer of repair work done, §55-24-209, of the arbitration procedure, §55-24-206(a); (b) Consumer — written notice by certified mail to the manufacturer by the consumer or his representative; opportunity to cure within ten days, §55-24-205(c); (c) Business entities that purchase fleets of new motor vehicles, and titles. Where the motor vehicle is in the name of a business entity, the seller must disclose in writing the remaining manufacturer's warranty to an individual purchaser. §55-24-212

5. *Repair requirements:* It is presumed that a reasonable number of attempts have been made if the same nonconformity is subjected to four or more repairs, or the vehicle is out of service for a cumulative total of 30 or more calendar days. §55-24-205(a)

6. *Affirmative defenses:* The nonconformity does not substantially impair the vehicle, or is the result of the consumer's abuse, neglect, or unauthorized modifications or alterations. §55-24-203(e) Time limit to action. §55-24-207.

7. *Replace/refund:* The manufacturer shall replace with a comparable vehicle (defined), or refund the full purchase price less a reasonable use allowance (defined). §55-24-203(a) For leases, see §55-24-204.

8. *Other reimbursement:* Collateral charges (defined). §55-24-203(b)(3). Refunds to the consumer and lienholder. §55-24-203(c)

9. *Other remedies:* There is no limit on other consumer remedies. §55-24-210(a). Attorney fees. §55-24-208

10. *Informal dispute mechanism:* For remedies under this section, a consumer must use an informal dispute settlement procedure established by the manufacturer provided the procedure complies with 16 C.F.R. 703. §55-24-206

Tex. Rev. Civ. Stat. Ann. art. 4413(36) (Vernon)

1. *Vehicles covered:* Every fully self-propelled vehicle with the primary purpose of transporting persons or property on public highways and having two or more wheels. §1.03(25). New vehicles which have not been the subject of a "retail sale" without regard to mileage. §1.03(26)

2. *Persons covered:* Owners on title, transferees and lessees during express warranty period, or any other person entitled to enforce the warranty. §6.07(a)

3. *Period covered:* Whichever is first: 24 months or 24,000 miles. §6.07(d)

4. *Notice requirements:* (a) Dealer — provide notice of complaint procedures and rights, §4.07(a); (b) Consumer — report the nonconformity to the manufacturer, distributor, agent or dealer. §§6.07(b), (c)

5. *Repair requirements:* It is presumed that a reasonable number of attempts have been made if the same nonconformity is subjected to four or more repair attempts, at least two of which were made within the first twelve months or 12,000 miles. If the defect creates a serious safety hazard. The presumption applies if the defect has been subject to two or more repairs, one of which occurred within the first twelve months or 12,000 miles. Presumption also applies if vehicle is out of service for 30 or more days and at least two repair attempts were made in the first twelve months or 12,000 miles. §6.07(d)

6. *Affirmative defenses:* The nonconformity does not substantially impair the use or value of the vehicle, or is the result of the consumer's abuse, neglect, or unauthorized modifications or alterations. §6.07(c) Time limit to action. §6.07(h).

7. *Replace/refund:* The manufacturer shall replace with a comparable vehicle, or refund the full purchase price less a reasonable use allowance. §6.07(c)

8. *Other reimbursement:* Refunds to the consumer and lienholder; reasonable incidental costs. §6.07(c)

9. *Other remedies:* There is no limit on other consumer remedies. §6.07(f)

10. *Informal dispute mechanism:* For remedies under this section, a consumer must use an informal dispute settlement procedure established by the Commission. §6.07(e)

11. *Resale of lemon:* Disclosure and warranty required. §6.07(j).

Utah Code Ann. §§13-20-1; 41-3-406

1. *Vehicles covered:* Vehicles, defined in Utah Code Ann. §41-1a-102, sold in-state. Excludes motorcycles, trucks, farm or road tractors, and vehicles over 12,000 lbs. §§13-20-2(4), 41-3-407(4)

2. *Persons covered:* Purchasers, lessees, transferees during express warranty period, or any person entitled to enforce the warranty. §§13-20-2(1), 41-3-407(2)

3. *Period covered:* Whichever is first: term of express warranty or within one year from date of delivery. §13-20-3

4. *Notice requirements:* (a) Manufacturer — none; (b) Consumer — report the nonconformity to the manufacturer, its agent or an authorized dealer. §13-20-3

5. *Repair requirements:* It is presumed that a reasonable number of attempts have been made if the same nonconformity is subjected to four or more repairs, or the vehicle is out of service for a cumulative total of 30 or more business days. §13-20-5

6. *Affirmative defenses:* The nonconformity does not substantially impair the use, market value or safety of the vehicle, or is the result of the consumer's abuse, neglect, or unauthorized modifications or alterations. §13-20-4(4)

7. *Replace/refund:* The manufacturer shall replace with a new comparable vehicle, or refund the full purchase price less a reasonable use allowance. §13-20-4

8. *Other reimbursement:* Collateral charges; refunds to the consumer and lienholder. §13-20-4(1)

9. *Other remedies:* There is no limit on other consumer remedies. §13-20-6(3) Attorney fees. §13-20-6(4)

10. *Informal dispute mechanism:* For remedies under this section, a consumer must use an informal dispute settlement procedure established by the manufacturer provided the procedure complies with 16 C.F.R. 703. §13-20-7

11. *Dealer liability:* None. §13-20-6(2)

12. *Resale of Lemon:* Full written disclosure in conspicuous manner of specified statement and branding of title required. §§41-3-408, -409. Violation is an unfair trade practice. §41-3-412

Vt. Stat. Ann. tit. 9, §4170

1. *Vehicles covered:* New vehicles purchased, leased or registered, including demonstrators. §4171(9) Excludes tractors, highway building equipment, road-making appliances, snowmobiles, motorcycles, mopeds, living part of recreational vehicles or trucks over 10,000 lbs. §4171(6)

2. *Persons covered:* Purchasers, transferees during express warranty period, or any person entitled to enforce the warranty. Excludes government entities and businesses with three or more vehicles. §4171(2)

3. *Period covered:* Term of express warranty or written warranties. §§4171(6)/-/4171(10), 4172(a)

4. *Notice requirements:* (a) Manufacturer — provide form at time the vehicle is delivered, §4180, itemized statement of repair work, §4172(d), and must display consumer rights, §4173(a); (b) Consumer — notify the manufacturer in writing on form provided by manufacturer after the third repair attempt or out of service for 30 days. §4173(a)

5. *Repair requirements:* It is presumed that a reasonable number of attempts have been made if the same nonconformity is subjected to three or more repairs, or the vehicle is out of service for a cumulative total of 30 or more calendar days. The first repair attempt must be within the express warranty period. §4172(g)

6. *Affirmative defenses:* The nonconformity does not substantially impair the use, market value or safety of the vehicle, or is the result of the consumer's abuse, neglect, or unauthorized modifications or alterations. §4172(f)

7. *Replace/refund:* At the consumer's option within 30 days, the manufacturer shall replace with a new vehicle of comparable worth, or refund the full purchase price less a reasonable use allowance (defined). §4172(e)

8. *Other reimbursement:* Credits, allowances, fees, charges, and incidental and consequential damages; refunds to the consumer and lienholder (file purchase and use tax refund with commissioner). §4172(e)

9. *Other remedies:* A consumer cannot pursue a remedy under this chapter if it has discontinued payment due to the manufacturer's breach. §4173(b). The manufacturer's failure to comply with the statute is an unfair or deceptive act or practice. §4177

10. *Informal dispute mechanism:* For remedies under this section, consumer must notify manufacturer if elects to use an arbitration procedure, either through the manufacturer's dispute mechanism or through the Vermont Motor Vehicle Arbitration Board. §4173(c)

11. *Resale of lemon:* Full disclosure required. §4181

12. *Dealer liability:* None. §4178

Va. Code §59.1-207.9 to 207.16

1. *Vehicles covered:* Passenger cars, pick-up or panel trucks, motorcycles, motorized portions of motor homes and mopeds, demonstrators, and lease-purchase vehicles. §59.1-207.11

2. *Persons covered:* Purchasers, transferees during express warranty period, or any person entitled to enforce the warranty, where vehicle used in substantial part for personal, family, or household purposes. §59.1-207.11

3. *Period covered:* 18 months from date of delivery. §59.1-207.11

4. *Notice requirements:* (a) Manufacturer — provide in the warranty or owner's manual clear and conspicuous notification of what the consumer is to do if there is a nonconformity, §59.1-207.13(D); (b) Consumer — written notification by the consumer or his representative to the address the manufacturer specifies in the warranty or owner's manual. §59.1-207.13(E)

5. *Repair requirements:* It is presumed that a reasonable number of attempts have been made if the same nonconformity is subjected to three or more repairs, the nonconformity is a serious safety defect subjected to one or more repairs, or the vehicle is out of service for a cumulative total of 30 or more calendar days. §59.1-207.13(B)

6. *Affirmative defenses:* The nonconformity does not substantially impair the use, market value or safety of the vehicle, or is the result of the consumer's abuse, neglect, or unauthorized modifications or alterations. §59.1-207.13(G)

7. *Replace/refund:* At the consumer's option, the manufacturer shall replace with a comparable vehicle acceptable to the consumer, or refund the full purchase price less a reasonable use allowance (defined). §59.1-207.13(A)

8. *Other reimbursement:* Collateral charges and incidental damages. §59.1-207.13(A)(2)

9. *Other remedies:* There is no limit on other consumer remedies. §59.1-207.13(F) Attorney fees and court costs. §59.1-207.14

10. *Informal dispute mechanism:* For remedies under this section, a consumer may choose to use an informal dispute settlement procedure established by the manufacturer provided the procedure complies with state and federal laws. §59.1-207.15

11. *Resale of Lemon:* Full written disclosure required. §59.1-207.16:1

Wash. Rev. Code §19.118.021

1. *Vehicles covered:* Leases or purchases made in-state and registered in-state, including demonstrators, motorcycles, and lease-purchases. Excludes business fleets with 10 or more vehicles, non-motor portions of motor homes, and trucks over 19,000 lbs. §19.118.021(11)

2. *Persons covered:* Consumers under agreement or contract for transfer, lease, or purchase of a new vehicle. §19.118.021(4)

3. *Period covered:* Whichever is first: two years or 24,000 miles. §19.118.021(22)

4. *Notice requirements:* (a) Manufacturer — to provide statement of rights, written statement of repairs after vehicle's return, §19.118.031; (b) Consumer — written request for replacement/refund. §19.118.041(1)

5. *Repair requirements:* a) Serious defect: two or more repair attempts; b) Same nonconformity: four or more repair attempts; or c) Out of service for a cumulative total of 30 or more calendar days, with at least 15 days during first year or first 12,000 miles. §19.118.041(2)

6. *Affirmative defenses:* The nonconformity does not substantially impair the use, value or safety of the vehicle, or is the result of abuse, neglect, or unauthorized modifications or alterations. §19.118.090(6)

7. *Replace/refund:* At the consumer's option, the manufacturer shall replace with an identical or reasonably equivalent vehicle, or refund the full purchase price less a reasonable use allowance. §19.118.041(1)

8. *Other reimbursement:* Collateral and incidental costs as defined in Wash. Rev. Code Ann. §19.118.021(2), (6). Refunds to the consumer and lienholder. §19.118.041(1)

9. *Other remedies:* There is no limit on other consumer remedies. §19.118.140. Violation of the chapter is an unfair or deceptive trade practice. §19.118.120. Attorney fees, costs, and treble damages. §19.118.100(3)

10. *Informal dispute mechanism:* For remedies under this section, a consumer may use an informal dispute settlement procedure provided the procedure complies with 16 C.F.R. 703 or with the new Motor Vehicle Arbitration Board procedure. §19.118.150

11. *Resale of lemon:* Full disclosure required. §19.118.061

12. *Dealer liability:* None. §19.118.041(3)

W. Va. Code §46A-6A-1

1. *Vehicles covered:* Passenger vehicles, pick-up trucks, vans, and motor portion of motor homes sold in-state, subject to registration. §46A-6A-2(4)

2. *Persons covered:* Purchasers, transferees during express warranty period, or any person entitled to enforce the warranty, where vehicle primarily for personal, family, or household use. §46A-6A-2(1)

3. *Period covered:* Whichever is later: term of express warranty or within one year from date of delivery. §46A-6A-3(a)

4. *Notice requirements:* (a) Manufacturer — provide specific separate statement of rights, 46A-6A-6; (b) Dealer — must provide notice if repairs have been made to a vehicle after receipt from the manufacturer if they cost more than $500, §46A-6A-3a; (c) Consumer — written notice of the nonconformity to the manufacturer, agent or authorized dealer. §§46A-6A-3(a), 46A-6A-5(c)

5. *Repair requirements:* It is presumed that a reasonable number of attempts have been made if the same nonconformity is subjected to three or more repairs, the vehicle is out of service for a cumulative total of 30 or more calendar days, or there has been one repair if the nonconformity is likely to cause death or serious bodily harm. §46A-6A-5

6. *Affirmative defenses:* The nonconformity does not substantially impair the use or market value, or is the result of the consumer's abuse, neglect, or unauthorized modifications or alterations. §46A-6A-4(c)

7. *Replace/refund:* The manufacturer shall replace the nonconforming vehicle with a comparable new motor vehicle. §46A-6A-3(b)

8. *Other reimbursement:* In a civil action, a consumer may be awarded refund of the purchase price, including taxes, fees, and expenses, loss of use, and attorney fees. §46A-6A-4(b)

9. *Other remedies:* There is no limit on other consumer remedies. §46A-6A-9

10. *Informal dispute mechanism:* For remedies under this section, a consumer must use an informal dispute settlement procedure provided the procedure complies with 16 C.F.R. 703, as determined by the attorney general, and if consumer receives timely notice of availability of procedure. §46A-6A-8

11. *Resale of lemon:* Full disclosure required. §46A-6A-7

12. *Dealer liability:* None. §46A-6A-4(e)

Wis. Stat. Ann. §218.015

1. *Vehicles covered:* Vehicles registered and purchased or leased in-state, including demonstrator or executive vehicles. Excludes mopeds, semitrailers or trailers used with trucks. §218.015(1)(d)

2. *Persons covered:* Purchasers or lessees, transferees during express warranty period, or any person entitled to enforce the warranty. §218.015(1)(b)

3. *Period covered:* Whichever is first: term of express warranty or within one year from date of delivery. §218.015(2)(a)

4. *Notice requirement:* (a) Manufacturer — none; (b) Consumer — notice to the manufacturer or authorized dealer. §218.015(2)(a)

5. *Repair requirements:* It is presumed that a reasonable number of attempts have been made if the same nonconformity is subjected to four or more repairs, or the vehicle is out of service for 30 or more calendar days. §218.015(1)(h)

6. *Affirmative defenses:* The nonconformity is the result of the consumer's abuse, neglect, or unauthorized modifications or alterations. §218.015(1)(f)

7. *Replace/refund:* At the consumer's option, the manufacturer shall replace with a new comparable vehicle, or refund the full purchase price less a reasonable use allowance (defined). §218.015(2)(b)

8. *Other reimbursement:* Taxes and charges; refund to the consumer and lienholder; other damages. §218.015(2)(b) Double damages and attorney fees. §218.015(7)

9. *Other remedies:* There is no limit on other consumer remedies. §218.015(5)

10. *Informal dispute mechanism:* For remedies under this section, a consumer must use an informal dispute settlement procedure established by the manufacturer provided the procedure complies with 16 C.F.R. 703. §218.015(3), (4)

11. *Resale of lemon:* Full disclosure required. §218.015(2)(d)

Wyo. Stat. Ann. §40-17-101

1. *Vehicles covered:* Every vehicle under 10,000 lbs. sold or registered in-state which is self-propelled. §40-17-101(a)(ii)

2. *Persons covered:* Purchasers, transferees during express warranty period, or any person entitled to enforce the warranty. §40-17-101(a)(i)

3. *Period covered:* Within one year from the date of delivery. §40-17-101(b)

4. *Notice requirement:* (a) Manufacturer — none; (b) Consumer — nonconformity must be reported to the manufacturer by or on behalf of the consumer; opportunity to cure. §40-17-101(h)

5. *Repair requirements:* It is presumed that a reasonable number of attempts have been made if the same nonconformity is subjected to three or more repairs, or the vehicle is out of service for a cumulative total of 30 or more business days. §40-17-101(d)

6. *Affirmative defenses:* The nonconformity does not substantially impair the use and market value of the vehicle, or is the result of the consumer's abuse, neglect, or unauthorized modifications or alterations. §40-17-101(g)

7. *Replace/refund:* The manufacturer shall replace with a new or comparable vehicle, or refund the full purchase price less a reasonable use allowance. §40-17-101(c)

8. *Other reimbursement:* Collateral charges; refund to the consumer and lienholder. §40-17-101(c)(ii)

9. *Other remedies:* There is no limit on other consumer remedies. §40-17-101(e). Civil suit for violation of the statute and attorney fees. §40-17-101(j)

10. *Informal dispute mechanism:* For remedies under this section, a consumer must use an informal dispute settlement procedure established by the manufacturer provided the procedure complies with state and federal laws. §40-17-101(f)

Index

Related Books
of Interest for Lawyers

The following seven NCLC legal practice manuals have especial relevance to automobile cases. These are detailed treatises designed to be an attorney's primary practice guide and legal resource when representing clients in all fifty states. The volumes are generally updated annually and include companion disks to bring sample pleadings and key primary source materials directly onto the attorney's wordprocessor:

Consumer Warranty Law (1997 with current Supplement and Companion Disk) (768 pp. plus Supp.): detailed treatment of new and used car lemon laws, the Federal Magnuson-Moss Warranty Act, UCC Articles 2 and 2A, mobile home warranty legislation, FTC Used Car Rule, negligence and strict liability theories, car repair and home improvement statutes, service contract and lease laws. Also includes sample pleadings and discovery, notice of revocation, and other practice aids.

Unfair and Deceptive Acts and Practices (4th ed. 1997 with current Supplement and Companion Disk) (944 pp. plus Supp.): the only practice manual that covers all aspects of handling a deceptive practices case in every state. Special sections on automobile sales practices, the federal racketeering (RICO) statute, and the FTC Holder Rule.

Automobile Fraud (1998 with current Supplement and Companion Disk) (464 pp. plus Supp.): detailed examination of odometer tampering, lemon laundering, hidden sale of salvage, wrecked, and flood-damaged cars, the failure to disclose damage to new cars, misrepresentations about demonstrators, program cars, and the number of prior users. Includes special chapters on fraud claims for punitive damages, investigating a car's prior history, and litigating automobile fraud claims. Appendices set out relevant legislation for each state, state procedures for title searches and numerous sample pleadings.

Repossessions (and Foreclosures) (1999 4th ed. with Companion Disk) (700 pp.): unique guide to car and mobile home repossessions, default remedies relating to automobile leases and rent-to-own transactions, home foreclosures, threatened seizures of household goods, and tax and other statutory liens.

Truth in Lending (1999 4th ed. with Companion Disk) (800 pp.): detailed analysis of all aspects of TILA, and the Consumer Leasing Act. Appendices reprint Reg. Z, Reg. M, their Official Staff Commentaries, and sample pleadings. The companion disk includes a program to compute APRs.

Consumer Law Pleadings With Disk (1994, 1995, 1997, 1998, 1999, all with Companion Disks) (368pp., 416pp., 368pp., 336pp., 424pp.): five volumes, each containing notable recent pleadings (ready to edit on the accompanying disk) from all types of consumer cases — including many pleadings related to lemon laws, car fraud, automobile financing and leasing, repossessions, and mobile homes.

Fair Credit Reporting Act (4th ed. 1998 with current Supplement and Companion Disk) (784 pp. plus Supp.): the key resource for handling any type of credit reporting issue, from cleaning up blemished credit records to obtaining credit despite negative information to suing reporting agencies and creditors under the FCRA for inaccurate reports.

Surviving Debt
A GUIDE FOR CONSUMERS
(3d edition 1999) (408 pp.) ($17.00)

Now, everything a non-lawyer needs to know about:
- Home foreclosures and evictions
- Dealing with debt collectors and credit card debt
- Which bills to pay first and when to refinance
- Managing credit card debt
- Stopping repossession of property
- Quick debt relief strategies.

"Surviving Debt *provides sound advice to consumers struggling with over-indebtedness.*" — Ralph Nader

"A gold mine on topics like how to handle collectors, which debts to pay first, and how collection lawsuits work." — U.S. News & World Report

"Outstanding manual ... Seldom is such useful, authoritative information available for so small a price!"
— *Booklist*, Magazine of the American Library Association

CONTENTS

National Consumer Law Center, 18 Tremont Street, Suite 400, Boston MA 02108
(617) 523-8089   Fax (617) 523-7398   www.consumerlaw.org

To Order

To order *Return to Sender*, contact your local bookstore, or order directly from National Consumer Law Center by sending $16 (shipping and handling included) for each copy. Please call (617) 523-8089 for MasterCard/Visa orders and for bulk discount orders of five or more. Send your check to:

**National Consumer Law Center
18 Tremont Street, Suite 400
Boston, MA 02108**

**(617) 523-8089
Fax (617) 523-7398
email: publications@nclc.org**

Visit National Consumer Law Center on the web:
www.consumerlaw.org